THE
AMERICAN
PROPHECIES

THE
AMERICAN
PROPHECIES

ANCIENT SCRIPTURES REVEAL
OUR NATION'S FUTURE

Michael D. Evans

New York   Boston   Nashville

Unless otherwise indicated, Scripture quotations are taken from the King James Version of the Bible.

Scriptures noted NKJV are taken from THE NEW KING JAMES VERSION. Copyright © 1979, 1980, 1982, Thomas Nelson, Inc., Publishers.

Scriptures noted NIV are taken from the HOLY BIBLE: NEW INTERNATIONAL VERSION®. Copyright © 1973, 1978, 1984 by International Bible Society. Used by permission of Zondervan Publishing House. All rights reserved.

Scriptures noted RSV are taken from the REVISED STANDARD VERSION of the Bible. Copyright © 1949, 1952, 1971, 1973 by the Division of Christian Education of the National Council of the Churches of Christ in the U.S.A. Used by permission.

Warner Faith
Time Warner Book Group
1271 Avenue of the Americas, New York, NY 10020

Visit our Web site at www.twbookmark.com.

Originally published in hardcover by Warner Books
Printed in the United States of America
First Warner Books Trade Edition: August 2005
10 9 8 7 6 5 4 3 2 1

The Library of Congress has cataloged the hardcover edition as follows:

Evans, Michael D. (Michael David), 1959–
    The American prophecies : terrorism and mideast conflict reveal a nation's destiny /
Michael D. Evans.
        p. cm.
    Includes bibliographical references and index.
    ISBN 0-446-52252-X
    1. Christianity—United States. 2. United States—Religion. 3. September 11 Terrorist Attacks, 2001—Religious aspects—Christianity. 4. Terrorism—Religious aspects—Christianity. I. Title.
    BR515 .E93 2004
    277.3'083—dc22   2004005809

ISBN: 0-446-69328-6 (pbk)
Cover design by Shasti O'Leary
Cover photograph by Jethro Soudant

Contents

THE
AMERICAN
PROPHECIES

The Second Coming

Turning and turning in the widening gyre
The falcon cannot hear the falconer;
Things fall apart; the centre cannot hold;
Mere anarchy is loosed upon the world,
The blood-dimmed tide is loosed, and everywhere
The ceremony of innocence is drowned;
The best lack all conviction, while the worst
Are full of passionate intensity.

Surely some revelation is at hand;
Surely the Second Coming is at hand.
The Second Coming! Hardly are those words out
When a vast image out of *Spiritus Mundi*
Troubles my sight: somewhere in sands of the desert
A shape with lion body and the head of a man,
A gaze blank and pitiless as the sun,
Is moving its slow thighs, while all about it
Reel shadows of the indignant desert birds.
The darkness drops again; but now I know
That twenty centuries of stony sleep
Were vexed to nightmare by a rocking cradle,
And what rough beast, its hour come round at last,
Slouches toward Bethlehem to be born?

William Butler Yeats
Written in 1920

CHAPTER ONE

In the Eye of the Prophetic Storm

You might be president one day. You will make mistakes, and God will forgive you. But God will never forgive you if you abandon the state of Israel.

> Rev. W. O. Vaught, Pastor
> Immanuel Baptist Church, Little Rock, Arkansas,
> to parishioner and then-Governor William Clinton[1]

For he that soweth to his flesh shall of the flesh reap corruption; but he that soweth to the Spirit shall of the Spirit reap life everlasting.

> Galatians 6:8
> Scripture used by President-elect William Clinton
> for his oath of office, January 20, 1993

On April 30, 1789, George Washington placed his hand on a Masonic Bible, randomly opened to Genesis 49. This chapter is a prophecy of blessing from a dying man—Jacob, whose name was changed to Israel—to his twelve sons. The prophecy concerned both their futures and the coming Messiah: Verse 10 reads, "The scepter shall not depart from Judah . . . until Shiloh come." With his hand on this portion of Scripture, Washington took the oath of office to become the first president of the American Republic.[2] Each president since Washington has followed the same pattern, most of them choosing to open the Bible to a particular passage of Scripture as they swear to preserve, protect, and defend the Constitution of the United States. The choice of Scripture has often proved to be prophetic of a president's term of office, and on occasion the chosen verses have uncannily reflected America's role in the plan of Bible prophecy.

I find it intriguing, for example, that in January 1993, President Bill Clinton took his oath of office with a Bible opened to Galatians 6:8 (quoted above). No doubt the president-elect intended for his administration to be characterized by the latter half of that verse, but can any honest observer question the conclusion that the Clinton presidency came to be characterized by the former instead?

During his second term in office, Bill Clinton was impeached, yet not on charges stemming from the sleazy scandals that consumed the public's attention. It wasn't his affair with Monica Lewinsky or Gennifer Flowers, nor was it his sexual harassment of Paula Jones, Kathleen Willey, or Juanita Broderick that brought the president of the United States before a congressional panel to face removal from office. No, Bill Clinton was impeached for placing his hand on the Bible, promising to "tell the truth, the whole truth, and nothing but the truth," and then lying to cover up his indiscretions. An American president had "sown to the flesh" and "reaped corruption"—with the entire world as witnesses. *And the fact that the United States Senate could not muster the moral courage to convict a president in the face of obvious perjury shows the degree to which our national leadership has succumbed to the dangerous doctrine of moral relativism.*

When I think of the significance of President Clinton's choice of Galatians 6:8 for his first inauguration, I cannot help contrasting it to President Reagan's first inauguration. On January 20, 1981, the warmest inaugural day on record—a crisp 55 degrees—he stepped to the podium to take the oath of office. As Chief Justice Warren Burger administered the oath, Ronald Reagan's left hand rested on a Bible prophecy—a prophecy that would decide the fate of the nation of which he was taking leadership, as well as the fate of the world. (Mr. Reagan's policies set the stage for the fall of the great "ism" of the twentieth century—communism.) That day the Bible was opened to 2 Chronicles 7:14, a prophecy given in the historic city of Jerusalem to King Solomon. God said to the king these words:

> If my people, which are called by my name, shall humble themselves, and pray, and seek my face, and turn from their wicked ways; then will I hear from heaven, and will forgive their sin, and will heal their land.

During the early years of the Reagan administration, I once had a meeting with a presidential aide who showed me around the Oval Office. There, I saw the family Bible that President Reagan had used at his inauguration. It was still opened to 2 Chronicles 7:14, and I saw that in the margin next to that verse his mother had written this note: "Son, this scripture is for the healing of the nations." I was moved that the president had been influenced by this ancient prophecy, especially as I recalled the momentous events of that inaugural day in 1981. That was a presidential inauguration I will never forget.

I was at home watching the television coverage of the swearing-in ceremony and the commentary that followed when the networks cut away from Washington, D.C., to show scenes of the release of American hostages who had been held captive for 444 days by the revolutionary terrorist government in Iran. While watching these simultaneous events unfolding, suddenly I heard my phone ring. It was a call from Israel.

"Mike, are you watching TV?" said Reuben Hecht, senior adviser to Israel's prime minister, Menachem Begin. "Harel's prophecy is coming to pass before our eyes."

Reuben Hecht and I had enjoyed dinner with Isser Harel (founder of Mossad, and head of Israeli intelligence from 1947 to 1963) at his home a few months earlier. Over dinner that night, I had asked Harel, "Who do you think will be America's next president?"

Harel responded, "The word on the streets is that terrorists might have a say about that. They are going to attempt to influence your elections by releasing the hostages precisely when Reagan is sworn into office."

Completely stunned, I responded, "What? Why?"

Harel said, "They want Carter out because of his passion to democratize Islam." The former intelligence head was referring to President Jimmy Carter's attempt to transform the shah's regime in Iran. Those actions destabilized Iran, and opened the door for Ayatollah Khomeini, for the Camp David accords, and to Carter's advice that Sadat give a speech in Egypt stating that religion and politics must be separate. This speech was heard by a blind cleric named al-Rahman, who issued the *fatwa* (decree) to assassinate Sadat; the same cleric was later indicted for his part in the 1993 bombing of the World Trade Center.

Reuben Hecht, Isser Harel, and I had quite a dinner conversation that evening. We talked about America's foreign policy and the tensions in the Middle East, Saddam Hussein's power play in Iraq, and how Carter manipulated the overthrow of the Iranian shah through the American embassy—contrary to the advice of Israeli intelligence, which asserted that instead of improving the country, it would give impetus to Islamic fundamentalists and provoke the Soviets to invade Afghanistan.

"They want to kill Sadat," Harel said. "Now they want to kill Carter's chances of reelection. They feel that if the hostages are released early, it would put Carter back in office."

Later on that same evening, I asked Harel another question: "Will terrorism ever come to America?"

"Will terrorism come to America?" he repeated my question back to me. "America has the power to fight terrorism, but not the will; the terrorists have the will, but not the power. But all of that could change in time. Oil buys more than tents. You in the West kill a fly and rejoice. In the Middle East, we kill one, and one hundred flies come to the funeral.

"Yes, I fear it will come in time."

"Where will it come?" I asked him.

He thought for a moment. "New York is the symbol of your freedom and capitalism. It's likely they will strike there first. At your tallest building, which is a symbol of your power."

That conversation took place in October 1980. Little did I know that Harel's predictions—the death of Sadat, the release of the hostages at the exact hour of President Reagan's inauguration, and the terrorist strikes against the tallest building in New York—would come to pass within a dozen years. And less than a decade after that, the United States would plunge headfirst into an apocalyptic tornado on September 11, 2001.

Where Is America Found in Bible Prophecy?

Is America in prophecy? Yes, it is. As a Middle East analyst and minister who has worked closely with leaders in that region for decades, I tended to be skeptical of attempts to come up with schemes to plug America into prophetic interpretations. I have often referred to such teachers as "Pop Prophecy Peddlers." But, after thousands of hours of research, I am totally convinced that America *is* found in prophecy, and I believe you will, too, after reading this book.

In a nutshell, here is how the United States fits into Bible prophecy. America has married two brothers, both descendants of ancient Abraham, who was told by God to get out of Ur of the Chaldees (modern-day Iraq).

> The LORD had said to Abram, "Leave your country, your people and your father's household and go to the land I will show you. I will make you into a great nation and I will bless you; I will make your name great, and you will be a blessing. I will bless those who bless you, and whoever curses you I will curse; and all peoples on earth will be blessed through you." (Genesis 12:1–3 NIV)

One of these marriages was based on America's guilt over its appeasement policies, which resulted in the deaths of millions of Jews during the Holocaust. America has attempted to use a tiny democratic state in the midst of a sea of instability in the Middle East—Israel—to assist in deterring communism, fascism, and terrorism. The marriage to the other brother, Ishmael, was one of convenience. A mortal enemy of the younger brother, Ishmael brought a dowry of black gold (oil) to the marriage, and then used it to blackmail America.

The Middle East is home to two-thirds of the world's global oil reserves. OPEC presently accounts for 40 percent of the world's oil imports. According to the International Energy Agency, by 2030 that figure is expected to rise to 60 percent. By that time, the Middle East will supply 50 percent of U.S. oil imports, 50 percent of European imports, 80 percent of China's imports, and 90 percent of Japan's imports.

While Middle Eastern oil flows to the West, we ship arms in their direction. In fact, the Middle East region is currently America's number one client in the world for weapons of war. The U.S. has sold Saudi Arabia alone more than $200 billion in weapons since the 1980s.

Even after September 11, petrodollars earned by countries such as Saudi Arabia, Iran, and Libya have been used to sponsor terrorism, produce weapons of mass destruction, and finance a gospel of hatred that is brainwashing millions of Islamic youth. Yet America has been unwilling to admit that it is being blackmailed, let alone draw a line in the sand against it. Many Islamic regimes know that while they have the oil, as Ariel Sharon once said, "We have the matches."[3] It's time for the U.S. to stand up to these bullies and quit capitulating to blackmail. Our future depends on it.

Presently, America's other marriage partner, Isaac (Israel), has developed the fourth largest nuclear arsenal in the world, knowing Islamic fundamentalists are hell-bent on annihilating the people of Israel. They are determined that what happened in the Holocaust, while the world kept silent, will never happen again. Israel has opened nuclear silos during three Middle Eastern wars, and has targeted cities such as Baghdad, Damascus, Cairo, and even some in the former Soviet Union.

While we know that Israel has had nuclear strike capabilities since at least the late 1960s, today Islamic nations are very close to having their finger poised over the red button as well. It appears that at least one of these nations may have suitcase nuclear bombs paid for by oil sales to America. In addition to this, the *Washington Post* reported the following on December 21, 2003:

Documents provided by Iran to UN nuclear inspectors since early November have exposed the outlines of a vast, secret procurement network that successfully acquired thousands of sensitive parts and tools from numerous countries over a 17-year period . . . While American presidents since Ronald Reagan worried that Iran might seek nuclear weapons, U.S. and allied intelligence agencies were unable to halt Iran's most significant nuclear acquisitions, or even to spot a major nuclear facility under construction until it was essentially completed . . . Iran's pilot facility, which is now functional, and a much larger uranium-enrichment plant under construction next door are designed to produce enough fissile material to make at least two dozen nuclear bombs each year.

Through these two political—and spiritual—marriages, America has stepped into the center of the prophetic storm. America now finds herself trying to accommodate an ancient Jew-hating older brother (Ishmael) who has refused to make peace with the younger (Isaac). In order to live with both, America has appeased them with bombs and bribes—(more than $400 billion in military equipment and $100 billion in aid).

The Bitter Root of Bigotry

During the Persian Gulf War in 1991, I had lunch one afternoon with the governor of Dhahran, Saudi Arabia, Prince Mohammed Khalid (commander in chief of the Saudi Royal Air Force and the Arab multinational forces). During the time he was head of the Syrian High Command and the Egyptian Third Army Commander, America paid Syria a billion dollars to support the Persian Gulf War—knowing Syria was a terrorist state. Syria went on to use that money to buy missiles from North Korea.

After we ate lunch, Khalid and I talked about Islamic fundamentalists and the threat they and their fanatical religion could be to the West. My words antagonized Khalid, and he said, "Listen, your country is a lot more dangerous than ours. You can walk our streets at two in the morning and nobody will bother you. You can't do that in L.A., New York, Chicago, or most of the big U.S. cities."

"You're right," I said. "But that's because you cut off people's hands and heads in public squares."

"Well, it works. What do you do? Put color televisions in your prisons and serve them Christmas dinner? And besides, don't insult our religion by exaggerating. Islam is a peaceful religion."

"Are you telling me Islamic fundamentalists are peaceful?" I asked.

"No," he said, "they're not. But they represent no more than 10 percent of Islam."

"Excuse me," I retorted. "That really comforts me to know that only a hundred million or so people want to kill me in the name of their religion."

I've heard the same argument about the impact of Islamic fundamentalism again and again. Liberal politicians and special-interest groups continue to propagate a myth that Islam is a peaceful religion. But think about this for a moment. Islam has around one billion adherents worldwide. The actual number is probably higher, but one billion is a nice, even number for the sake of argument. Now, even if 90 percent of the Islamic world is peaceful, as Prince Khalid assured me, it still places the planet at the brink of the greatest crisis of history. Even if 99.9 percent of the Islamic world is completely nonviolent, we are still in grave danger. If only one-tenth of 1 percent of all Muslims were radical Islamists, that is still a staggering number: It means that one million people are intent on killing us. *It took only nineteen hijackers to wreak massive destruction on the United States on September 11. Each one of those men believed he was on a divine assignment from God.*

The terrorists' war against America and Israel is rooted in this radical religious doctrine called Islamic fundamentalism. This distorted Islamic belief is very difficult for Americans to comprehend, partly because our modern secular world is still getting past the long conflict between science and religion—which most assume was won long ago by science and secularism. Suddenly, a religious adversary is attacking mighty secular America. It's no longer just the streets of Jerusalem that are threatened, but those of New York and Washington.

In April 2003, while the U.S. was in the midst of the Persian Gulf War, I wrote a book that ultimately became a *New York Times* best seller, *Beyond Iraq: The Next Move*. In the book, I stated my belief that weapons of mass destruction were in Syria. I also stated that, compliments of the Syrian government and the Iraqi embassy in Damascus, money and key Iraqi leaders were being moved through Syria. This, in my opinion, explains why President Bush had to move so quickly— Saddam Hussein was moving the WMDs and the funds to disseminate them out of Iraq.

There is no question in my mind that the U.S. must quickly close the borders of Syria to contain Saddam Hussein's money and weapons of mass destruction. I believe America will ultimately have to go to war against Syria, a much more dangerous terrorist-harboring state than Iraq. Hopefully, that war can be fought through economic and diplomatic means without the shedding of American blood. If not, America will still have to shut down the engine of terror in Syria.

Numbers of Americans have died because Syria allowed Islamic martyrs to use their country as a pipeline from other Arab states into Iraq to attack the "infidels" (American soldiers). There is no doubt that Israel will have to go into Iran and take out their nuclear reactor, and do it quickly (in the same way they did in Iraq). America will likely encourage Israel to do so, and then deny any involvement, as they did in the 1980s.

America will have to allow Israel to fight their war against terrorism that has never been fought. Israel must root out the terrorist organizations in the territories, and they will have to do it themselves. The war on terrorism will never be won as long as the Palestinian territories remain the point of exportation for suicide bombers. The dissemination of media propaganda that enrages the masses in the Palestinian territories must also be stopped.

True hope for peace lies in discerning the truth and acting on it, not in believing myths propagated by liberal power brokers and in ignoring bigotry. Yet too many people in America view the real enemy as the "narrow-minded, right-wing, Bible-thumping Christians" who believe in black and white, right and wrong. The same people who see conservative Christians as the enemy often legitimize the acts of cold-blooded murderers as steps to obtain freedom and peace. These apostles of appeasement have raised the hopes of the Islamic fanatics so high that the national security of America is now at stake. Equally as important, our very freedoms are at stake. We can echo the prayer of Dietrich Bonhoeffer: "Death, throw off our grievous chains and demolish the thick walls of our mortal body and our blinded souls, so that at last we may behold what we have failed to see in this place. Freedom, long we have sought you through discipline, through action and through suffering. Now that we are dying we see you there in the face of God."[4]

Why do they hate us? Everyone wants to know the answer to that question. Here's the answer: Simply because they hate us!

The more important question is this: What is fueling that hatred, and how can the engine of hate be derailed? If you don't think bigotry is at the root of it all, you're dead wrong. It is no coincidence that the World Conference on Racism in Durban, South Africa, turned into a "World Conference on Jew-Hatred," and ended three days before September 11, 2001. Is there zero correlation between the U.S. and Israel walking out of the conference, and September 11?

Many believe that the current Palestinian crisis has much to do with the issue of "Jew-hatred." They are right, it does. *The entire Palestinian crisis comes down to two things: refugees and terrorism.*

Is there a refugee crisis anywhere on earth that has drawn the world into such a mess? The answer is, clearly, "No." Civilized countries solve refugee crises on their own. The truth is that the Arab world has fueled and fed the Palestinian refugee crisis, using it to exploit Jew-hatred. Their attitude is: "Blame the Jews for all the problems, just as Hitler did, and we will not be shot for our brutality." Since their "thugocracies" are run by the bullet, and not the ballot, someone needs to bear the blame . . . why not the Jews and the "crusaders." State-controlled media that brainwash the masses are the root of the problem.

America has done nothing to address this danger. It must be stopped. The U.S. must use every means possible to shut down the

"Baghdad Bobs" who are recruiting children to kill in the name of Allah.

How did Israel solve its refugee crisis in Europe at the end of the Holocaust? How did they solve the crisis in Arab countries where Jewish citizens were being killed simply because they were Jews? They took care of their own.

Why did the Arab League tell the Arabs to leave Palestine and fight Israel, then turn their backs on the very refugees they created? Why did they make up the myth that Israeli Arabs must have a state inside Israel, even though they never had such a thing in three thousand years of history? Or that an Egyptian-born billionaire terrorist by the name of Yasser Arafat is their "George Washington"?

I believe there is a direct correlation between current events and prophecy. I am firmly convinced that President Jimmy Carter unlocked Pandora's box in the Middle East, and President Bill Clinton stepped into the maelstrom that was unleashed. I also contend that America has made a conscious decision to tolerate bigotry perpetrated in the name of Islam, a bigotry that is presently polluting and poisoning the peace of the world. *The war on terrorism cannot be won without a war against racism and bigotry.*

If America had maintained moral clarity, Iran might have continued to be a pro-Western country. Iraq might never have gone to war against Iran, a war that took the lives of 1.2 million Arabs. The U.S. certainly would not have assisted them in doing so. The U.S.S.R. might not have invaded Afghanistan, and America would not have armed and trained thousands of terrorists throughout the Middle East to fight the Soviets. These same American-trained and American-armed terrorists—Osama bin Laden's *al Qaeda* being the most infamous example—have now turned on America. The truth is, America might never have ended up in this mess if we had maintained our conservative policies of not negotiating with terrorists.

Has America Abandoned Israel?

At the beginning of this chapter I placed a quote from Rev. W. O. Vaught, who was Bill Clinton's pastor while he was governor of

Arkansas. Reverend Vaught, who made more than forty trips to Israel during his lifetime, told Clinton that God would forgive him for mistakes he made while in office. "But if you abandon Israel," Vaught said, "God will never forgive you."

That quote turned out to be as prophetic as Galatians 6:8 for the Clinton presidency. Barely a month into his first term, President Clinton received a wake-up call from bin Laden's organization: the February 26, 1993, truck bombing of the World Trade Center. While this first WTC attack went relatively unnoticed, in it were seeds of the eventual September 11 attacks, and not only in the fact of its New York City location. The actual aim of the bombing was to topple the towers and kill as many as 250,000 people.[5] If they had succeeded in even 1 percent of this instead of killing only seven people, we would be remembering February 26, 1993, not September 11, 2001. Instead, because our president at the time was more occupied in implementing his economic program than keeping America safe, no one else paid much attention to the bombing either. In his regular radio address the day after the bombing, President Clinton mentioned the "tragedy" (he never once used the word "bomb" or "terrorist" in the address) and never brought up the incident in public again. Nor did he ever visit the site of the blast. As the author of *Losing bin Laden*, Richard Miniter, said about Clinton's inability to deal with bin Laden throughout his presidency:

> In 1993, bin Laden was a small-time funder of militant
> Muslim terrorists in Sudan, Yemen, and Afghanistan. By
> the end of 2000, Clinton's last year in office, bin Laden's
> network was operating in more than fifty-five countries and
> already responsible for the deaths of thousands [including
> fifty-five Americans].[6]

Clinton was tested by historic, global conflict, the first phase of America's war on terror. He was president when bin Laden declared war on America. He had many chances to defeat bin Laden; he simply did not take them. If, in the wake of the 1998 embassy bombings, Clinton had rallied the public and the Congress to fight bin Laden and smash terrorism, he might have been the Winston Churchill of his generation. But, instead, he chose the role of Neville Chamberlain (whose appeasements of Hitler in Munich in 1938 are credited with paving the way to the Nazi invasion of Poland that began World War II the next year).

In October 1993, the same year as the first World Trade Center attack, U.S. troops were sent on a humanitarian mission to Mogadishu, Somalia. I was there shortly after two Blackhawk helicopters were shot down and a roughly twenty-hour firefight ensued, in which nineteen American soldiers and more than a thousand Somalis were killed. Shortly after this, President Clinton made the decision to pull out of Somalia. Evidence was later found that the Somalis who shot down the helicopters had received training from bin Laden's forces, which had become adept at bringing down advanced Soviet helicopters in their fighting in Afghanistan with rocket-propelled grenades. Bin Laden eventually admitted his involvement in Somalia in an interview on CNN. The terrorists considered it a glorious victory.

In September of that same year, I sat in the audience as President Clinton held a celebration on the White House lawn for what he called "a brave gamble for peace." I watched as he forced—standing with his thumb in the Israeli prime minister's back—Yitzhak Rabin to shake hands with PLO Chairman Yasser Arafat. They shook hands over a sheet of paper that represented the Declaration of Principles—or Oslo Accords—which led to Israeli concessions to the Palestinian Authority (the PLO, a terrorist organization), which would only be answered with more terrorist bombs in Jerusalem and Tel Aviv. The paper lay on the same table over which President Jimmy Carter had presided as Menachim Begin and Anwar Sadat had signed the Peace Treaty between Israel and Egypt in 1979. President Clinton later described it as one of "the highest moments" of his presidency as the two "shook hands for the first time in front of a billion people on television. It was an unbelievable day."[7]

It was indeed an "unbelievable day" and a defining moment for the forty-second president of the United States, but hardly in the terms that he described. The much vaunted "peace process," the foreign policy focus of Bill Clinton's presidency and the issue that was supposed to secure his historic legacy, has brought anything but peace to the Middle East. I believe that is because America has abandoned Israel at key moments. As Reverend Vaught said, God will not forgive that.

America is the mightiest nation on earth and has long been a partaker of God's blessings. It's time to ask ourselves, "Why?" America comprises only 7 percent of the world's population and is in possession of more than half the world's wealth. America has 63 percent of the world's manufacturing goods, 74 percent of the world's automobiles, 52 percent of the world's trucks, 56 percent of the world's telephones, 47 percent of the world's radios, 46 percent of the world's electrical output, 52 percent of the world's steel, 35 percent of the world's petroleum, and consumes 35 percent of the world's energy.

Yet, during the past few decades, America has seen her "culture polluted, God dethroned, and her heroes defiled."[8] Bible-believing Americans have been demonized as bigots and extremists. God has been taken out of schools, courts, and town squares, and even our Pledge of Allegiance—"one nation, under God"—has been challenged. The same moral compromise that has infected our domestic policy has also infected our foreign policy. In the 1990s, terrorists could clear customs and set up shop inside our borders.

There is absolutely no question that God's hedge of protection was lifted from America. September 11 was a curse on our beloved nation, but worse is the fact that most Americans don't understand why it happened. I believe it will happen again, and again and again, and much worse, if Americans do not wake up to the truth.

I am on a quest for the truth, and I trust you will join me as I attempt to stare into the depths of God's eternal Word and search for His purpose and plan in the midst of all the chaos on the planet.

America Needs Marriage Counseling

Today, America's secular political engine is on a collision course with prophecy. Many believe that there is nothing we can do about it. If it is foretold, then it must just come to pass. However, if that is our attitude, then we are missing the true point of prophecy. The Bible doesn't tell us what the future holds so that we can sit back and let disaster strike; but rather so that we can prepare, and take any necessary actions to make sure we are on the prophetic side of blessing, and not cursing. It is up to God-fearing Americans who are willing to step out and make a difference to keep our country headed in the right direction, whether that be in our domestic policy or our foreign policy. This is why I have always done whatever I could to see that our government acts with moral clarity, whatever the issue.

This is also why, in 1981, I was willing to use what I knew about the Middle East to help President Reagan's staff act with moral clarity concerning the issue of that region. In that role, I was asked to attend a high-level briefing with U.S. generals and admirals over the sale of AWACS planes to Saudi Arabia. I challenged the White House staff over the decision, stating that those planes could eventually end up in the hands of Islamic fundamentalists and pose a major threat to America's and Israel's security. My arguments were mostly pragmatic, but I had so much intelligence information that they let me speak. When I inserted a Scripture into my short speech, I was flagged with this question: "What does God know about foreign policy?"

I replied to the question, "He is foreign policy!"

Do we truly think we can push our government forward without His guidance? Our forefathers certainly didn't! I don't think we should either!

Several months later, a small U.S. delegation and I were invited to have lunch with the president and his cabinet. Chuck Colson sat next to me. It was his first time back in the White House since the Nixon days. I said to Mr. Colson, "I imagine you're thinking all about the White House strategy that's going on in this room." He smiled and said, "Not at all, Mike. I'm thinking about one thing . . . eternity!"

His statement really struck me. Sooner or later everyone on the planet—rich and poor; skeptic and religious; presidents and paupers—will all be thinking about only one thing . . . eternity. Can we really think that we can plan the future of our nation—of our world—without considering it as well? While democracy may have been invented in

Greece, it was not until Bible-quoting, God-fearing people joined together to form a United States of America that it rose to the ideal we know today. Our system may not be perfect, but it is the best our world has seen yet, and that is because it was a system defined by moral clarity and based on the principles of the Bible.

Dr. Martin Luther King Jr. said, "Nothing in the world is more dangerous than sincere ignorance and conscientious stupidity."[9] America stepped into the twenty-first century with a terminal case of both.

America is in this position primarily because we are the only nation today in alliance with both the historical brothers of prophecy—Ishmael and Isaac. The Bible begins and ends with the struggle between these two sons of Abraham. Today, their descendants are still in a Cain-and-Abel struggle for dominion, and America has stepped right into the middle of it.

The ancient Scriptures of the Bible have a great deal to say about the two spirits behind these brothers who are fighting it out through the nations of the earth. Ishmael was not the son of promise, but the son of a man trying to work the will of God in his own way. God had promised Abraham a son, but his wife, Sarah, was barren. At her request, Abraham took Hagar, her maidservant, and impregnated her. The result was the son Ishmael. Though a man of faith, Abraham acted in his own wisdom and lust, not God's direction—he justified a foolish action through moral relativism, tradition, and human reasoning, trying to get God's blessing on his own terms. It was not until some years later when the son of promise, Isaac, was born that Abraham fully realized the gravity of his mistake. Rejecting the "son of human reasoning," God blessed and cut covenant with the "son of faith." Ishmael went on to be the father of the Arab race, and Isaac a patriarch of the Hebrews. However, the battle continues, for the Qur'an teaches that Ishmael, not Isaac, was Abraham's son of promise, and that he inherited the land and the title deed to Jerusalem.

Today, America is caught in the same battle. Some want to try to "do good" without God, making our halls of government secular, amoral, and irreligious. Instead, we are making them immoral and blind. Instead of looking to God for blessings and prosperity, we are looking to our own reasoning and logic. For this reason, we are willing to trade almost anything to get the black gold—oil—that keeps our economy lubricated and running smoothly. Moral Americans are called bigots; yet, on the other hand, real bigotry is overlooked in other areas to keep America's economy "flowing with blessings."

America knows that Ishmael, the older brother in this struggle, believes the lies Hitler used to twist the minds of the Germans: that the Jews are the reason for the ills of the world and of the Arabs in particular, and if they are simply gotten rid of, the whole world will sleep easier. Yet, America does nothing to counteract this vile doctrine. Instead, we reward those who preach the same things by calling them "diplomats"—terrorist organizations such as the PLO and terrorist states such as Syria, Iran, and Saudi Arabia—and through "negotiations" force the other brother, Isaac, to make more concessions to an implacably angry Ishmael. However, Ishmael will never be appeased with a Palestinian state; that is only a hoped-for first step. While al Qaeda may wave the Palestinian flag as they cry, "Death to Americans," we cannot believe that they will suddenly start to love us if Palestine becomes a state, any more than Hitler allied with the rest of Europe when Chamberlain and others allowed him to annex the Sudetenland.

Dr. Yossef Bodansky and I spent considerable time in Jerusalem discussing this matter. In his book *The High Cost of Peace,* he states that the Palestinians' "step-by-step" plans to retake Palestine actually came from the experience of the Vietnamese in dealing with the U.S.:

> Abu-Iyad detailed how he brought up the question of why the Palestinian armed struggle was considered terrorism whereas the Vietnamese struggle was lauded and supported throughout the West. His host attributed this phenomenon to the different ways the two liberation movements had packaged their goals. The Vietnamese team agreed to sit with the PLO delegation and help them develop a program that would appear flexible and moderate, especially in dealing with the United States, the Vietnamese explained, one

must "sacrifice the unimportant if only in order to preserve the essential."[10]

They emphasized that the PLO must remain committed to its ultimate objective—namely, "the establishment of a unified democratic state in the entire Palestine"—in the near term, it would be politically advantageous to accept transient phases and even interim solutions. The Vietnamese suggested accepting "the division of the land between two independent states," without making it clear that this was only an interim phase.

The Hanoi team also introduced the Palestinians to such issues as dealing with the U.S. media and with liberal political circles and institutions, and they provided insight on the power of the Jewish community. Disinformation and psychological warfare experts assisted the Palestinians in formulating a "moderate political program accepting the establishment of a small Palestine" in the territories. The result was the "Phase Plan" adopted as the resolution of the twelfth Palestinian National Council in Cairo on June 19, 1974.

We can never win the war on terrorism by appeasing terrorists on one hand and trying to root them out with the other. This is a sure guarantee for another September 11—or worse. We will never be able to turn this tide without getting to the root of the terrorists' hatred for Israel and for us, and exposing it at its source.

Why must the teaching of jihad be outlawed in America? Islamic fundamentalists use religion to recruit *shahids*—martyrs who are willing to kill themselves for the "cause." When Yasser Arafat delivers his speeches calling for one million shahids to liberate Jerusalem, he is not simply humoring the crowds. Jerusalem has experienced more terrorist attacks than any city in the world. When Islamic fundamentalist clerics call for shahids in the mosques, it is not just religious jargon. Islamic fundamentalism is a religion that kills.

It's not only critical that we understand why these people hate us, it is absolutely vital that we understand why they act on that hatred. The shahids believe they are performing a holy ritual for Allah. From childhood, Muslims are taught that to be a shahid, one must be chosen by

Allah. It is the greatest honor in life. Shahids are taught that a martyr does not have a funeral, but rather a wedding. This is the reason families do not hold funerals when a child commits an act of martyrdom. Instead, a wedding celebration is held.

The prospective shahid is told that when the holy and religious act is performed:

- He will feel no pain or fear. In essence, the sting of death is removed.

- He will not die. All souls go into the ground awaiting resurrection except the souls of the shahid. They go directly to paradise; his own personal and immediate resurrection.

- He will be honored when he arrives in paradise with a crown of glory that has a jewel of the wealth of the world set in the center of it. (In Christianity, the crown is placed on the head of Jesus, and the saints lay their crowns at His feet.)

- He will attend his own wedding with seventy-two black-eyed virgins. The word "black-eyed" does not denote eye color; it denotes that they are incorruptible—an interesting word. (It is the same word in the Scripture used by Bill Clinton when he was sworn into office.) This belief is so strong that before the act of martyrdom, the shahid shaves all pubic hair and tapes his private parts. This is symbolic of what is to come.

- He will pave the way for seventy relatives to go to paradise and be exempt from the horrors of hell. In essence, the blood of the shahid atones for sin. It certainly would make for a horrible childhood to have all of your relatives lobbying for a spot on your "paradise list."

The insane aspect of this is that this diabolical battle for the minds of the children begins in kindergarten. Cartoon characters similar to our Mickey Mouse or Donald Duck are used with a message incorporated to seduce and recruit these small children as shahids. Kindergarten camps are used to teach the principles of jihad. Bridges, roads, parks, and buildings are named after the martyrs, and posters of their photos are everywhere. (Thousands upon thousands of children were used to clear the minefields during the Iran-Iraq war. "Keys to heaven" were placed around their necks and a martyr's badge was pinned to their clothing.)

The war on terrorism that we have today is fueled by Stone Age hatred—the same hatred Cain had for Abel, Ishmael had for Isaac, and Satan had for Jesus. Terrorists wage a spiritual war of fear and bigotry beyond what we understand—such a war cannot be won with tactical weaponry alone.

The holy grail of understanding is this: Islamic fundamentalists are the reason for September 11 and the terrorism war that America is fighting. Their ideology is as lethal as fascism or Nazism. As long as godless liberals attempt to dumb-down God-fearing Americans with a "don't ask, don't tell" policy on bigotry, the war on terrorism will not only survive, but thrive. In order to win this war, America must speak out on bigotry the same way Abraham Lincoln and Martin Luther King Jr. did.

I've already stated my thesis that America has married these two brothers; Ishmael (the Arab nations) out of convenience and Isaac (Israel) out of guilt. America knows that the older brother, Ishmael, believes the lies Hitler used to twist the Germans' minds against the Jews. *Yet America does nothing to counteract this vile doctrine.* Instead, in order to appease one ally, our other ally—the only true pro-Western democracy in the Middle East—was denied a place in the coalition forces during two wars in Iraq. Instead, America aligned itself with Islamic terrorist-funding regimes. And America is arming Islamic terrorist-harboring states whose citizens have been baptized in bigotry. This is a sure guarantee for another September 11—or worse. Bigotry is an equal opportunity employer; bigots will kill Christians with the same justifications they use to kill Jews. Someone needs to scream out, "It's about racism, stupid."

The war on terrorism we are waging today is part of the struggle between these two brothers. Terrorists wage a spiritual war of fear and hatred—such a war cannot be won with tactical weaponry alone. There has never been a more urgent time for Americans to act with moral clarity than today, yet there has also never been a time in which we have seemed more duplicitous. The future of our nation, as well as our world, hangs in the balance between our action and our apathy.

The Final Battle

Though William Butler Yeats was not a Christian prophet, his poem, which I placed at the front of this book, expresses the tensions of our times. We have rejected the foundation of our culture that has traditionally held us together—God and the Holy Scriptures—and as our culture drifts away from that center, we—the falcon—no longer hear His voice. As a nation our innocence is being drowned. Things are falling apart. In our halls of justice, in our pulpits, and in the political arenas, those who would speak for God not only lack the conviction to be effective, they are being systematically silenced because of a perverted interpretation of "separation of church and state." First Amendment rights are denied to those who would speak for God, while those who fight for self, special interest, and immorality are passionately intense as the *Spiritus Mundi*—the "spirit of the world"—takes over. Since Yeats wrote this poem, in fact, we have witnessed this spirit's being more active in our world than ever before through the "isms" of fascism, Nazism, communism, and terrorism—the greatest threats to human liberty we have ever faced.

The final battle in prophecy will take place in Israel. It is a battle line drawn through the heart of the city of Jerusalem, whose disposition has repeatedly thwarted peace efforts in the Middle East. Palestinians have been offered their own state time and again—first in 1947 by the United Nations, then in 1991 at the Madrid Conference after the Gulf War, then at the Wye River talks, and then again in a desperate President Bill Clinton's final days in office. But the major stumbling block on the way to peace has always been the control of East Jerusalem, the historic City of David where the Temple Mount rests—the very spot where heaven and earth met, and will meet again, and where the most dangerous prophecies concerning the nations of the world are written in the stones. It all begins with, "But now I have chosen Jerusalem for my Name to be there, and I have chosen David to rule my people Israel."[11]

As the twenty-first century has dawned, no nation stands as prominently between these two brothers, Isaac and Ishmael, as the United States of America. Since Israel's declaration of statehood on May 14, 1948, when the U.S. was the first nation to recognize its existence, to Israel's defense in the Yom Kippur War of 1973, and the defense aid we have given ever since, no nation has stood by Israel as we have. On the other hand, since 1945, when President Franklin Delano Roosevelt met with Hitler-supporting King ibn Saud of Saudi Arabia and promised that no U.S. decision regarding the Middle East would be made without first consulting the Arabs, neither has any nation been more closely linked to the Muslim nations in that region. I wonder if his death within weeks of making this decision was simply a coincidence.

Our influence on both sides goes much farther back. What these relationships have done is to make the United States the only nation that is the honest/dishonest broker trusted by both Ishmael and Isaac to barter peace between them. *And this has placed America squarely in the eye of the storm of biblical prophecy.*

America is thus caught in a tug-of-war between these two brothers—between oil, political expedience, and conscience in many ways—and it is our decisions and policies concerning these two brothers that will determine whether the United States will survive or go the way of the Roman Empire. Only the "People of the Book"—and I mean the Bible, not the Qur'an—can tip the scales in the right direction.

However, America remains complacent about such issues, even though we have already had many warnings. In the last century, we have seen three dress rehearsals for Armageddon: World War I, World War II, and the Cold War. For several decades we fought the "isms" of fascism, Nazism, and communism, and now we are the fighting the "ism" of terrorism. The issues surrounding it are rapidly delineating the sides in this battle, just as these earlier "isms" delineated the sides of World War II and the Cold War. *Yet we have totally missed the fact that the spirit that drove Hitler and Stalin is the same spirit that is driving terrorism today*—although you won't hear anyone else talking about it. It is the spirit of hatred, which always begins in the same way: It first starts by hating Jews (anti-Semitism) and then moves on to hating Christians.

Today, we see the same hatred in the extreme Islamic fundamentalists who carry out horrific acts of terror. In fact, if you read some of the Islamic papers today, they are eerily reminiscent of newspapers from the early years of Nazi Germany. Hitler's gospel is back. It started with killing Jews, and spread to the killing of Christians (between the Nazis and the Soviets, roughly six million Christians were martyred during World War II, though not in death camps as the Jews were murdered).[12]

America can ill afford to continue to ignore the first sign that another world war could soon be upon us: the increase of rabid anti-Semitism in the Arab world that is now returning to Europe. Do you believe there is no way America can be destroyed by terrorists because it is too mighty a nation? Then let me ask you a simple question: If America were to experience the equivalent number of suicide attacks in our malls, movie theaters, restaurants, and even churches and synagogues that Israel experiences per capita—and that would mean hundreds of attacks a week in our nation—would it not be better to declare all-out war on bigotry now, before bigotry declares all-out war on our cities?

The Arab leaders are at the tip of a pyramid whose base rests on the bloodlust of millions of fanatics, sympathizers, and potential terrorists who lionize the bin Ladens of the world. As Yale professor David Gelernter wrote in the *Wall Street Journal*:

> Terrorists evidently control large segments of Arab opinion the way the Nazis once controlled Germany—by swagger and lies, by dispensing a dangerous hallucinogenic ideology for the masses, and by murdering opponents.[13]

Why is the U.S. turning a blind eye to, and even funding, anti-Semitic, terrorist-harboring regimes? Have we learned nothing from September 11? Have we forgotten the mobs screaming "Death to Israel" and "Death to America"? The goal of an Arab conquest of Israel is another Holocaust. As for America, Islamic extremists hate everything about us; but their greatest hatred is our Christian majority and biblical principles by which we live our lives—our emancipation of women, our freedom, our wealth, our power, and our culture. They want to kill Americans because of all we represent in their oppressed and twisted minds.

Questions for America

While researching this book in both America and the Middle East, I experienced some eye-opening revelations about America's role in prophecy—past, present, and future. Below are some of the questions I have had answered while researching and writing this book:

- Why does America continue to feed and fuel Islamic regimes that are more racist than the KKK and whose population is taught terrorist-breeding ideologies?
- Why is America afraid to arrest a terrorist-murderer who has killed dozens of Americans, including American diplomats, a terrorist who keeps on his desk one of Hitler's best-loved books, *The Protocols of the Elders of Zion*, and quotes from it with pride?
- Why has America not allowed Israel to fight a real war against terrorism, such as we have done in Afghanistan and Iraq?
- Why did the State Department keep FBI agents from arresting three terrorists who were part of a Saudi entourage on its way to meet with President Bush in Crawford, Texas, seven and a half months after the attacks of September 11?
- Why did both President Clinton and President Bush disregard a report from the United States Commission on National Security that stated: "Americans will likely die on American soil, possibly in large numbers," which they both received well in advance of the September 11 attacks?
- Why is no one talking about the missing suitcase nuclear bombs from the former U.S.S.R., or the weapons of mass destruction Saddam moved out of Iraq through Syria before Operation Iraqi

Freedom? Who has them, and what are they planning to do with them?

- Why did the nations of the world call for a 2001 conference on racism and work themselves into a rage against the Jews? Why was America attacked just seven days after the United States and Israel walked out of this conference in protest?

- Why is Hitler's *Mein Kampf* a best-selling book throughout the Muslim world more than fifty years after Hitler's death? And why is it used as a textbook in Muslim schools in the Middle East?

- Why did Hitler want the Jews out of Germany, and why did America do everything in its power to keep them there until six million perished?

- Why did the rest of the world also close their doors to the Jews when they most needed help on the eve of the Holocaust?

- Why did Franklin Delano Roosevelt refuse to recognize what was happening in the death camps until it was too late? Why, even after he had publicly condemned these mass executions, did Roosevelt refuse to bomb the gas chambers in Auschwitz, when Allied planes were flying routine missions near them nearly every day in the last months of the war?

- Why did a pair of brothers who aided the Nazis through the end of World War II later become secretary of state and director of the CIA under President Eisenhower?

- Why did a terrorist kill a presidential candidate two weeks after the assassination of Martin Luther King Jr., on the anniversary of the Six-Day War? Why did another terrorist take two American diplomats hostage, and eventually kill them, because a U.S. president would not release that assassin? Why, instead of being arrested, was that second terrorist later elevated to diplomatic status, invited repeatedly to the White House, and awarded the Nobel Peace Prize?

- Why did we fund, arm, and train terrorists who shot down our own helicopters in Mogadishu?

- Why is America promising a terrorist regime half of Jerusalem, when prophecy pronounces a curse on those who divide this city?

- Why is America spending billions of dollars to rebuild ancient Babylon, when 62 percent of the population are Shi'ites who would guarantee another Iran in time? The scriptures pronounce an end-time curse upon ancient Babylon more than upon any country in the world. Is America blessing what God has cursed?

Our nation's fate will be determined in a final test. Will America's first war of the twenty-first century, the conflict in Iraq, continue until it terminates in the most climactic prophetic event in history? This brings to mind an unnerving question: *Will America choose God's side of the prophetic battle, or will it fight God? If America chooses the latter, it will end up on the ash heap of history.*

I believe that we can never win against such apocalyptic hatred without first dealing with, and changing for the better, four key issues:

1. **America is willfully ignoring the virus that is the growing plague of the Middle East**—Jew-hatred (anti-Semitism such as the world saw in the 1930s)—coupled with Adolf Hitler's teaching that the Jews rule the world (as evidenced by such things as the World Muslim Conference in Malaysia during October 2003). Because of this, America is pouring billions of dollars worth of war weaponry into Jew-hating Arab regimes that are using these Hitlerian myths about the Jews to recruit a new generation of suicide terrorists to strike their greatest enemies—Israel and the United States.

2. **September 11 would never have happened if America had fought the same bigotry in the 1990s rather than trying to appease it.** Millions of Jews would be living today if anti-Semitism had not been ignored in the 1920s and 1930s. The Great Depression, as well as other American tragedies, happened because of America's pride and challenge to God Almighty's plan.

3. **The war on terrorism has been fueled by America's support for Islamic terrorists in Israel.** The Arab world also feeds it to save their "thug-ocracies." They never wanted to take care of their own

as the rest of the world has done concerning refugees. It has in-fected Osama and in fact the entire world (as evidenced by the 2001 Durban Anti-Racism Conference, which blamed all the world's problems on Israel and no other nation). If that support continues, the war on terror cannot be won.

4. **America is under a biblical curse that can be reversed. Jerusalem is the final compromise.** If America divides Jerusalem, there will be no forgiveness. America will tragically end up on the ash heap of history.

America has been weighed in the balance and found wanting. The graveyard of history testifies that God rejects nations that reject Him and His Word. Is God getting ready to reject us once and for all? Or, will God-fearing Americans stand in the gap and turn America around by standing for, and speaking, the truth? The following words are etched into the wall in the main lobby of the original CIA headquarters build-ing to characterize the intelligence mission of a free society: "And ye shall know the Truth and the Truth shall make you free" (see John 8:32).

I now believe that we are very close to the coming of Christ, and that not only is America in prophecy, but the tragic events of September 11 are, as well. I believe that America was attacked because of its unholy covenant with the descendants of the oldest son of Abraham, Ish-mael—the Arab nations, specifically the nations led by or heavily in-fluenced by Islamic fundamentalist populations. These regimes are, in great numbers, intolerant, barbaric bigots still living in the Dark Ages, and they are completely dedicated to the destruction of Israel, Amer-ica's other covenant partner.

America's fate will be determined in a final test. It is time to REPENT!

Everyone speaking on the subject of what we face today gives us the sense that events are accelerating toward some unknown outcome. "September 11 was a wake-up call from hell that has opened our eyes to the horrors that await us tomorrow if we fail to act today," said Binyamin Netanyahu, then prime minister of Israel, speaking before the U.S. House of Representatives Government Reform Committee on September 20, 2001.[14]

CHAPTER TWO

America and the Fig Tree

Nothing equals the misery and suffering of the Jews who are the constant objects of Muslim oppression and intolerance.

Karl Marx
New York Daily Tribune
April 18, 1854

For this is what the LORD Almighty says: "After he has honored me and has sent me against the nations that have plundered you—for whoever touches you touches the apple of his eye."

Zechariah 2:8 NIV

The river of prophecy is filled with rapids, obstacles, eddies, and undercurrents. It often has more to do with milestones we will see along the way than it does with the details of how something foretold comes about. Events tend to collide and conflict in the currents as prophecy moves toward fulfillment, sometimes seeming to move ahead briskly, other times coming to a stagnant halt, flowing backward for a time as its energy builds, or even disappearing from sight only to reemerge farther downstream. This often makes finding ourselves at any one point in the river rather confusing—it is easy to get lost if you look only at the currents; you can't tell what progress you have made downstream unless you gauge your progress in relation to the bank. This is why God gave us mile markers along that river to let us know what to watch for next. Thus if we look at where we have come from—noting how we arrived at the markers we have already passed—it can be easier to see how to handle the rapids and undertows on the way to the next marker. By understanding the flow of prophecy of the last few centuries, and seeing how those events relate to the pattern of events happening today, we can begin to clearly see what Bible prophecy holds for America.

America is here today in full strength and regarded as a world leader—as such it is present in the events that will shape the world during the end times. The keys to America's future are not buried in bureaucratic babble, but in understanding the Word of God and what God is doing and saying as He awaits the final battle that will put evil away for a thousand years.

Many look at prophecy and think that because certain things are ordained to come to pass, it gives them reason to sit back and wait. I disagree. As in the days of Noah, too many continue to eat and drink, marry and give in marriage, and yet disaster—or deliverance—is at the door. Which one will be allowed to enter is clearly up to us.

While many may think that the fulfillment of biblical prophecy is a sovereign act of God, the Scriptures themselves indicate that we can choose to be on the blessing or cursing side of prophecy. When God was about to destroy Sodom and Gomorrah, He said to Himself, "Shall I hide from Abraham that thing which I do?"[1] God felt He should take no action of judgment without giving His friend Abraham the right to intercede on the people's behalf.

As Daniel was reading in the book of Jeremiah one day in his old age, he came across a Scripture that said, "After seventy years be accomplished at Babylon I will visit you, and perform my good word toward you, in causing you to return to this place."[2] Daniel did some quick counting—more than seventy years had already passed, and Israel was still in captivity under Babylon! So he set himself to praying God's promise back to Him. Thus was the heart of Babylonian King Cyrus turned, and Nehemiah was given permission to rebuild Jerusalem and the temple.

As Jesus Himself said:

> You are my friends if you do what I command. I no longer call you servants, because a servant *does not know* his master's business. Instead, I have called you friends, *for everything that I learned from my Father I have made known to you.* (John 15:14–15 NIV, emphasis added)

As Jesus' friends, we should know what He's planning concerning the events for our nation. We should be involved with praying them through. As it was with Daniel, God needs someone to agree with Him, pray His promises into reality, and carry out His plan on the earth.

In the parable of the fig tree (Matthew 24:32–44), Jesus told His disciples that when we begin to see the events He foretold earlier in Matthew 24, they would be indications of the "season" of the end of this age—just as new leaves on the fig tree would indicate that summer was coming—and that the generation that saw these things would also see end-time prophecy fulfilled. Look for a moment at what Jesus said would mark the final age and His return:

• Many would come in His name setting themselves up as Christ and establishing their own religions (Matthew 24:5, 11).

The twentieth century witnessed a dramatic decline in membership in the mainline Protestant denominations. Not only has there been a decline in church membership and attendance, the last few decades have seen a departure from the historic faith. American studies show that between two and five million young adults between the ages of eighteen and twenty-five are involved in approximately two thousand to five thousand cult groups today.[3]

Many churches and entire denominations have abandoned biblical truth wholesale. The most recent example is the ordination of an openly gay bishop in the Episcopal Church, a controversial move that threatens the unity of the entire denomination. I have no doubt that Rev. Gene Robinson of New Hampshire is sincerely committed to his faith and wants to help the people of his diocese. The problem is that he is living a lifestyle that directly contradicts the clear teaching of Scripture. God does not hate gays—far from it—but He does not want practicing homosexuals *mis*-leading His church.

This is not a new problem, by the way. The church at Corinth had homosexuals, adulterers, and drunkards. The difference is that they had all given up their former lifestyles when they accepted Christ as their Savior.

> Do you not know that the unrighteous will not inherit the kingdom of God? Do not be deceived. Neither fornicators, nor idolaters, nor adulterers, nor homosexuals, nor sodomites, nor thieves, nor covetous, nor drunkards, nor revilers, nor extortioners will inherit the kingdom of God. *And such were some of you.* But you were washed, but you were sanctified, but you were justified in the name of the LORD Jesus and by the Spirit of our God. (1 Corinthians 6:9–11 NKJV, emphasis added)

- There would be wars and rumors of wars; and nations will rise up against nations (Matthew 24:6–7).

  All we need to do is turn on any 24-hour news channel to hear of these wars and their rumors. How long have 24-hour news channels been around? The first, CNN, began broadcasting in 1981. Now, terrorist strikes and the ongoing battle on terrorism are reported daily.
- There will be famines, epidemic diseases, and earthquakes all over the world (Matthew 24:7).

  An entire continent, Africa, is suffering from drought, war, poverty, and plagues.

  Despite longer life expectancy, new diseases such as AIDS and other sexually transmitted diseases are devastating nations. Viruses such as the West Nile and SARS have thrown many into panic. We have more knowledge than ever before about disease and better technology and techniques, yet at the same time we also face epidemic increases in cardiovascular disease, diabetes, and Alzheimer's disease.

Since 1900, the world has experienced more than a hundred different earthquakes where a thousand or more were killed, and of the twenty-one earthquakes in the history of the world where more than 50,000 were killed, more than half of them have taken place in the last century.[4] In December 2003 an earthquake hit Iran that killed as many as 30,000, injured another 30,000, and left more than 100,000 homeless. On the same day, several other earthquakes above 5.0 on the Richter scale hit in the world's "ring of fire," all reported to be unrelated.

- Persecution shall increase (Matthew 24:8–10).

More than 65 percent of the nearly 69.5 million Christians who have died for their faith, died in the twentieth century. Today, an average of 435 Christians die for their faith *every day*.[5]

- Sin shall flourish and Christian love will grow cold (Matthew 24:12).

I have seen this prophesied "falling away" in my lifetime, and it is rapidly increasing. There is a modern disconnect between personal spirituality and the traditional church or synagogue. Polls consistently show that more than 90 percent of Americans profess a belief in God, and more than 60 percent say that religion is very important to their own lives; yet only 43 percent attend church or synagogue on a regular basis.[6]

Liberals have used "freedom of speech" to legalize every form of perversity. What used to be unseen and spurned is taking to the streets and growing. At the same time, Christians in the U.S. seem less and less sure of themselves, and the culture has turned against God. Christian expression is being increasingly limited in our schools and society.

Meanwhile, our pews are filled with people who are biblically illiterate. Why? Because churches have abandoned Christian education in favor of a feel-good faith! We pay more attention to the music we sing than the gospel we preach. We attempt to gently introduce sinners into the church environment. Don't get me wrong. I'm all for reaching out to those who don't know the Lord—it's our Great Commission—but there is a fine line between building a bridge to the lost and compromising biblical truth. Our marching orders are to go into the world and "make disciples . . . baptizing them . . . teaching them to observe all things"[7] that God commanded. The goal is not converts; it is disciples. And making disciples requires more than a "don't-worry-be-happy" gospel. It requires faithful preaching of all of Scripture, including the parts that are difficult to hear and that convict our hearts.

- But there shall also be an honored remnant of believers who will not grow cold, but will become more diligent, and they will see that the gospel of God's kingdom will be preached in every nation (Matthew 24:13–14).

While there are other signs of the end times foretold in the Bible, I think these are enough to make us see that the season Jesus spoke of is upon us. While we don't know the day or the hour, the leaves of the fig tree definitely are sprouting and flourishing. It is time that we understood the significance of today's events and our nation's precarious position between the two sons of Abraham, so that we know what to do in the days to come.

In order to do that, we must first know the milestones for which to watch. According to Bible prophecy as it has been interpreted by those who have dedicated much of their lives to studying and understanding it, here are the most significant biblical prophecies, past and present, with respect to the salvation of God's people:

- Jesus' first coming (Isaiah 53; Psalms 41:9; 55:12–14; Zechariah 9:9; 13:7).
- Jesus' death on the cross and resurrection (Jeremiah 31:15; Psalm 22).
- Jesus' ascension to the right hand of the Father and the gift of the Holy Spirit to the church (John 20:17).

- The destruction of the temple and Jerusalem (Matthew 24:1–2).
- The scattering of the Jews to the nations of the earth (the Diaspora) (Genesis 49:7; Leviticus 26:33; Nehemiah 1:8).
- The reestablishment of the nation of Israel (Isaiah 11:1; 35:10; Jeremiah 31:10).
- The Rapture (1 Corinthians 15:51–52; 1 Thessalonians 4:16; Luke 17:34).
- The Antichrist's seven-year peace pact with Israel (marking the beginning of the Tribulation) (Daniel 9:27).
- Gog and Magog (most commonly seen as representing Russia or a coalition of forces led by Russia or perhaps some of its former Soviet Republics) attack Israel, but are thwarted by a supernatural intervention of God (Revelation 20:8).
- The rebuilding of the temple (Ezekiel 43:2–5; 44:4; Acts 15:13–17).
- The temple's desecration by the Antichrist (marking the beginning of the three and a half years of Great Tribulation) (Daniel 9:27).
- The Battle of Armageddon (Revelation 18).
- Jesus' second coming (1 Thessalonians 4:16–17; Acts 1:11; Matthew 24:30; 1 Peter 1:7; 4:13).
- The Millennium (Revelation 20:1–5).
- Satan again loosed for a season (Revelation 20:6–10).
- The Great White Throne Judgment (Revelation 20:11–15).
- Eternity.

In looking at these prophetic mile markers, there are a couple of keys to notice—namely where we are in this series of events today, and when and how they have occurred. One is that, since the destruction of the temple and Jerusalem by the Romans in AD 70, the single most significant event of prophecy was the reestablishment of the nation of Israel on May 14, 1948.

A second thing to notice is that America's future is on the doorstep of one of the next two events: (1) The blessed hope, the Rapture, followed by (2) the cursed hell of the Tribulation. If we are reading the signs of the time correctly, these events are even likely to happen soon, possibly within our generation. Though we have been told this to the point where its urgency is lost for many of us, it is nevertheless true if we are reading these Scriptures correctly. Since Jesus said, "When you see all these things, know that it is near—at the doors! . . . This generation will by no means pass away till all these things take place,"[8] it seems very likely that the events we are currently seeing in the Middle East are setting the stage for what will happen in the world during the Tribulation.

Another thing to notice is that there are two currents of salvation flowing in the river of prophecy—one according to the Old Testament and one according to the New, because there are two currents that represent God's people—Jews and Christians; Israel and the church. As these two currents often flow together and intermingle, many have made the mistake of thinking that there is only one, but with respect to the prophecies of final events, the differences between them become enormous. Certainly they are one in the end and in heaven, but, until that point, God still has an obligation to deal uniquely and differently with the people of Isaac because of His covenant with Abraham. Though the new covenant supersedes and fulfills the old, it has not voided it.

This is why there are so many things on this list that apply uniquely to Israel. This makes sense as once those who know the Lord are gone in the Rapture, the rest of the salvation for the world's population centers on the Jews. This is also visible in the fact that the spirit of antichrist that has been so active in the last century is also, not surprisingly, rabidly anti-Semitic. While the twentieth century was the greatest period of Christian persecution in the history of the world, it was also the time of the Holocaust and czarist and Soviet pogroms designed to rid Russia of the Jews. Today, the greatest persecution of Christians happens in fundamentalist Muslim countries under *shari'a* law (the religious criminal code set forth by the Qur'an), whose news media are also filled with disdain for the Jews. These are the white-hot ember beds that keep the fire of anti-Semitism and terrorism ablaze. This spirit of antichrist, which will one day possess what John called the Antichrist, has also been behind the greatest threats to freedom we have seen in the last century: fascism, Nazism, communism, and now Wahhabism—the form of fundamentalist Islam that is fueling terrorist rage. If we read trends correctly, it is also the spirit behind much of liberalism's secular relativism that is trying to silence God's voice in America today. Though this spirit has also infected blocks of the church from time to time, and turned it toward apostasy (as it seems to also be doing today) and anti-Semitism (as it has often done in the past), we should not be confused by this seeming crossover. The true church will always be the one following the Spirit of Christ, exhibiting His true fruit and gifts, not those who have turned to political correctness rather than the love of God to rule them.

While America is clearly in this river of prophecy, it is clear to see that nations such as Jordan (represented by the ancient peoples and lands of Ammon, Moab, and Edom), Egypt, Iran (biblical Persia), Iraq (biblical Babylonia), the EU (the reunited "ten toes" of the Roman Empire), Russia (Rosh), and Saudi Arabia (Sheba and Dedan), among others, also are specifically mentioned in the Bible. Some have also proposed that America is in prophecy disguised as the "tall and smooth-skinned" people who are "feared far and wide, an aggressive nation of strange speech, whose land is divided by rivers"[9] or as a young lion of Tarshish,[10] the "two wings of the great eagle,"[11] or even the spiritual Babylon of the end times. In fact, highly respected evangelical leaders such as Rev. David Wilkerson, pastor of Times Square Church in New York City, believe that America is the Babylonia of Revelation 18, with New York City the spiritual city of Babylon. Look for a moment at how he describes the nation that will be spiritual Babylon:

1. It is a nation of immigrants (Revelation 18:15).
2. It is a cultural city (Revelation 18:22).
3. It has a deep water port (Revelation 18:17–19).
4. It has the wealth of the world (Revelation 18:15–19; Jeremiah 51:13).
5. It is the last superpower on the earth (Babylon the Great) (Revelation 17:5).
6. The world's leaders will assemble there (Jeremiah 51:44).

7. It will be a world policeman (Jeremiah 50:23).
8. A military of land and airpower and a land of air travel (Isaiah 18:1).
9. It would seem to be connected to outer space (Jeremiah 51:53).
10. Would have some amazing stealth-type technology (Isaiah 47:10–13).[12]

However, while this may be a possibility, I believe America may presently have another course. As the Bible says, "Blessed is the nation whose God is the LORD,"[13] and "Righteousness exalts a nation, but sin is a disgrace."[14] Our politics and the course of our nation are a result of what is in our hearts—they do not determine what is in our hearts. If God is to truly heal our land, it is not just a question of correct foreign and domestic policy, but also an issue of the church of the United States kicking relativism out and earnestly seeking God and His ways above all else. Our battle is not a conflict between Christian and secular *culture*, but between good and evil, between the Spirit of Christ and the spirit of antichrist, between revealing Jesus to our world and being satisfied with complacency and lukewarm spirituality. America's roots were firmly established in the moral clarity of the Bible and prayer. If we call on our God to heal our land, America might well be aligned with Israel and aid in its revival in the end times, not swallowed up in the spirit of the world that will put us on the wrong side of the Battle of Armageddon.

While the rapture of the church may not happen tomorrow, the Bible admonishes us to "occupy till I come" (Luke 19:13). There are things we can do to have peace in our time, win the war on terrorism, and continue to maintain moral clarity in our dealings with Ishmael, while refusing to compromise principles for petroleum. With the help of God, we can accomplish what no other nation on earth could even hope to do, but we can't do that without a major course correction. It is time to realign our moral compass to its proper headings. The church needs to be an eternal purpose-driven body of believers, determined to preach the truth from the pulpits in America, determined to be salt and light to a dark and hopeless world.

We stand as Nineveh did at the message of Jonah—we have the choice to either continue as we have and leave God behind, or we can repent and experience revival. We are at a crossroads, but more significant even than that, we are in the crosshairs of those who hate Christians and Jews and all that the nations of the United States and Israel stand for. To these we must respond both spiritually and naturally—with Christian love and compassion, and with political wisdom based on clarity of vision and moral integrity. It is a worthy calling, far more powerful than the call to martyrdom of the suicide bombers. Yet until we live with greater conviction than they die with, our generation will see nothing of what God wants to do in it.

Had the church obeyed the Great Commission to be a witness unto Him in Jerusalem, Judea and Samaria, Islamic fundamentalists such as Hamas would not have been able to corrupt the minds of the children with hatred for Jews and Christians. Instead, they would be Christians, filled with love. The truth is: Palestinian Christians do not blow up Jews. Revival would be spreading across the Middle East, and the events of September 11 may never have happened.

Did the church fail this nation, and our Lord? Is the church guiltier in the eyes of God than Bill Clinton? Is it too late? No, it's not too late; but if ever the church of Jesus Christ plans to repent and obey the Great Commission, rather than continuing to pursue the "Great Omission," now is the time!

I pray that pastors will begin to preach on the second coming of the Lord. The Bible tells us that we are to "live soberly, righteously, and godly, in this present world, looking for that blessed hope, and the glorious appearing of the great God and our Savior Jesus Christ" (Titus 2:12–13). There never was a time in history when God dwelt in a church with an earthly perspective. It is time to proclaim this message. Why? The world has taken over the church. Abortions, divorces, pornography, drugs, alcohol, and even homosexuality are alive and well in the church. Many pastors allow fear of retaliation to keep them from preaching against these matters.

As a minister of the gospel, God has placed one message on my heart to preach in this hour: Jesus is coming! The Bible says, "I know your deeds, that you are neither cold nor hot. I wish you were either one or the other! So, because you are lukewarm—neither hot nor cold—I am about to spit you out of my mouth" (Revelation 3:15–16 NIV).

The Shepherd is calling for spiritual warriors—will we answer His call? If so, we need to understand the currents of American prophecy from our beginnings so that we know how to navigate the waters that lie ahead of us.

CHAPTER THREE

A Christian Nation

We have no government armed with power capable of contending with human passions unbridled by morality and religion. Avarice, ambition, revenge, or gallantry, would break the strongest cords of our Constitution as a whale goes through a net. Our Constitution was made only for a moral and religious people. It is wholly inadequate for the government of any other.

John Adams[1]

Where the Spirit of the LORD is, there is liberty.

2 Corinthians 3:17

From the charters drafted by the Pilgrims who first colonized what would one day become the United States of America, our forefathers purposed in their hearts to be a force for good on the earth as defined by the Bible and its prophecies. As stated in the Declaration of Independence, they believed these truths to be "self-evident, that all Men are created equal, that they are endowed by their Creator with certain unalienable Rights, that among these are Life, Liberty and the Pursuit of Happiness." Thomas Jefferson, one of the writers of that Declaration, further said: "Can the liberties of a nation be secure when we have removed a conviction that these liberties are the gift of God? That they are not to be violated but with his wrath?"[2] From this first declaration and by invoking the blessings of God in its foundations, the United States of America placed itself in the hands of God for its existence and its future.

Bible prophecy begins and ends with the nation of Israel. By founding itself and its values on these same Scriptures, America stepped into an alliance with God's chosen people. This decision would eventually lead America to be a key player in bringing about the most significant prophetic event in nearly two millennia—the rebirth of the nation of Israel.

Though some scholars seem to debate whether or not the United States was founded as a Christian nation, it is difficult to look at the writings of our founding fathers and not hear their faith. There are many books that do a better job of proving this than I can in the limited space I have here, but let's suffice it to say that up until the latter half of the twentieth century, this debate would never have been raised. In fact, in 1892, in the case of *Church of the Holy Trinity vs. United States*, the Supreme Court ruled that the church has precedent over state and federal law, because "this is a Christian nation." In the court opinion written by Mr. Justice Brewer, the court felt that

> no purpose of action against religion can be imputed to any legislation, state or national, because this is a religious people. This is historically true. From the discovery of this continent to the present hour, there is a single voice making this affirmation.[3]

Brewer then went on to give various examples of America's connection to Christianity from documents ranging from the foundational principles set forth for the colonies to the constitutions of several of the states to a myriad of court cases supporting biblical principles, all of which supported Christianity as the basis of our laws and government. One argument from the state of Pennsylvania even went as far as saying that the defense of Christianity was a necessity, while the defense of the religions of the "impostors" Muhammad and the Grand Lama, were not. From these precedents, Mr. Justice Brewer had this to say in his concluding remarks:

> These and many other matters, which might be noticed, add a volume of unofficial declarations to the mass of organic utterances that this is a Christian nation.[4]

If the Supreme Court of our nation found this to be "a Christian nation" even 116 years after the Declaration of Independence, then it is odd that we should find otherwise today. Somewhere along the way we have lost contact with our roots—our moral compass was replaced by moral relativism, and the ship of our great nation started to drift off course.

Considering these roots, it is not surprising to see that the Christian men who set the foundations of our nation felt an ingrained bond with the displaced and disbursed nation of Israel in their day. They were the other people of the Bible, and we seemed to feel a kinship to the people of Isaac from the beginning—and with good reason.

For one instance, near the beginning of the American Revolution, when the colonial soldiers were poorly armed, starving to death, and on the verge of defeat, a Jewish banker from Philadelphia, Hyman Salomon, went to the Jews in America and Europe and gathered a gift of $1 million for the support of the American troops. He gave this money to General George Washington. Washington used it to buy clothes and arms to outfit the American soldiers. To show his appreciation, Washington had the engravers of the U.S. one-dollar bill include a memorial to the Jewish people over the head of the American eagle. It is still there today. If you look at a one-dollar bill closely, you will see thirteen stars over the eagle's head that form the six-pointed Star of David. Around that is a cloudburst representing the glory in the tabernacle in Jerusalem. President Washington specified that this was to be a lasting memorial to the Jewish people for their help in winning the war.[5]

American history textbooks used to carry a story that showed where Washington's heart was concerning God and how God's hand was on him. On July 9, 1755, in a battle of the French and Indian War near

A CHRISTIAN NATION | 43

Fort Duquesne in Pennsylvania, Washington was the sole mounted officer to survive the battle uninjured, despite the fact that he had four bullet holes in his coat and two horses were shot out from under him. That day, more than half of the nearly thirteen hundred American and British troops with him had been killed or wounded, including their commanding officer, British General Edward Braddock. History eventually dubbed Washington as "bulletproof" because of this incident and the fact that he was never wounded in battle.[6] God needed a godly man to be the first president of the godly nation of the United States, so it appears that His hand of protection was on Washington throughout his life.

Washington was not alone in his faith or feelings of brotherhood for the Jews. At the Continental Congress of 1776, Benjamin Franklin suggested that the Great Seal of the United States bear the likeness of a triumphant Moses raising his staff to divide the waters of the Red Sea, with the waters crashing in on the armies of Pharaoh in the background. Thomas Jefferson, on the other hand, preferred an image that showed more perseverance: that of the children of Israel marching through the desert following rays from the pillar of fire.[7] The final design of the Great Seal included a pyramid (Egypt), eagle (protection), and rays of fire and a cloud (divine leadership). All were symbolic of the Red Sea experience of the children of Israel.

As president, Washington welcomed the Jews as partners in building our new nation. In a letter to the Jews of Newport, Rhode Island, in 1790, Washington wrote, "For happily the Government of the United States, which gives bigotry no sanction, to persecution no assistance, requires only that they who live under its protection should demean themselves as good citizens . . . May the Children of the stock of Abraham, who dwell in this land, continue to merit and enjoy the good will of the other Inhabitants; while every one shall sit under his own vine and fig tree, and there shall be none to make him afraid."[8]

The United States was built on Christian principles, with the Ten Commandments and the laws of the Bible as the basis for its own laws. The newly born nation refused tyranny, creating a constitution of checks and balances to control government power, and also refused to embrace old-world struggles—such as that of Christian against Jew—as part of its culture. The fledgling government took literally the Scripture "Old things are passed away; behold, all things are become new."[9] This admonition was the true source of the idea of "separation between church and state," that all faiths would have the right to the freedom of religious gathering, worship, and expression, and that the state would not dictate what church was attended, nor would it silence anyone from expressing their faith in public office or the halls of government.

It may be well that the writings of Georg Hegel were not then available to our forefathers. Hegel, born in 1770, conceived the dialectical philosophy that would inspire Karl Marx. Marx preached that the state was "God walking on earth . . . and had the foremost right against the individual."[10]

The founding fathers saw no conflict between these freedoms and wearing their religious beliefs on their coat sleeves as they went about their daily business as citizens and civic leaders, nor would they silence any religion for the sake of those who chose not to believe in God at all. The government was not to be antireligious, amoral, or secular as the courts seem to think today—but rather full of the Judeo-Christian virtues of love and a dedication to pray for others rather than try to force them to change.

The second president of the U.S., John Adams, had an equal admiration for the people of Israel. He wrote Jefferson, "I will insist that the Hebrews have done more to civilize man than any other nation." He also once expressed to a Jewish petitioner his wish that

> your nation be admitted to all the privileges of citizens in every country of the world. This country has done much. I wish it may do more, and annul every narrow idea in religion, government, and commerce.[11]

Near the end of his life, Adams even expressed, "For I really wish the Jews again in Judea an independent nation." This later became a slogan among the early Jewish nationalists, though they did not add the rest of his desire in this—that this gathering of Jews might also be an opportunity for them to find peace and be more open to taking steps toward Christianity.[12]

Yet this feeling of kinship of spirit with the Jews by early American founders would be taken to a deeper, more active, and more prophetic loyalty in just a few decades. In 1814, at a dire point in the midst of the War of 1812, America caught a glimpse of what it would grow to be just over a century later: a nation integral to the rebirth of Israel. This happened when a Presbyterian pastor in Albany, New York, named John MacDonald made a startling discovery while teaching on Old Testament prophecy to his congregation. He had been teaching on the subject for some time and especially focusing on the prophecies in the book of Isaiah, which spoke of the restoration of the nation of Israel and the subsequent redemption of humankind. One day while poring over Isaiah 18 he read a challenge to "the land shadowing with wings, which is beyond the rivers of Ethiopia: that sendeth ambassadors by the sea."[13] In this he saw that "beyond Ethiopia" meant a nation far to the west of Israel, which was where Isaiah spoke these words. It was a nation shadowed by wings—a nation whose symbol was a great bird, like the bald eagle, perhaps—who sent its ambassadors by the sea. "What other nations were forced to send their ambassadors across the sea besides those on the continent of America? In MacDonald's eyes, this prophetic notion took shape—it had to be the United States! And what was the challenge to this nation? "Go, ye swift messengers, to a nation scattered and peeled, to a people terrible from their beginning hitherto; a nation meted out and trodden down, whose land the rivers have spoiled! . . . In that time shall the present be brought unto the LORD of hosts . . . to the place of the name of the LORD of hosts, the mount Zion."[14] In Isaiah 18, MacDonald heard a clear clarion call from God for the great nation of the United States to send ambassadors to help reestablish a kingdom for the Jewish people upon Mt. Zion—the city of Jerusalem![15]

While Washington and other founding fathers had called the Jews a friend and ally of our nation and seen the founding of America as a parallel to the Jews' coming to possess their promised land of Canaan, MacDonald had seen in the Scriptures a divine call to champion the

Jews in regaining their own nation, not just anywhere in the world as was initially projected by early Zionists, but in the original Holy Lands, with Jerusalem as its capital. In his eyes, America was the nation of prophecy that would "send their sons and employ their substance in his heaven-planned expedition"[16] to reestablish the nation of Israel.

Thus MacDonald sounded a prophetic trumpet: "Jehovah . . . dispatched American messengers to the relief of his prodigal children. Rise, American ambassadors, and prepare to carry the tidings of joy and salvation to your Savior's kinsmen in disgrace!"[17]

It was not long after this that a flamboyant New York Jew by the name of Mordecai Manuel Noah stepped into the pulpit of the synagogue Shearith Israel in New York on April 17, 1818, and struck a similar note that would resonate for more than a century and a quarter. In his address that day, he stated that the Jews

> will march in triumphant numbers, and possess themselves once more of Syria, and take their ranks among the governments of the world . . . This is not fancy . . . [Jews] hold the purse strings, and can wield the sword; they can bring 100,000 men into the field. Let us then hope that the day is not far distant when, from the operation of liberal and enlightened measures, we may look towards that country where our people have established a mild, just, and honorable government, accredited by the world, and admired by all good men.[18]

This image of one hundred thousand Jews marching to Palestine was that note—in April of 1948 it was *this exact number* of possible European Jewish refugees who had been displaced by the Holocaust that diplomats discussed returning to Palestine.

Retired President John Adams even picked up this figure in writing to support Noah in his efforts: "If I were to let my imagination loose, I could find it in my heart to wish that you had been at the head of a hundred thousand Israelites and marching with them into Judea and making a conquest of that country and restoring your nation."[19]

Noah's efforts, however, didn't peak until some years later in 1844, just seven years before his death. During this year, he seized upon the same passage that MacDonald had, though with a somewhat different emphasis. He continued to call for American Jews to work for the restoration of a state for their people in Palestine, but added to this a rallying cry from Isaiah 18 for the American Christians to join them in this quest. "Christians can thus give impetus to this important movement," Noah declared in an address at the Broadway Tabernacle in New York to an overflow audience, "and lay the foundation for the elements of government and the triumph of restoration. This, my friends, may be the glorious result of [our] . . . promoting the final destiny of the chosen people."[20]

It is quite possible that the Damascus incident of 1840 had opened the American ear—that of both Jew and Christian—to the need for the Hebrew people of the world to have a homeland within whose borders they could finally find security from persecution. The incident was such an epitome of old-world prejudices the United States had been trying to escape that it is the first and only time our government, especially the State Department, acted on behalf of the Jews without first being prodded by the American people.

What brought the affair to the attention of President Martin Van Buren and his secretary of state, John Forsyth, was a dispatch from the American consul in Beirut describing the massacre in Damascus of Jewish men, women, and children who had been accused of ritual murder in order to obtain Christian blood for their Passover services—something known as "blood libel." The accusations were used as a justification to destroy Jewish property and murder Jews in the streets. In the end, it was found that French agents had started the rumor to incite the Muslims in that region against the Jews and to enhance France's position as the protector of Christians in the area. While the issue was undeniably a gross violation of basic human rights, the end result was that it placed the United States unequivocally and officially on the side of the Jews, forcing the U.S. to express itself through formal diplomatic channels in support of the Jews. This action was so fast, in fact, that by the time the American public raised the issue to the government, the formal protests had already been lodged.[21]

The British foreign secretary at the time, Lord Henry John Temple Palmerston, also supported the Jews, being one of the first government officials to step out to endorse the Jews in Palestine by extending consular protection to them. Another Englishman, Sir Moses Montefiore, took a series of journeys about this time and became a new "Nehemiah" in his charitable work aimed at helping the Jews living in Palestine.

The 1830s and 1840s also saw a great influx of Jews into the United States from Central Europe. The unrest that incited these families to seek new hope in America was also a herald of what would happen during the next century. "The Jewish Problem" (i.e., the displaced nation of Israel scattered among the nations without a land to call their own) would be an issue of debate that would fuel the Zionist movement and eventually lead to Hitler's attempted "final solution to the Jewish problem" in the death camps.

Young Adolf Hitler was convinced that he had been anointed to rid the world of "undesirables" and to establish a superrace that would rule the world. At the age of twenty-five, he volunteered for service. He later told an acquaintance that he was so overcome with emotion, he fell to his knees, "and thanked heaven from an overflowing heart for granting me the good fortune of being allowed to live at this time."[22] When he swiftly and successfully conquered Austria, Hitler addressed the jubilant German crowds: "I believe that it was God's will to send a youth from here to the Reich, to raise him to be the leader of the nation . . . I felt the call of Providence. And that which took place was only conceivable as the fulfillment of the wish and will of this Providence."[23] He was consumed with the certainty that he was providentially chosen. Following an early failure in his rise to power, Hitler affirmed, "We knew we were carrying out the will of Providence, and we were being guided by a higher power . . . Fate meant well with us."[24] To Benito Mussolini he stated: "It is obvious that nothing is going to happen to me; undoubtedly it is my Fate to continue on my way and bring my task to completion."[25] And following an assassination attempt, Hitler opined, "I regard this as a confirmation of the task imposed upon me by Providence."[26]

In 1937, five years into his campaign to obliterate the Jews, Hitler was still convinced of his calling and his invincibility: "Yet at the moment when [the individual] acts as Providence would have him act he becomes immeasurably strong . . . When I look back only on the five years which lie behind us, then I feel justified in saying: this has not been the work of man alone."[27] Fortunately for the Jewish people, biblical prophecy triumphed over Hitler's "Providence."

Thus, roughly a century before Israel's rebirth, the groundwork had already been laid in the American conscience for its support of and relationship with the nation of Isaac. The call had begun for America to be an international ambassador to help the Jews reestablish a land and a state for themselves. Over the next century, almost every American president would be faced with the issue of being part of or ignoring the prophecies stating that the people of Isaac would again have their own land and government. Amazingly, the battle continues despite Arab hatred for the Jews and the abounding conspiracy myths that the Jews blew up the World Trade Center towers. Such myths are propagated by the "Baghdad Bobs" of the Islamic world.

CHAPTER FOUR

Presidents in Prophecy

That there seem to be many evidences to show that we have reached the period in the great roll of the centuries, when the ever-living God of Abraham, Isaac and Jacob, is lifting up His hand to the Gentiles . . . to bring His sons and His daughters from far, that he may plant them again in their own land . . . Not for twenty-four centuries, since the days of Cyrus, King of Persia, has there been offered to any mortal such a privileged opportunity to further the purposes of God concerning His ancient people.

> William Eugene Blackstone
> In his letter to President Benjamin Harrison
> that accompanied Blackstone's memorial for the reestablishment
> of a Jewish state in Palestine[1]

I heard another out of the altar say, Even so, Lord God Almighty, true and righteous are thy judgments.

> Revelation 16:7
> Abraham Lincoln's Inaugural Scripture of 1865

Virtually every American president has in some way been impacted by prophecy. From Washington's divine protection, to every other president's decisions concerning the direction of our nation and its relationship to Isaac and Ishmael, our leaders have navigated the murky waters of foreign policy to decide America's role in world affairs. As our domestic conscience has elected men into office, it has also directed how America will account for its stewardship of the power entrusted to us. It seems that though we were prophetically called on to be used of God in the world, we will also have much to answer for because of our sluggishness in responding to that call and taking our appointed place of leadership.

While the American heart seemed dedicated to helping the Jewish people find a place of peace and security on the earth as the second half of the nineteenth century dawned, its hands were occupied with westward expansion and solving its own greatest internal moral dilemma, namely the end of slavery and maintaining its Union through a bloody Civil War. While Jefferson had warned that God's justice would not sleep forever concerning the issue of slavery,[2] America would still be caught in its bloodiest conflict ever because of its moral relativism. It took a man with great moral resolve to see the U.S. through this time of division. History can only speculate how events may have turned out had it not been Abraham Lincoln who placed his hand on the Bible in 1861 to be sworn in as the sixteenth president of the United States. It is quite likely that a man of lesser moral fiber would not have seen his country whole again at the conclusion of his presidency. "My great concern is not whether God is on our side," Lincoln was quoted as saying. "My great concern is to be on God's side."

While Lincoln's hands were full with the issues surrounding the Civil War, he did at least express sympathy concerning the establishment of a Jewish homeland. In fact, Lincoln even received a prophetic appeal from Henry Wentworth Monk in March 1863. When one of the president's public addresses was opened for questions, from the back rows of the room Monk stepped forward, introduced himself as a visitor from Canada, and asked the president: "Why not follow the emancipation of the Negro by a still more urgent step, the emancipation of the Jew?"

Lincoln faltered at this. "The Jew—why the Jew? Are they not free already?"

"Certainly, Mr. President, the American Jew is free, and so is the English Jew, but not the European. In America we live so far off that we are blinded to what goes on in Russia and Prussia and Turkey. There can be no permanent peace in the world until the civilized nations . . . atone for what they have done to the Jews—for their two thousand years of persecution—by restoring them to their national home in Palestine."

"That is a noble dream, Mr. Monk," Lincoln responded, "and one shared by many Americans. I myself have a high regard for the Jews . . . But the United States is at the moment a house divided against itself. We must first bring this dreadful war to a victorious conclusion . . . and then, Mr. Monk, we may begin again to see visions and dream dreams. Then you will see what leadership America will show the world!"[3]

However, despite what intentions Lincoln may have had in his heart concerning this issue, he was assassinated before he could act on any of them. Yet God still held the U.S. in His hand as a tool to fulfill prophecy. A new call for American support of replanting Israel in its ancient lands would soon come from a Christian businessman of Oak Park, Illinois, who would pick up the torch that MacDonald and others had lit.

Again the push toward a Jewish homeland came from a Christian and not a Jew, but given the Jewish perspective of the time, perhaps this is not so remarkable. From 1881 to about 1920, the United States saw the greatest period of immigration, among which were three million Jews from Eastern Europe. It was the time of America's Open Door and the Great Melting Pot. It is not surprising that a Jewish poet, Emma Lazarus, would write the words emblazoned in bronze on the pedestal of the Statue of Liberty:

> Here at our sea-washed, sunset gates shall stand
> A mighty woman with a torch
> Whose flame is the imprisoned lightning, and her name
> Mother of Exiles . . .
>
> "Keep ancient lands your storied pomp," cries she
> With silent lips. "Give me your tired, your poor,

Your huddled masses yearning to breathe free,
The wretched refuse of your teeming shore.
Send these, the homeless, tempest-tost to me,
I lift my lamp beside the golden door!"

Palestine at the time was a desert wasteland in the hands of the un-friendly Turks—America held much greater promise to Jews than re-turning there. In fact, the Jews in the United States came to view America as their promised land. They were comfortable in America's graces and felt no need to seek peace elsewhere. This great sentiment was not without its repercussions, however. As the poor Jews of Europe flooded to America, it not so much answered "the Jewish Problem" as brought it to America. The United States felt it could not hold them all, and sought some other answer.

As a result, in 1921 Congress passed a quota targeting mostly Euro-peans who were unskilled workers. Another law was passed in 1921 that limited each country to sending the equivalent of only 3 percent of its nationals already living in America in 1910. This law limited im-migration to 357,000 people. Three years later, the Johnson-Reed Im-migration Restriction of 1924 lowered this quota to 2 percent, while also lowering the base year to 1890—when only 150,000 people were allowed in. The government's restrictive immigration policy thus cut immigration from 800,000 in 1921 to 23,000 in 1933. Ellis Island's role quickly changed from a depot to a detention center. In 1915, Ellis Island admitted 178,000 immigrants; by 1919 that number had fallen to 26,000. Something different would have to be done to solve the Jew-ish problem in Europe rather than shipping Jews to the United States.

However, before any of this even really started, God had appointed someone to step forward with a solution—William Eugene Blackstone. Blackstone was born into a Methodist home in upstate New York in 1841, but followed his fortunes west to Oak Park, Illinois, after the Civil War. Though he was not an ordained minister, but rather the founder of a construction and investment company, Blackstone was an ardent student of the Bible from his boyhood. In 1878, he published a book called *Jesus Is Coming*, which sold more than a million copies (no small feat in a nation of only about fifty million—roughly a sixth of what America's population is today). While the book was offensive to many who had grown comfortable in their American Christianity and were content to live the American dream, it was welcomed by such men as Dwight L. Moody and Cyrus I. Scofield, who appreciated his more literal interpretation of the Scriptures and welcomed a more active and evangelical, missions-minded Christianity. It so touched the American conscience that it "in a large measure set the tone for this period of history."[4]

Blackstone's book was so well documented that it was actually more Scripture than commentary, listing hundreds of Bible passages for the reader to review on their own because of the limited space. It was a hard book for any true believer to ignore. Suddenly, once again, an American was becoming a beacon to the world pointing to Bible prophecy. The book was eventually translated into forty-eight languages, including Hebrew, and is still in print today.

Chapter 15 of the book is titled simply "Israel to Be Restored," and starts with this passage:

> Perhaps you say, "I don't believe the Israelites are to be restored to Canaan, and Jerusalem to be rebuilt."
>
> Have you read the declarations in God's Word about it? Surely nothing is more plainly stated in the Scriptures.[5]

From here he goes on to list eighty-nine different Scripture passages that support this assertion. Later in the chapter he further states:

> It would seem that such overwhelming testimony would convince every fair-minded reader that there is a glorious future restoration in store for Israel . . .
>
> I could fill a book with comments about how Israel will be restored, but all I have desired to do was to show that it is an incontrovertible fact of prophecy, and that it is intimately connected with our Lord's appearing.[6]

Perhaps Blackstone's remarks seem somewhat overstated to us some six and a half decades after the birth of Israel as a state, but to those of his time, some six and a half decades before the event, the confidence of his statements was no less than prophetic. Few in America's churches seemed to give any real credence to the possibility that the Jews would ever again have their own land and state, let alone in their ancient homeland with Jerusalem as their capital. For their part, the Jews overall had little interest in the idea themselves. By the outbreak of World War I, only about 20,000 of the 2.5 million Jews in the U.S. belonged to any type of Zionist organization.[7] American Jews were quite happy where they were.

However, Blackstone looked on Israel as "God's sun-dial." He even went so far as to say, "If anyone desires to know our place in God's chronology, our position in the march of events, look at Israel."[8] For Blackstone, it was the next milestone along the river of prophecy.

In what light did the American churches interpret the Scriptures that Blackstone was quoting? How could they have missed the obviousness of these prophecies concerning the rebirth of Israel? They interpreted them as referring to "spiritual Israel"—as the church of the modern day. Wisely, Blackstone had a few things to say about this as well—a subject that would touch on some of the darkest episodes for the descendants of Isaac in the next century. He saw quite plainly that Israel and the church were separate entities with separate futures as applied to their different covenants. God had not forsaken one for the other, but rather had a unique plan for each.

However, by replacing literal Israel in the Bible with the church, Christians of the time no longer had to feel any responsibility to the Jews as God's chosen people. This "Replacement Theology" would be exactly what would quiet the church in Germany during World War II as the death camps sped into full swing. They had no obligation to the Jews. They were "suffering for their sins of rejection of the Messiah." It was as if Jesus' death cut them free from these people rather than grafted them into their tree. However they saw it, this insidious virus—an invisible anti-Semitism—allowed the mainstream German church to look the other way as the most horrific and ungodly things were done. As Victor Frankl, a Holocaust survivor, wrote: "The gas chambers of Auschwitz were the ultimate consequence of the theory that man is nothing but the product of heredity and environment—or, as the Nazis liked to say, 'of blood and soil.' I'm absolutely convinced that the gas chambers of Auschwitz, Treblinka, and Maidanek were ultimately prepared not in some ministry or other in Berlin, but rather at the desk and in the lecture halls of nihilistic scientists and philosophers."[9]

Blackstone's words did not fall on deaf ears in the United States, however. As his popularity rose, so did his activity. In 1888, he and his daughter, Flora, visited Palestine, and concluded their trip in London. The trip took about a year.

When he returned, he was more zealous for the cause of reestablishing the state of Israel than ever before. Shortly thereafter, the burden of his heart was to initiate a conference between Jews and Christians to discuss this very topic. The "Conference on the Past, Present, and Future of Israel" took place November 24–25, 1890, at the First Methodist Episcopal Church in Chicago. It was attended by some of the best-known Christian and Jewish leaders. The assembly passed resolutions of sympathy for the oppressed Jews living in Russia, and copies were forwarded to the czar and other world leaders. However, Blackstone knew that it was not enough to beg mercy from these leaders— the Jews needed a land to call their own within whose borders they could find peace and security. He wanted these world leaders to grant the Jews permission to return to Palestine and establish just such a state. Out of these meetings came the inspiration for the document that would eventually be known as "The Blackstone Memorial."

On March 5, 1891, Secretary of State James G. Blaine introduced William Blackstone to President Benjamin Harrison. Blackstone personally handed the president his memorial, originally titled "Palestine for the Jews." President Harrison seemed like a man who would favor Israel as well, since he chose Psalm 121:1–6 as the Scripture on which he would place his hand as he took the oath of office as the twenty-sixth president of the United States:

I will lift up mine eyes unto the hills, from whence cometh my help. My help cometh from the LORD, which made heaven and earth. He will not suffer thy foot to be moved: he that keepeth thee will not slumber. Behold, he that keepeth Israel shall neither slumber nor sleep. The LORD is thy keeper: the LORD is thy shade upon thy right hand. The sun shall not smite thee by day, nor the moon by night.

The first paragraph of Blackstone's memorial began simply, "What shall be done for the Russian Jews?" and the second, "Why not give Palestine back to them again?"[10] It was signed by 413 prominent Americans including John D. Rockefeller, J. P. Morgan, Cyrus McCormick, the chief justice of the Supreme Court, heads of several major newspapers, the Speaker of the House, among other members of Congress, the mayors of Chicago and Philadelphia, and several other businessmen, ministers, and clergy. It called for a conference to discuss the possibilities of a Jewish homeland—a first step on the road to a Jewish state—and copies were also sent to the head of every European nation. The letter that accompanied Blackstone's memorial ended with these words:

> That there seem to be many evidences to show that we have reached the period in the great roll of the centuries, when the ever-living God of Abraham, Isaac, and Jacob, is lifting up His hand to the Gentiles (Isaiah 49:22), to bring His sons and His daughters from far, that he may plant them again in their own land (Ezekiel 34, &c). Not for twenty-four centuries, since the days of Cyrus, King of Persia, has there been offered to any mortal such a privileged opportunity to further the purposes of God concerning His ancient people.
>
> May it be the high privilege of your Excellency, and the Honorable Secretary, to take a personal interest in this great matter, and secure through the Conference, a home for these wandering millions of Israel, and thereby receive to

> yourselves the promise of Him, who said to Abraham, "I
> will bless them that bless thee," Genesis 12:3.[11]

While most Americans have probably never heard of William E. Blackstone, the same could not have been said of American presidents from Harrison through Truman. As Blackstone believed that the church could well be raptured at any moment, he became increasingly preoccupied with "God's sun-dial"—the Jewish people and their promised return to Palestine. He kept the issue before the eye of every U.S. president until his death in 1935. Blackstone not only handed the memorial to Harrison, but would also see it presented to Presidents William McKinley, Grover Cleveland, Theodore Roosevelt, and Woodrow Wilson—William McKinley even signed it.[12] Blackstone's words so saturated these presidents that in 1949, some fourteen years after Blackstone's death, Harry Truman, who made the U.S. the first nation to recognize the newborn state of Israel, virtually quoted Blackstone's letter. When he was introduced to some Jewish scholars that year as "the man who helped create the State of Israel," Truman responded with, "What do you mean 'helped create'? I am Cyrus, I am Cyrus!"[13]

Blackstone's memorial was written five years before the father of modern-day Zionism, Theodor Herzl, published his book *The Jewish State* and founded the Zionist movement. In fact, when Blackstone discovered that Herzl's book was practical and political, not prophetic, he marked all the prophecies in the Old Testament concerning Israel's rebirth in a Bible, and sent it to Herzl. Blackstone informed Herzl that his proposal to have the Jewish state in Argentina, Uganda, or any other country was unacceptable—it had to be in the promised land of Palestine with Jerusalem as its capital. Blackstone so greatly influenced Herzl that the Bible containing those marked prophecies is displayed in Herzl's tomb in Israel.

Because of his zeal, Blackstone is perhaps the most famous American in Israel today. While righteous Gentiles such as Corrie ten Boom and Oskar Schindler have a tree dedicated to them for saving lives in the Holocaust, Blackstone has a forest named after him and is mentioned in most textbooks discussing the history of Israel.

Despite his presence before these presidents and his popularity, however, Blackstone would be to these presidents what Moses was to Pharaoh—a voice calling from God, "Let My people go!" but also one that, for the most part, would be unheeded. As Pharaoh vacillated in his decision to release the Jews to go to Canaan (ancient Palestine) after the plagues, so would the American presidents. However, it was not God who hardened presidential hearts as He had done with Pharaoh; it would be the State Department.

It was the State Department that incited U.S. protests against the murder of Jews in Damascus in 1840, but now the State Department would silence the U.S.'s response to Blackstone's plea, and eventually welcome America's apathy toward the murder of Jews during the Holocaust. The death knell that sounded over the Blackstone Memorial came in a penciled note from Alvey A. Adee, who was the assistant secretary of state from 1886 to 1924, an incredible thirty-eight-year stint in the office that left his fingerprints everywhere in America's foreign policy throughout his tenure and beyond. If Adee felt one way, then it was a good indication of the way any up-and-coming young State Department officers should feel if they hoped for advancement. His note read:

> For thirty years and I know not how much longer, Turkey
> has writhed under the dread of a restoration of the Judean
> monarchy. Every few months we are asked to negotiate for
> the cessation of Palestine to the Jewish "nation." The whole
> project is chimerical [fanciful].[14]

While, in fact, the project was not an impossible and foolish fancy as Adee suggested, his note was enough to infect the State Department with the idea that any action toward helping Israel become a nation again was not only a waste of time, but also not in the interest of peaceful relations with the powers that controlled the region at the time— namely the crumbling Ottoman Empire. A tone was also set in these intellectual halls that the simplistic, black-and-white values and ideas of evangelical Christians such as Blackstone were naive and quixotic. Well-informed diplomats knew more about the values and cultures of the regions involved, so they were in a better place to make policy regarding the issues concerning them.

Slowly the State Department was starting to make its decisions based more on what other nations thought than using the values on which our country was founded. This trend away from the moral clarity of our forefathers and toward the relativism of humanistic secularism is what has turned the State Department into the friend of the United Nations and globalization—more than the friend of their own nation—that it has become today.

A further prophetic insight was realized when William Blackstone's friend Cyrus Scofield published his famous study Bible in 1909. It was greatly inspired by Blackstone's interest in Bible prophecy and his simple, straightforward interpretation of Scripture. In his notes, Scofield interpreted Ezekiel 38 and 39 to mean that Russia would invade Israel during the end times. That interpretation was challenged and even mocked. Many said, "How can you possibly say that? Russia is a Christian Orthodox nation, and Israel doesn't even exist . . . nor is there any possibility that Israel will exist." Scofield answered simply, "I don't understand it, and I can't explain it, but the Bible says it, and I believe it." Today no one doubts that Russia would attack Israel—especially since it has been known to regularly target Israeli cities with nuclear missiles—and Scofield's interpretation is almost taken for granted.

William Blackstone was God's voice to a generation. He raised the call for Zionism before the Zionist movement was even founded. Through Blackstone, God was calling on the conscience of America, which had called on Him to save it from the tyranny of the British and from its own divisive internal strife over the issue of slavery. God answered us willingly and faithfully, in both instances keeping America whole through each of these as well as other conflicts. Now God was calling on America to act on behalf of His chosen people, the Jews— and for more than fifty years, His call went ignored. The fact of the matter was, had any of the presidents who received Blackstone's memorial acted on it—in other words, if they had acted on prophecy instead of disregarding it—it could well have saved the lives of the six million Jews who died in the Holocaust, as well as the lives of those persecuted in Russia and elsewhere in the world. America's inaction during this time is as responsible for the Holocaust as the silence of the German church in the 1930s and 1940s.

CHAPTER FIVE

A Prophetic Struggle

Principle—particularly moral principle—can never be a weather-vane, spinning around this way and that with the shifting winds of expediency. Moral principle is a compass forever fixed and forever true.

Edward R. Lyman[1]

Surely the LORD GOD does nothing,
Unless He reveals His secret to His servants the prophets.

Amos 3:7 NKJV

The fulfillment of prophecy concerning God's people has never been a unilateral act of God. First, God informs His prophets what is to come to pass (which can mean quickening His Scriptures to them as happened with Daniel), then His people begin to pray, and God moves in the hearts of leaders to fulfill His Word concerning these things. This seems exactly the pattern that happened with William Blackstone and the leaders of his day. Blackstone saw what biblical prophecy said, he and others began to pray over it, and suddenly, leaders all over the world began to pick up their standards in support. As America, England, and the rest of Europe directed global politics at this time, so these nations were in the thick of fulfilling the prophecies Blackstone had found.

Interestingly, although at least three of the men God used to work toward this cause were Jews, all three were also the most un-Jewish of Jews.

The first of these was Theodor Herzl. Though Herzl took part in many of the Jewish traditions as he grew up, his mother raised him more as a cultural German than a Jew. Because of this, it is not surprising to note that Herzl's zeal for a Jewish state did not grow out of his religious convictions, but in reaction to the blatant European anti-Semitism of the time. He had read the anti-Semitic literature of his day, but always dismissed the idea that the formation of a Jewish state was needed to remedy this malaise in Europe. However, he soon saw that it was more than a simple malaise, when what he thought was a simple espionage trial of a French officer accused of stealing confidential papers of the French general staff turned ugly because the accused, Alfred Dreyfus, was a Jew. Herzl became convinced of Captain Dreyfus's innocence and later wrote of that December 1894 trial:

> The Dreyfus case embodies more than a judicial error; it embodies the desire of the vast majority of the French to condemn a Jew, and to condemn all Jews in this one Jew. Death to Jews! Howled the mob . . . Where? In France, in republican, modern, civilized France, a hundred years after the Declaration of the Rights of Man. The French people, or at any rate the greater part of the French people, does not want to extend the rights of man to Jews. The edict of the great revolution had been revoked . . .
>
> Until that time most of us believed that the solution of the Jewish question was to be patiently waited for as part of the general development of mankind. But when a people which in every other respect is so progressive and so highly civilized can take such a turn, what are we to expect of other peoples, which have not even attained the level which France attained a hundred years ago?[2]

Herzl saw that anti-Semitism was buried deep in the European psyche, and there would be no rooting it out for many, many years. The Dreyfus case transformed Herzl into a Zionist.

Thus came Herzl's *Der Judenstaat* in 1896, a book originally in German, but eventually translated into English with the title *The Jewish State: An Attempt at a Modern Solution of the Jewish Problem.* The book was short and to the point, and ended with these words:

> The Jews who wish for a State will have it.
>
> We shall live at last as free men on our own soil, and die peacefully in our own homes.
>
> The world will be freed by our liberty, enriched by our wealth, magnified by our greatness.
>
> And whatever we attempt will react powerfully and beneficially for the good of humanity.[3]

Herzl's book found considerable support among Christians of the day, though Herzl's call for a Jewish state was totally based on secular reasoning. The Reverend William Hechler, who was the chaplain for the British embassy in Vienna when Herzl wrote his book and later authored a pamphlet titled *The Restoration of the Jews to Palestine According to the Prophets,* did what he could to help Herzl. This included introducing him to the grand duke of Baden and his nephew Kaiser Wilhelm II, whom Reverend Hechler knew because he had once tutored the grand duke's son.

Herzl also organized the First Zionist congress in Basel, Switzerland, which met August 29–31, 1897. It had 197 delegates (Reverend Hechler was among these), plus representatives of the press who came from all over Europe, America, and Algeria. At the end of the congress, Herzl wrote in his diary, "At Basel I founded the Jewish State . . . Perhaps in five years, and certainly fifty, everyone will know it."[4] Sure enough, fifty years later, in November 1947, the United Nations authorized the creation of a Jewish state in Palestine.

Zionism now had a leader whose grounds seemed purely practical and political and a voice in Europe. It also had a center for raising funds for the cause of starting a Jewish state. Though Herzl lived only eight years beyond the publication of his book, his influence would continue.

The second of these three Jews was a man who would be appointed to the Supreme Court of the United States by Woodrow Wilson, and would turn just as radically toward Zionism, though more mysteriously. His name was Louis Dembitz Brandeis, a first-generation American whose father had bought wholeheartedly into the freedom promised by the American dream. In fact, when he wrote to his fiancée, who was soon to join him in the U.S., he said:

> In a few months you will be here yourself. To your own surprise you will see how your hatred of your fellow man, all your disgust at civilization, all your revulsion from the intellectual life, will drop away from you at once.[5]

He and his wife entered the United States during the great influx of Jewish immigrants in the 1830s and 1840s, and Louis Dembitz Brandeis was born in 1856.

Within this new freedom found in America, Brandeis grew up with little to no connection to his Jewish roots. He was unschooled in the Talmud, had no religious training, and did not even attend synagogue. He was as likely to quote a Scripture from the New Testament as from the Old. In fact, when the opportunity arose that he might be selected as a member in Woodrow Wilson's cabinet, he was not recognized as the type of man other Jews would claim as a "representative Jew," meaning he would not curry support for Wilson from the Jewish voters. For this reason, Brandeis was passed up for a position with Wilson, though he had been at the top of the list of candidates for attorney general.

Through his uncle's influence, Brandeis became a lawyer, the type referred to in those days as a "people's attorney"—champion of the working class. He attended Harvard and graduated in 1877. By the time he was thirty-four years old, he was financially independent and able to devote much of his time to causes that interested him. It was around the time Brandeis first met Wilson that he seemed eager to take a step toward greater influence in American life.

In August 1912 on Cape Cod, where Brandeis spent almost every August of his adult life, a conversation with journalist Jacob De Haas about Zionism lit a spark in him where there had been no fuel. Brandeis had no reason to support Zionism or pick it up as a cause given his interests and background, yet for some reason he did. Roughly a month and a half after learning he had been passed over for a cabinet position, Brandeis formally joined the Zionist Association of Boston and threw his influence into the cause. The day was April 17, 1913.[6] Because of his sudden advocacy for Zionism, when Wilson brought up his name in 1916 as a possible associate justice of the Supreme Court, the Jewish community gave him warm support. He was thus the first Jewish member of the Supreme Court.

Brandeis maintained a good relationship with President Wilson, and in May 1917, Brandeis met with His Britannic Majesty's secretary of state for foreign affairs at a White House Luncheon: a man by the name of Arthur James Balfour. Balfour turned out to be a Christian who supported Zionism as a student of history. In his mind, the Roman destruction of Jerusalem and the temple in AD 70 and the subsequent scattering of the Jews was one of the greatest wrongs of all time. This made him sympathetic to the Zionist cause, though he seemed to know little of the movement or its people. They met a few days later for breakfast.

What Brandeis didn't know was that Balfour was on a mission to fulfill a promise to Chaim Weizmann by the British government. The previous year the war had been going rather poorly for the British because of the superiority of the German machine guns, among other weapons. England was desperate to find a more rapid method of manufacturing TNT and smokeless gunpowder to help their weapons catch up. Dr. Weizmann provided this formula and literally changed the course of the war for the British. In return, the British told Dr. Weizmann to name his price for his services. Weizmann refused money and asked instead that Palestine be declared an international homeland for the Jews once it was liberated from the Turks. Balfour's name would be on that answer to the promise in the Balfour Declaration. (It is interesting to note here that it was another Jew, Albert Einstein, who would help the United States develop the atomic bomb, which turned the tide of the Second World War in the Asian theater for the Americans. Two Jews were used by God Almighty to save the lives of millions of Americans.)

Thus this occasion turned out to be more than a friendly get-together. At this point in World War I, Britain had Turkey on its heels and was very near victory on the Middle Eastern front. Balfour had some weeks before received a telegram from one of the chief Jewish leaders of Zionism in Great Britain, James de Rothschild, further discussing the possibility of extending the British Empire with former Turkish provinces, namely Palestine as a Jewish state. Balfour wanted to know what Brandeis thought of a Jewish Palestine under British protectorate. Or perhaps even as an American protectorate. If Brandeis and the American Zionists supported the idea, could Brandeis get the endorsement of it from President Wilson as well?

Brandeis was actually a bit stumped at the proposal. It was as if, despite all the talking and fund-raising, no one had considered possible plans for an actual Jewish state. They were more comfortable with the dream than the reality, but it didn't take long to make the switch. Brandeis met with his Zionist colleagues, then with President Wilson, and again with Balfour.

Brandeis let the foreign secretary know that America was not interested in being a protectorate of any of the former Ottoman lands, but was very open to the idea of a British protectorate of a Jewish state in Palestine. It wasn't a stretch for Wilson to agree to this. As the son of a Presbyterian minister, Wilson had always sensed God's hand on him for the purpose of doing great good. For the Scripture on which he would place his hand to take the oath of office in 1917, Wilson chose:

> The heathen raged, the kingdoms were moved: he uttered
> his voice, the earth melted. The LORD of hosts is with us;
> the God of Jacob is our refuge. (Psalm 46:6, 11)

Britain's ambassador had in fact noted this, stating that "he believes God sent him here to do something." Peter Grose, author of *Israel in the Mind of America*, had this to say about Wilson's support of the idea:

> Finally, the prophetic stream of Christian thought had its effects on Wilson, with his daily Bible readings, his romantic visions of the people of the Book. The evangelist Blackstone, undeterred by the lack of interest of previous Presidents, persisted in his campaigns for the Jewish State; in 1916 he persuaded the Presbyterian General Assembly, governing body of Wilson's own church, to endorse the Zionist goal. "To think that I, the son of the manse, should be able to help restore the Holy Land to its people," Wilson once remarked.[7]

The idea of a Supreme Court justice meeting with a foreign secretary of state and influencing the president in matters of U.S. foreign policy is, to say the least, rather unusual. Yet it also appears no one else in the Wilson circle of influence could have convinced Wilson to support the idea, even if they had been inclined to attempt to do so. Wilson had already somewhat turned his back on the State Department and his own secretary of state, Robert Lansing, for making decisions concerning U.S. policy at the time, instead turning to a reservist colonel named Edward M. House to help him decide what to do about this Zionist proposal. Even House was cautious and suspicious at first about British aims in the matter and urged deferment of his decision. However, when the British presented the president with intelligence that the Germans were also close to endorsing a Jewish homeland, he concurred with the British plan. Thus the Balfour Declaration was the first official step by a world government toward giving the Jews a homeland again in Palestine.

Foreign Office
November 2nd, 1917
Dear Lord Rothschild,

I have much pleasure in conveying to you, on behalf of His Majesty's Government, the following declaration of sympathy with Jewish Zionist aspirations, which has been submitted to, and approved by, the Cabinet.

"His Majesty's Government views with favour the establishment in Palestine of a national home for the Jewish people, and will use their best endeavours to facilitate the achievement of this object, it being clearly understood that nothing shall be done which may prejudice the civil and religious rights of existing non-Jewish communities in Palestine, or the rights and political status enjoyed by Jews in any other country."

I should be grateful if you would bring this declaration to the knowledge of the Zionist Federation.

Yours sincerely,

Arthur James Balfour[8]

On December 11, 1917, the British General Edward Allenby, a Christian, liberated Jerusalem from Turkish control. On that day, the Jews lit their candles to celebrate the feast of Hanukkah. Allenby, later knighted Lord Allenby of Megiddo, swept through the Middle East and defeated the Ottoman Turkish Empire. A Christian general had conquered Islam and restored the Middle East to Christian rule. To this day, Islam refers to this as the Great Catastrophe.

I wrote of this in my book *Israel: America's Key to Survival*:

> It was not until 1917, when under the British General Allenby, Jerusalem was set free from the Muslim Turkish rule, that the long Diaspora of the Jews was over.
>
> General Allenby's capture of Jerusalem fulfilled a 2500-year-old prophecy by the prophet Isaiah. This is what he had predicted, "As birds flying, so will the Lord of Hosts defend Jerusalem; defending also he will deliver it, and passing over he will preserve it" (Isaiah 31:5). With the prophecy in mind, compare what actually happened.
>
> In 1917, in his campaign to oust the Turks from Pales-

tine, General Allenby reached the gates of Jerusalem; not the far-spreading city of today, but the tiny walled city of those days. If he shelled this city, some holy place would inevitably be damaged, and then the Christian, Jewish and Muslim world would be up in arms. What should he do? In his perplexity, the general dispatched a cable to the War Office in London, but the reply brought him little comfort. It merely said, "Use your own discretion." But, that was just what he did not want to do. So, a second cable was sent to King George V who replied, "Make it a matter of prayer."

After that, Allenby hit upon the idea of printing leaflets, which called on the Turks to surrender. He would send up a little open-cockpit bi-plane to drop them on the city. The order was duly executed but with no immediate or visible results. The next morning, their effect was discovered in the most down-to-earth way. One of the British army cooks was facing what, to him, was a major disaster. He found that he had no eggs for the traditional British breakfast of bacon and eggs. Then, to his infinite relief, he heard the crowing of a cock, and with his native Cockney common sense, and a traditional disregard for his aitches, he said to himself, "Where there's cocks, there's 'ens, and where there's 'ens, there's 'heggs." Sallying forth hurriedly, intending to go to the nearby village of Lifta, he missed his way, and found himself instead on the outskirts of Jerusalem. To his surprise, he saw a group of Arabs carrying a white flag approaching him. In their midst was the Arab mayor of the city, who ceremoniously proceeded to offer him the keys of Jerusalem. Never having been initiated into the formalities of receiving the surrender of a city, he abruptly refused the keys, saying with some indignation, "I don't want no keys; I want heggs for me hofficers."

"As birds flying"—Isaiah could not use the word "airplanes"; neither he nor his hearers knew the word, so—"as birds flying shall the Lord of Hosts defend Jerusalem." The little bi-planes "defended" the city by those harmless but strangely potent leaflets. While defending, they also "delivered" it, for the 400-year oppression of the city by the Ottomans was now over, and the "passing over" of the planes certainly "preserved" it, for not a shot was fired or a holy place harmed. Incidentally, the motto of the Fourteenth Bomber Squadron, which flew over the city of Jerusalem that day was "I spread my wings and keep my promise."

There is yet another prophecy which has been fulfilled in living memory. The twelfth verse of the twelfth chapter of Daniel [says], "Blessed [happy] is he that waiteth, and cometh to the thousand three hundred and five and thirty days." "What," asked the students of prophecy, "did these obscure words mean?" The period mentioned, 1335 days, did not fit into any of those neat charts and graphs so beloved by those who investigate the prophecies in hopes of understanding what the future holds.

It remained a mystery until that day when General Allenby entered Jerusalem and set it free from times of the treading down of the Gentiles, an event which Jesus had predicted two thousand years before, and which Daniel had concealed in his prophecy hundreds of years before Christ.

The year Jerusalem was set free from four hundred years of Turkish rule was 1917, which was the date stamped on the Turkish coins minted that year. On the other side of the coins was the year 1335 according to the Turkish calendar.[9]

That same month, Secretary of State Lansing sent a letter to Wilson recommending the U.S. show no support for the Balfour Declaration, not knowing that the president had already endorsed it. He cited three reasons for this: (1) The U.S. was still at war with Turkey and should not be appearing to divide Turkey prematurely, (2) that there was very little overall Jewish support for Zionist hopes in the U.S. at the time, and (3) "many Christian sects and individuals would undoubtedly resent turning the Holy Land over to the absolute control of the race credited with the death of Christ."[10] The president returned the letter to his secretary of state the next day when they met in cabinet. Obviously, Wilson did not want such an inflammatory document found in his own files. When the document was found in Lansing's personal files some years later, it had a note attached to it that read: "very unwilling" and that the secretary had the "impression that we had assented to the British declaration."[11]

The details of the end of the war, the Bolshevik Revolution in Russia, forming the League of Nations, and President Wilson's physical collapse in September of 1919, however, kept him from ever really contributing more than his initial support to the Balfour Declaration. He never removed his support, however, and even ordered Lansing to support a pro-Zionist position at the peace tables in February 1920. His presidency ended when the Democratic Party lavished great praise on him at the 1920 Democratic Convention, and went on to nominate James M. Cox as their candidate for president in the upcoming elections. Physically spent, Wilson retired to a house in Washington, D.C., where he died in 1924.

The Balfour Declaration was in fact little noticed in the events of its day, coming in the midst of the First World War and within the same week as the Bolshevik overthrow of their provisional government on the eve of the Second All-Russia Congress of Soviets. Because of this coincidence in timing, among other factors, the State Department seemed to link the growth of communism and Zionism in their minds and had a growing distaste for each.

Through the peace negotiations that ended World War I, President Wilson and his secretary of state, Robert Lansing, were barely on speaking terms. Despite the president's endorsement of the Balfour Declaration, the State Department had committed itself to do what it could to undermine it. As far as they were concerned, the United States had never supported—and would never support—the declaration. The State Department had set its mind to back the children of Ishmael in the dispensation of political control over Palestine. Yet, regardless of this, Palestine would be given to Britain with the plan that Balfour's principles would be carried out. However, for the next quarter century, with little international support pushing for or action taken to implement those principles, little happened to create this safe haven for Jews until after the Holocaust.

The period between the end of World War I and the beginning of World War II was marked by an odd lethargy concerning the state of Israel. While the Balfour Declaration had seemed to win international support, and a similar resolution supporting a new Israel was adopted by the League of Nations in 1922, when its strongest supporters, namely Balfour himself and Wilson, stepped out of the limelight, no one moved forward to pick up where they had left off. The Jewish problem was on the world stage more than ever, but its accepted solution in reestablishing a Jewish state in Palestine was barely moving forward. In fact, other than some limited Jewish immigration into Palestine, it could be said that nothing at all was happening.

With his part in the declaration now over, and his involvement in it having been rather small in his own eyes anyway, Brandeis went on with his push for social reform as a Supreme Court justice, though at night he still spent much of his time contemplating what the community and government of a Jewish state in Palestine might look like. He even visited Palestine in 1919 and met once more with Balfour on the way back, urging further protection for the Jews already in Palestine. He saw no real rivalry between immigrating Jews and the Arabs who already lived there, as he saw the new state would be a place "where Western science and technology would cross-fertilize Eastern mysticism and religion, . . . a country where Jew and Arab would live peacefully side by side as they developed a common culture drawn from the distinctive heritage of each."[12] Perhaps Brandeis was too American-melting-pot in his thinking to grasp the real issues and undercurrents that this struggle would birth between the children of Isaac and Ishmael.

Brandeis would, however, have only limited influence in the cause of Zionism after that. In the months to follow, he would lose a rather divisive struggle for control of the world Zionist movement to Chaim Weizmann. Brandeis's views were, in fact, too American for the general group—his drawing of a parallel between the New England Puritans and the new Jewish settlers in Palestine was unpalatable to the overall followers of the movement. After this, Brandeis played no further direct part in world Zionist politics. However, David Ben-Gurion, who had contact with Brandeis through a banking enterprise Brandeis had helped establish, said this of him: "Brandeis was the first Jew to be great both as an American, quite apart from what he did for the Jews, and great as a Jew, quite apart from what he did for America."[13]

On an interesting side note, it was around this time that Colonel P. C. Joyce, an officer who had been attached to the Arab revolt against Turkey as T. E. Lawrence had been, escorted Weizmann to meet with Prince Feisal. According to Joyce's report:

> Feisal really welcomed Jewish cooperation and considered it essential to future Arab ambitions though unable to express any very definite views in absence of authority from his father. It is Colonel Joyce's opinion that Feisal fully realizes the future possibility of a Jewish Palestine, and would probably accept it if it assisted Arab expansion further north.[14]

After the meeting, the two had their picture taken together, with Weizmann wearing an Arab kaffiyeh. Later that summer, King Hussein sent word to meet with Weizmann, but the trip was never arranged for logistical reasons.

Despite his lack of overt participation in the Zionist movement in America after this, Brandeis's private court—the one he held over tea and watercress sandwiches in his Washington apartment—would have further influence on the future formation of the state of Israel through the men who would occasionally join him there, notably a young Jew named Henry Morgenthau Jr., who would become secretary of the Treasury, and a junior senator from the state of Missouri, Harry S. Truman. Brandeis was also in the heart of the New Deal elite and had access to President Roosevelt's ear on issues. Roosevelt always seemed friendly to Brandeis's talk of Zionist aims in private, but in public his silence on such issues has been one of the greatest slurs on history's analysis of his presidency.

The third of these influential and not-so-Jewish Jews was Henry

Morgenthau Jr. He and his wife, Elinor, had no love for being Jewish, though they were keenly aware of other people's prejudices about their ethnicity. His eldest son, Henry III, would describe his father as a man who wished to be thought of as "one hundred percent American."[15] The elder Henry was an ambitious and successful man who wanted badly to be a Washington insider. However, the farthest he ever got was his nomination as the ambassador to Turkey by Woodrow Wilson, thanks to a generous donation he had made to his campaign fund. The younger Henry spent much of his life trying to escape his father's shadow. As the only son, however, this was hard to do. It would be a strange set of circumstances and a strong sense of conscience that would eventually distinguish Henry as his own man.

Henry Morgenthau Jr. found that he had no taste for the financial world of his father, who had been quite successful in the real estate business, but that he did like farming, so he used some of his family's wealth to buy a farm in upstate New York, where he would probably have been quite content to live out his days in obscurity. However, Elinor was a rather outgoing wife who balanced his introversion and made friends with their neighbors quite easily. Two of those neighbors were Franklin and Eleanor Roosevelt. Elinor and Eleanor became fast friends, and the husbands followed suit. Because of the paralysis that started to sideline Franklin in 1921, he spent a good deal of time on his farm and with his new friend, Henry Morgenthau Jr.

Thus Morgenthau eventually found himself in a rather surprising place at the dawn of the Second World War—as secretary of the Treasury in Roosevelt's presidential cabinet. It was a quirky irony that he had fulfilled his father's greatest ambition by trying to go in the exact opposite direction. However, his places in this cabinet and in history show that he, too, was part of biblical prophecy, as his moral conscience was to make him a key player in what efforts America would eventually make to stop the Holocaust.

CHAPTER SIX

A Deadly Lack of Conviction

Though I speak with the tongues of men and of angels, and have not charity, I am become as sounding brass, or a tinkling cymbal.

And though I have the gift of prophecy, and understand all mysteries, and all knowledge; and though I have all faith, so that I could remove mountains, and have not charity, I am nothing.

And though I bestow all my goods to feed the poor, and though I give my body to be burned, and have not charity, it profiteth me nothing.

1 Corinthians 13:1–3
President Franklin D. Roosevelt's Inauguration Scripture

First they came for the Jews and I did not speak out because I was not a Jew. Then they came for the Communists and I did not speak out because I was not a Communist. Then they came for the trade unionists and I did not speak out because I was not a trade unionist. Then they came for me and there was no one left to speak out for me.

Pastor Martin Niemöller
Founder, Confessing Church, with Dietrich Bonhoeffer[1]

A s both Hitler and Roosevelt took power in 1933, it is important to see the position the United States held in the world at that time.

William Blackstone was still alive and vocal (he would pass away in 1935), and this marked the forty-second year that U.S. presidents had his memorial for giving Palestine back to the Jews before them. America had been through two wars (the Spanish-American War and World War I), experienced one of its greatest times of prosperity in the 1920s (a ray of hope that came after the Wilson years), and was plunged into its deepest economic failures in the Great Depression. Franklin Delano Roosevelt would be the tenth president to have a chance to respond to Blackstone, but as the others before him, he would not.

Why would he not take steps to save Jewish lives? Many times, things are not as they appear. Franklin D. Roosevelt's grandfather, Warren Delano Jr., was the chief of operations of Russell and Company in Canton, China. Russell, whose fortune was built on the opium trade, was the founder of Yale's Skull and Bones secret society. Two prominent members of that society were Nazi bankers, H. J. Kouwenhoven and Johann Groninger. Could it be the grandson and namesake of Delano Roosevelt was influenced by people who had other agendas . . . people who were directly involved in supplying Hitler with the materials needed to rebuild a German war machine? Is that why Roosevelt turned a deaf ear to the cries of millions of Jews in Europe? (It is interesting to note that George Herbert Walker Bush, George W. Bush, and John F. Kerry are all members of this secret society. The 2004 presidential election pitted a Skull and Bones member against another—Bush versus Kerry.)[2]

Roosevelt would also be the last American president that could have taken action that might have prevented the Holocaust, yet even into the middle of the war, when more than three million had already been executed, he was still eerily silent on the matter. It appears that the man considered America's greatest Democratic president was also part of our darkest hour as a nation in relating to the children of Isaac.

What was going on in Nazi Germany was surely no mystery to FDR. Hitler had never been quiet regarding his anti-Semitism, and his book *Mein Kampf* ("My Struggle") spoke eloquently about his hatred for the Jews, blaming them for communism among other problems in the world. It is said that Hitler could not go more than ten minutes without talking about the Jews. Almost as soon as Hitler took office, laws were passed barring Jews from government employment, boycotting Jewish businesses, and restricting their admission to universities. Hitler quoted from anti-Semitic writings of Martin Luther and Friedrich Nietzsche to support his actions. (Nietzsche's bitter assaults were not confined to anti-Semitic ranting; he attacked Christianity as well. In his *Antichrist*, he wrote: "I call Christianity the one great curse, the one enormous and innermost perversion, the one moral blemish of mankind . . . I regard Christianity as the most seductive lie that has yet existed."[3]) This was the first test of how the nation would react to Hitler's anti-Semitic legislation. According to German historian Klaus Scholder: "During the decisive days around the first of April [1933], no bishop, no church dignitaries, no synod made any open declaration against the persecution of the Jews in Germany."[4]

How greatly was the church influenced by the pen of Nietzsche? He wrote: "The strong men, the masters, regain the pure consciousness of a beast of prey; monsters filled with joy, they can return from a fearful succession of murder, arson, rape, and torture with the same joy in their hearts . . . To judge morality properly, it must be replaced by two concepts borrowed from zoology: the training of the beast and the breeding of a specific species."[5]

The German church's silence during this time is one of the greatest indictments against Christianity in its entire history, but it also shows the incredible subtlety of the virus of anti-Semitism. One can have it and not even know it. It had been in the German culture for some time, as evidenced by Martin Luther's own writings. In one pamphlet of 1543 titled, "On the Jews and Their Lies," Luther wrote:

> In truth, the Jews, being foreigners, should possess nothing, and what they do possess should be ours. For they do not work, and we do not give them presents. Nonetheless, they keep our money and our goods and have become our masters in our own country and in their Dispersion. When a thief steals ten guldens, he is hanged; but when a Jew steals ten barrels of gold through his usury, he is prouder than the

Lord himself! He boasts of it and strengthens his faith and his hatred of us, and thinks: "See how the Lord does not abandon His people in the Dispersion. We do not work, we are idle, and we pass the time pleasantly; the cursed goyim must work for us, and we have their money: thus we are their lords and they our servants!"

To this day we still do not know what devil brought them into our country; surely we did not go to seek them out in Jerusalem![6]

Even hero of the faith Dietrich Bonhoeffer seemed somewhat infected, though he later got involved in trying to stop Hitler by conspiring to assassinate him, for which he was hung in 1945. He declared in regard to the 1933 boycott, "In the Church of Christ, we have never lost sight of the idea that the chosen people who nailed the Savior of the world to the Cross must bear the curse of the action through a long history of suffering."[7]

Some Christians did respond, however, but there were very few in Germany. Reece Howells, a Christian Zionist and a great intercessor who headed a Bible school in Wales, had students praying for the Jews for a long time. In September 1938, Howells received a special burden from the Lord when he heard that all the Jews had to leave Italy within six months, and that anti-Semitism was rising rapidly in Germany. He turned his thoughts toward the return of the Jews to their homeland. Reece Howells was one of hundreds, if not thousands, who were crying out to the world to allow the Jewish people a homeland. There were many others, but not enough. In Holland, Corrie ten Boom and her family were among those angels. Her forebears began a prayer meeting in their home in 1844 that continued until 1944, when all the family was sent to the death camps for saving Jews. (Her famous "Hiding Place" in the ten Boom clock shop in Haarlem, Holland, is part of our work.)

Over the years, however, German laws continued to become increasingly harsh, as Jews were deprived of citizenship, systematically excluded from employment, forbidden to own cars, thrown out of public schools, and stripped of their property.[8] At first, the idea was to drive the Jews out of Germany—that Germany would become *Judenrein*, "free of Jews." One example of this is the so-called *Haavarah* (Hebrew for "transfer") Agreement of August 27, 1933, between the German ministry of the economy and Zionist representatives from Germany and Palestine. It allowed Jewish emigrants to indirectly transfer part of their assets to Palestine and facilitated the exports of goods from Nazi Germany to Palestine. Because of this, some one hundred million reichsmarks found their way to Palestine, and most of the sixty thousand German Jews who arrived in that country during 1933–39 thus found a minimal basis for their material existence waiting when they arrived.[9]

In early 1933, Baron Leopold Itz Elder von Mildenstein visited Jewish settlements in Palestine. As they visited Eretz Israel, Kurt Tuchler, a leading member of the Berlin Zionist Organization, and his wife accompanied him. As a result, a series of highly positive articles, titled "A Nazi Visits Palestine," appeared in Goebbels's *Der Angriff* ("The Attack"). A commemorative medallion was also cast with a swastika on one side and a Star of David on the other.[10]

At first, however, most of the German Jews were reluctant to leave, but events escalated to a new height on November 9, 1938, when mobs turned on the Jews after reports that a young Jew had assassinated a German official in Paris. During the *Kristallnacht* ("Night of Broken Glass"), dozens of Jews were killed in riots, with the windows of Jewish shops and homes smashed and synagogues set on fire. Thousands of Jews were arrested.

It is difficult to arrive at an exact figure for the number of Jews who were able to escape from Europe prior to World War II, since the available statistics are incomplete. Many countries did not provide a breakdown of immigration statistics according to ethnic groups during this time. From 1933 to 1939, 355,278 German and Austrian Jews left their homes. (Some immigrated to countries later overrun by the Nazis.) In the same period, 80,860 Polish Jews immigrated to Palestine and 51,747 European Jews arrived in Argentina, Brazil, and Uruguay. During the years 1938–39, approximately 35,000 emigrated from Bohemia and Moravia (Czechoslovakia). Shanghai, the only place in the world for which one did not need an entry visa, received approximately 20,000 European Jews (mostly of German origin) who fled their homelands. According to author Friedlander Saul:

> By the end of 1938, fifteen hundred refugees had arrived; seven months later the number had reached fourteen thousand, and if the Japanese had not begun curtailing access to the city because of local conditions, the total would have mushroomed. On the eve of the war, the Jews who had reached the safe shores of the China Sea numbered between seventeen and eighteen thousand.[11]

When Germany invaded Poland in 1939, the two million Jews there were subject to even harsher laws as they were forced into ghettos surrounded with walls and barbed wire. When the Nazis invaded the Soviet Union in June 1941, special units called *Einsatzgruppen* ("action squads") were dispatched to kill Jews on sight. Before long, rumors of the killings were arriving in capitals around the world. Orders had already been issued by second in command Herman Göring to prepare for the Nazi's "final solution to the Jewish question." In September 1941, Russian Jews were already being forced to wear the yellow star that distinguished them from the Aryans, and in the following months, tens of thousand were deported to the ghettos of Poland. Only months before, in November 1940, when American Jews in France were forced to wear the stars, the United States protested but received no response from Germany. This time, America said nothing. Hitler had for years attempted to pressure America, and the world, into taking the Jews. He wanted them out of Germany. Neither America nor the world would budge. Hitler attempted to send Eichmann to Palestine. In the early years before his alliance with the Arabs, Hitler was willing to send the Jews to Palestine. Again, America offered no support to that solution. Hitler finally realized that the Jews meant little to others as well and that his anti-Semitic beliefs were embraced in some form by the rest of the world.

In that same month, the gassing vans—trucks that were sealed and used to suffocate those inside with carbon monoxide gas—began being used. These were eventually replaced by the first of the death camps, Chelmno, which began operation in late 1941. After the death camps were in operation, full-scale deportation began from the ghettos to the camps. The heaviest deportations took place in the summer and fall of 1942.[12]

There appears little doubt that the U.S. knew of Hitler's oppression in these early years, though at the time there were no plans in Germany for the "final solution." The U.S. ambassador to Germany, whom Roosevelt replaced with William E. Dodd, warned the Germans that there would be an ill reception in the United States if the Nazi government took to mistreating the Jews. It took Dodd himself less than a year to see that he was dealing with a government filled with unscrupulous men. "It was definitely the aim of the [Nazi] government . . . to eliminate the Jews from German life," one State Department officer wrote. By 1937, it was clear that the Nazi persecution was systematic and progressing toward an unwelcome end. They made things as uncomfortable as possible for the Jews to stay in Germany, and though they left by the tens of thousands, there were still millions who stayed. The problem was that no one else wanted to let them into their country even if they did want to leave Germany. The doors were slowly closing to German Jews everywhere; and by 1939, all doors were basically shut. For the U.S., the "Great Door" period of welcoming the world into its liberties was over. The Immigration Acts of 1921 and 1924 had developed strict quotas for immigration that were discriminatory to the Jews of Eastern Europe. Even those who did enter had trouble finding work, and Jews were being let go from jobs when non-Jews could be found to replace them.

Roosevelt was in many ways absorbed by a desire to help form a state for the Jews, but this was also, perhaps, more intellectual and more of an outgrowth of his love for geography than it was practical. As a boy, his Christian instruction had carried with it at least a touch of the hope prophecy held for the Jews but, as president, his discussion of it always carried more of the energy of brainstorming to solve a problem than a prophetic vision or a moral call to action. Over the years of Hitler's rise, Roosevelt's geographic task forces came up with no fewer than 666 possible sites to relocate "European refugees." An international conference was even held in July 1938 in Evian, France—which could still have prevented the Holocaust—but the responses from all the possible host countries seems easily summed up in one sentence: "As much as we would really like to welcome these people, in the end, we regret that we cannot." However, the conference seemed doomed from the start as countries invited by the United States and Great Britain were told: "No country would be expected to receive a greater number of emigrants than is permitted by its existing legislation."[13] Moreover, the British agreed to participate only if Palestine were not considered. Another conference on the subject was held in Bermuda in 1943, but the delegates did not deal with the fate of those still in Nazi hands, only those who had already escaped to neutral countries.

Thus, with the doors closed to Jews leaving Germany, the Germans began turning to their own "final solution for the Jewish problem" after the *Kristallnacht*. Even this early, it was clear that the Jews were doomed one way or the other. As Roosevelt said in a cable dated January 14, 1939: "The fact must be faced that there exists in Central and Eastern Europe a religious group of some seven million persons for whom the economic and social future is exceedingly dark."[14] However, again, he refused to call them Jews or substantially act to help them.

Despite the closed doors, with German persecutions increasing, Jews left anyway. Those who could move to Palestine did so, but the quotas were tight and the reception of the Arabs to Jewish immigrants was anything but friendly. Guerrilla fighting had broken out in 1936 between the Jews and the Arabs, and Britain could not keep the peace. Britain was also increasingly preoccupied with Hitler's influence in the Middle East. Nazi propaganda was playing heavily on the anti-Zionist fears of the Arabs. The British had been able to enlist the Arabs on their side in the First World War; but now Germany was trying to marshal the Arabs of Palestine to their side. Hitler was so confident that he was chosen by God as *the* world leader, not only of the Christian, but also of the non-Christian world, he commented, "I'm going to become a religious figure. Soon I'll be the great chief of the Tartars. Already Arabs and Moroccans are mingling my name with their prayers."[15]

Nazi broadcasts into the Middle East increased greatly during 1937. Zionism was portrayed as the handmaiden of French and British imperialism. Arab unrest kept increasing. Following the Peel Commission report, the Arab mufti of Jerusalem, Haj Amin al-Husseini, dropped in to see the German consul general in Jerusalem. He wanted to tell this Nazi official how much he admired the Third Reich, and how much he would appreciate a little help from them in his struggle against the British and the Jews. From there the negotiations progressed, until the head of German intelligence delivered quantities of weapons from German manufacturers to the mufti by way of Iraq and Saudi Arabia.

England's response was to become increasingly friendly toward the Arabs in an attempt to win their favor. One of the chief ways they did this was to impose restrictions on Jewish immigration. So, in an effort to appease the Arab population and keep them from totally turning to the Germans' side in the war, the British government was to issue the infamous White Paper on May 28, 1939. This document closed the official door of immigration to Palestine for any Jews. As usual, though, the British appeasement only served to spur the Arabs to more aggression until after the war, though roughly seventeen thousand managed to enter illegally from 1939 to the outbreak of the war.[16] Friedlander also reported:

> On September 2, 1939, off the beach at Tel-Aviv, a Royal Navy ship fired at the *Tiger Hill*, which was carrying fourteen hundred Jewish refugees, two of whom were killed. As Bernard Wasserstein ironically noted, "these were probably the first hostile shots fired by British forces after the [previous day's German] attack on Poland."[17]

Just five days before the White Paper was signed, a shipload of 925 Jews—including families with small children, some of them toddlers— left the port of Hamburg aboard the SS *St. Louis* for Cuba on May 23, 1939, grateful to be escaping the Nazi discrimination. Though every one of them carried a visa for Cuba, none of them were admitted. When the ship turned its prow toward America, hoping to find a safe harbor there, they found that door closed as well. Michael Barak, one of the small children aboard the ship, described the U.S. "welcome" at a 2002 reunion of the passengers in Jerusalem:

> When approaching Miami of the "free" country, Roosevelt sent the U.S. navy to prevent any entry. On top of that he warned any country in the region from letting any of the "damned" Jews to land safely on their soil. In Canada, the head of immigration said, after being asked how many Jews of that ship could be accepted, "None is too many."[18]

The ship sailed along the coast of Florida for five days, doing what it could to find an open door somewhere in the world. In all, it spent three weeks trying to find refuge. Urgent cables were sent to every level of the U.S. government, including two personal appeals to President Franklin D. Roosevelt. He never replied. Instead, Coast Guard boats patrolled to prevent anyone from swimming to shore. On June 7, 1938, the *St. Louis* was forced to recross the Atlantic, where it was able to scatter its cargo between England, Holland, France, and finally Belgium. Of the passengers aboard the *St. Louis*, most of the families were separated when the Nazis took control of Holland, Belgium, and France the following year (1940). About 260 were deported immediately to killing centers,[19] and nearly half of them died in the Holocaust.

Harry Fuld, another of the passengers on the *St. Louis*, was ten years old when he boarded the ship. His father had been killed in the *Kristallnacht*. He was on the *St. Louis* with his mother and thirteen-year-old brother. While he was at the reunion in Jerusalem in 2002, his daughter from New Jersey called to ask about his safety in a city where suicide bombings were happening with regularity. Fuld answered, "My ship has finally docked in Israel. I see a country which is determined to defend its people . . . If Israel had existed in 1939, every passenger on the SS *St. Louis* would have been saved."

In December 1939, Roosevelt appointed Breckenridge Long to the position of determining who would and would not receive American entry permits from Nazi Germany. His philosophy was simple: Keep them all out; they are all troublemakers. When once questioned about what should happen with the Jews trying to escape Hitler, Breckenridge replied by strafing the room, using his hands as an imaginary machine gun. In the end, despite the White Paper and strict British sanctions against Jewish immigration into Palestine, Palestine would still allow more refugees into is borders (258,000) between 1931 and 1942 than the United States would (169,000) during that same period of time. From 1933 on through the war, the State Department had such strict immigration policies that quotas for immigrants from Germany and Austria were never more than half filled. Between 1933 and 1938, for example, only 27,000 German Jews entered the United States, while the quotas would have allowed 129,875.[20] If the issue was ever raised about what was happening to Jews in Nazi-controlled lands, as it was in 1941 by Rabbi Stephen Wise and a delegation of Christian liberals, the president simply referred them back to his friend "Breck" Long.[21]

From the start of these struggles, the otherwise reserved Henry Morgenthau Jr. began to find his backbone. Though he considered himself "one hundred percent American," something struck a chord in him about what was happening to the Jews in Hitler's Germany. He knew, however, his friend President Roosevelt was not keen on the issue. Morgenthau told an aide that "Roosevelt was not the greatest—let's put it that way—on this Jewish problem."[22]

Morgenthau, however, would quietly and cautiously do what he could. In 1938, he suggested to the president that the U.S. acquire British and French Guiana to use as a sanctuary for the Jewish refugees in exchange for their World War I debt. Roosevelt passed it off, responding, "It's no good. It would take the Jews five to fifty years to overcome the fever."[23] The president did, however, investigate the possibility of Paraguay's harboring the Jews in exchange for money, but a plan was never formulated to present to possible donors.

Meanwhile, in 1941, Haj Amin al-Husseini was the honored guest of Adolf Hitler in Berlin. He was convinced that the Nazis held the key to the two great goals of his life: to destroy the Jews and to drive the British out of the Middle East.

In 1942, Haj Amin succeeded in getting both Hitler and Mussolini to agree in a secret document to "the abolition of the Jewish National Homeland in Palestine." But his greatest zeal was spent in destroying Jews. When the "final solution" was invoked, the mufti was one of its most enthusiastic supporters. He worked assiduously to ensure that none of the Jews intended for the gas chambers and ovens were mistakenly diverted to Palestine or other places of refuge. He personally lodged a complaint with Von Ribbentrop, the Nazi foreign minister, when he got word that almost seven thousand Jewish children and eight hundred Jewish adults were going to be exchanged for German, Romanian, and Hungarian citizens living in Palestine. Thanks to Haj Amin, none of these Jews ever left Europe.

Evidence supports the notion that Roosevelt and the State Department knew something definite about Hitler's "final solution to the Jewish problem" sometime in 1942. With the United States already in the war, it seems likely that either the U.S. would have done something to find a safe haven for the Jews, or at least have used the information about German atrocities against the Jews as a rallying cry for the war. Neither happened!

In July 1942, American Jewish Congress President Rabbi Stephen Wise asked Roosevelt for a statement that would be read at a Madison Square Garden rally against Hitler's treatment of the Jews. Wise suggested the president say that the Axis powers "will not succeed in exterminating Jews, as they have repeatedly threatened to do, and any more than they will succeed in enslaving mankind." Instead, Roosevelt said that Americans "sympathize with all victims of Nazi crime."[24] The crimes against the Jews seemed not to be in the president's vocabulary. In a conversation in December of that same year, when the president eventually admitted to Wise that the government knew many of the facts of what was happening to the Jews, he also stated it was hard to know what to do about it. It was in that same month that the British initiated a statement by the Allies against the Nazi "mass executions" of "many hundreds of thousands of innocent men, women, and children." America added nothing to that.

During this time, America seemed trapped in a mire of prejudice and inactivity concerning the fate of the Jews. In the half century since Adee's scribbled note condemning Blackstone's memorial, State Department regulars had solidified themselves into an isolationist and relativist mind-set. If peace could be bartered for other people's freedom, so be it. What right did we have to interfere in the affairs of other governments? Why even make a formal protest? It would just be ignored. We would keep ourselves clear of such entanglements, even if it meant ignoring the genocide being perpetrated by our enemies while we were at war with them. And even if we could help by just harboring the refugees fleeing that genocide, forget it. Let them go elsewhere.

Surprising as this attitude may seem, it was the stance of the U.S. until at least halfway through the war, when one man had the moral fiber and conscience to take on Washington's anti-Semitism as his own personal crusade.

When Rabbi Wise could find no more than sympathy from President Roosevelt or the State Department, he looked elsewhere for someone to begin taking action. His attention fell on the somewhat unlikely champion of Secretary of the Treasury Henry Morgenthau Jr. Rabbi Wise had known him for some time, having celebrated Morgenthau's marriage to his wife, Elinor. On the surface, Morgenthau did not seem the man to pick up the banner of any cause and plant it on the top of the mountain of Washington bureaucracy. Though he was Jewish, he considered himself more a generic American. He was also a somewhat fragile man. He suffered from migraines and spasms of nausea all his life, and spent hours and days stretched out in dark rooms trying to recover from them. Rabbi Wise's stories of what was happening in the death camps and through other Nazi pogroms could not have helped these bouts much. As Wise told him of the millions murdered and that the Nazis were making soap from the remains and lampshades from the skin of the Jews, Morgenthau's confidential aide Henrietta Klotz recalled that he "grew paler and paler, and I thought he was going to keel over." Morgenthau had even cried out for Rabbi Wise to stop, "I can't take any more!"[25]

But in Morgenthau, Wise had found his David to take on the Goliath prejudice of the State Department and the Washington career-path bureaucrats. When Morgenthau learned of Breckenridge Long's hostility to refugees, especially to Jews, and that he was deliberately hindering the funds, information, and passports that could save Jews from Hitler's "final solution," he decided to confront him. In December 1943 Morgenthau told Long, "Breck, we might be a little frank. The impression is all around that you particularly are anti-Semitic." When Long denied this, Morgenthau continued, "Breck, the United States of America was created as a refuge for people who were persecuted the world over, starting with Plymouth. And as Secretary of the Treasury for 135 million people, I am carrying this out as Secretary of Treasury, and not as a Jew."[26]

Morgenthau took the matter to Long's superior, Secretary of State Cordell Hull, whose wife happened to be half Jewish, though Hull had done everything he could to keep that fact quiet. Morgenthau, however, would now pull no punches. He told Hull that if he "were a member of the Cabinet in Germany today, you would be, most likely, in a prison camp, and your wife would be God knows where."[27]

However, Morgenthau got no more than bewilderment from either of these men. He determined he had to take the matter to President Roosevelt. Knowing the president's previous attitudes on these issues, Morgenthau knew that the matter could well cost him his position in the cabinet, as well as his friendship with Roosevelt. It no longer mattered to him, though; his conscience would not let him off the path he had started down. He had to see it through to the end, one way or the other.

So it was that Morgenthau made an appointment with President Roosevelt on Sunday, January 16, 1944. By this time, roughly four million Jews had already been murdered, and America had yet to publicly say a word about it.[28] The president had been suffering from the flu he had picked up on his trip to Tehran, so he met with Morgenthau and his aide in the upstairs Oval Room in the family quarters of the White

House. They gave the president a report Morgenthau had commissioned two aides (who were both Christians) to write titled, "Report to the Secretary on the Acquiescence of This Government in the Murder of the Jews." It indicted the State Department for "gross procrastination and willful failure to act, but even of willful attempts to prevent action from being taken to rescue Jews from Hitler," as well as stating:

> The tragic history of the Government's handling of this matter reveals that certain State Department officials are guilty of the following:
>
> (1) They have not only failed to use the Governmental machinery at their disposal to rescue Jews from Hitler, but have even gone so far as to use this Government machinery to prevent the rescue of these Jews.
>
> (2) They have not only failed to cooperate with private organizations in the efforts of these organizations to work out individual programs of their own, but have taken steps designed to prevent these programs from being put into effect.
>
> (2) They not only have failed to facilitate the obtaining of information concerning Hitler's plans to exterminate the Jews of Europe but in their official capacity have gone so far as to surreptitiously attempt to stop the obtaining of information concerning the murder of the Jewish population of Europe.
>
> (2) They have tried to cover up their guilt by:
>
>   (a) Concealment and misrepresentation;
>
>   (b) The giving of false and misleading explanations for their failures to act and their attempts to prevent action; and
>
>   (c) The issuance of false and misleading statements concerning the "action" which they have taken to date.[29]

It also quoted a Senate report "favoring the appointment of a commission to formulate plans to save the Jews of Europe from extinction by Nazi Germany."[30]

After skimming the report and listening to their summary of it, Roosevelt tried to defend his State Department, but his arguments seemed ill-founded. The meeting lasted about forty minutes in all, and despite his lack of apparent reasons, the president refused to commit. It was finally Eleanor who ended the meeting by coming in and reminding her husband that he had not been well and needed rest.

Morgenthau left the meeting extremely nervous and uncertain about the outcome. By evening, he was so concerned that he called the president under the pretext of getting his advice about a speech he was to give. Was the wording "ringleaders of hate" appropriate for a reference to the German leadership?

"Fine," the president responded. After further prompting, "But you might add the word 'proven' before ringleaders."[31] His old friend seemed his old friend again. The president joked and kidded with Morgenthau.

Six days later, President Roosevelt created the War Refugee Board. Morgenthau's confrontation seems to have tipped the president's scales in the direction of finally doing something about the Holocaust. By the end of the war, the Refugee Board may have saved as many as two hundred thousand lives.[32] In the subsequent months, the White House also seemed to have lost its hesitancy to publicly discuss the atrocities of the Nazis toward the Jews. On June 12, 1944, in an address to Congress, the president stated that America would now "manifest once again in a concrete way that our kind of world and not Hitler's will prevail."[33] From now on, the drive to end the war quickly would also involve discussion of how best to end the Nazi's "final solution."

It was not so much that Morgenthau had converted the president as that he revealed something already on Roosevelt's heart yet was never really acted on with full conviction. From the beginning of his presidency, he had intellectually toyed with the "refugee problem" as he called it, but for some reason was not willing to openly tie it to the one people group it most expressed—the European Jews. Perhaps this was his quandary in the first years of the war as well, when there was still time to act and save people from being executed in the gas chambers— he wanted to keep things general, not willing to recognize one people group over another, and therefore feeling that the best way to help everyone was to simply "win the war."

This does not go far enough, however, to explain the U.S. unwillingness to help those in the death camps. While Allied forces were pressing in on Berlin, American bombers were still making runs to take out factories to further hamper the German war machine. These bombers regularly hit targets near Auschwitz. Roosevelt and his chiefs of staff knew full well what was happening there. Even one bombing run to take out the gas chambers or the railways leading to the camp could have saved tens of thousands of lives, but Roosevelt and his staff voted against it. The fact that they would not even spare one bomb to try to help those being mass-murdered there still weighs as one of the greatest blots on Roosevelt's record as president.

Another interesting development as the war was drawing to a close was that the Germans started negotiating with various groups to trade the Jews for needed supplies. One example came to be known as "Blood for Trucks." On April 25, 1944, Joel Brand, a member of the Jewish Relief and Rescue Committee of Budapest, was summoned to a meeting with Adolf Eichmann, who presented him with the offer. Eichmann told Brand that the highest SS authorities had approved the terms, in which Eichmann would barter "a million Jews" for goods obtained outside Hungary, including ten thousand trucks for civilian use or, as an alternative, for use on the eastern front.

The one million Jews would have to leave the country—since Eichmann had promised that Hungary would be *Judenrein,* the German policy to make an area "free of Jews"—and that they might head for any destination other than Palestine, because he had promised the mufti of Jerusalem that no Jews would be allowed to immigrate there. To negotiate the implementation of the deal, Eichmann let Brand leave Hungary.

Although Brand was unaware of it at the time, the offer was evidently connected with an attempt by Himmler to drive a wedge between the Western Allies and the Soviet Union, and to conclude a separate peace with the former. Brand did go to Ankara, Jerusalem, and Cairo, and he negotiated with American officials and leaders of the Jewish Agency for Palestine. However, he was arrested by the British and imprisoned in Cairo, and the rescue scheme was never implemented.

Roosevelt still had his grand plans for the rebirth of Israel in Palestine, however. At one point he even proposed that two to three hundred thousand Arabs be moved to Iraq from Palestine and compensated at a cost of somewhere around $300 million. He also proposed that a political deal be cut with Arab nationalists and a barbed-wire fence be erected around what he described as "exclusive Jewish territory" so the Arabs could not "cut the throats of the Jews." As the war in Europe was drawing to a close, he even attempted to convince King Abdul Aziz ibn Saud of Saudi Arabia to assist him in resolving the problem; however, the Arabian king expressed no interest in having the Jews anywhere in the Middle East and refused to even consider the president's musings on the subject. Their meeting together, though it took place on Valentine's Day of 1945, was no lovefest.

Despite his lack of success, an important revelation came out of Roosevelt's meeting with King ibn Saud. In his own words, as Roosevelt shared them in his last address to Congress (in a sentence added to his formally prepared address): "On the problem of Arabia, I learned more about that whole problem, the Moslem problem, the Jewish problem, by talking with ibn Saud for five minutes than I could have learned in the exchange of two or three dozen letters."[34] What he had learned was that Arabs hated Jews, and he knew what that would mean for the future of any Jewish state in the Middle East, even if he had no idea what to do about it. It would be Truman, not Roosevelt, who would finally muster the resolve to act. Roosevelt lived less than two months beyond his meeting with ibn Saud, dying on the afternoon of April 12, 1945.

Thus it was not for lack of ideas or passion that Roosevelt failed to help the Jews—it was that he lacked the resolve to take definitive action. His apathy cost millions of lives. When he suggested his plans for a new Jewish state, it seemed as if he were waiting for someone else to step forward to champion the cause so that he could throw his support behind them. On his own, he would not push such plans through. Perhaps this is what he saw in Morgenthau: someone who would finally step up to the plate and do something. Thus Morgenthau was a Mordecai who ultimately did more toward the prophetic rebirth of Israel than the State Department ever dreamed of doing. With Roosevelt's death, however, Morgenthau's influence would wane, and the pressing issues of the end of World War II and the disposition of the Jews would fall to the Midwestern values of a new president, Harry S. Truman.

CHAPTER SEVEN

The Olive Tree Replanted

I had faith in Israel even before it was established. I knew it was based on the love of freedom, which has been the guiding star of the Jewish people since the days of Moses.

Harry S. Truman[1]

Whatever the part of America may be in world affairs, in our own affairs she may certainly be decisive.

David Ben-Gurion
Palestinian Labor Leader
Spoken a few months before Pearl Harbor[2]

And if some of the branches were broken off, and you, being a wild olive tree, were grafted in among them, and with them became a partaker of the root and fatness of the olive tree, do not boast against the branches. But if you do boast, remember that you do not support the root, but the root supports you.

Romans 11:17–18 NKJV

For now we see through a glass, darkly; but then face to face: now I know in part; but then shall I know even as also I am known.

1 Corinthians 13:12
Truman's Scripture of choice when taking the oath of office

The rebirth of the nation of Israel in 1948 has been the most significant prophetic event to happen in our generation. Many believe that it is the doorway through which we will enter before the final trumpet sounds:

> For the LORD himself shall descend from heaven with a shout, with the voice of the archangel, and with the trump of God: and the dead in Christ shall rise first: Then we which are alive and remain shall be caught up together with them in the clouds, to meet the LORD in the air: and so shall we ever be with the LORD. Wherefore comfort one another with these words. (1 Thessalonians 4:16–18)

As a nation, the heart of whose leadership has historically been turned by the hand of God, America's commitment to Israel has made our country a key to the door of prophetic events.

Harry S. Truman was sworn in as vice president of the United States on January 20, 1945. He was an odd choice for Roosevelt as a running mate as they had been on opposite ends of several issues while Truman was a senator. However, he made good political sense to the party since Roosevelt's prior vice president was seen as being too liberal. Because of his record for honesty and efficiency in facing tough issues (he was credited with saving the country roughly $15 billion in defense contracts through the toughest years of the Second World War), his name rose to the top of the list. Roosevelt and Truman, however, conferred little, and when Roosevelt died just eighty-two days into Truman's vice presidency, the new president knew very little of the old president's plans for the end of the war and its aftermath, let alone anything about Roosevelt's grandiose dreams for a Jewish state in Palestine.

However, Truman's Midwestern values and ability to meet hard issues head-on seemed to see him through. His love for the Bible (he had read it twice through by age twelve) gave him a natural inclination to favor "God's chosen people" in their quest for a safe homeland, and a communication from the State Department some six days into his presidency seemed to seal that leaning. The State Department sent him a memo outlining the "highly complex" issue of Palestine as being one that "involves questions which go far beyond the plight of Jews in Europe" and one the new president "would probably want to call for full and detailed information on the subject before taking any particular position."[3] The State Department was certain in their pro-Arab stance. Perhaps it was Secretary of Defense James Vincent Forrestal who best summed up their views, however, when he said, "You don't understand. There are four hundred thousand Jews and forty million Arabs. Forty million Arabs are going to push four hundred thousand Jews into the sea. And that's all there is to it. Oil—that is the side we ought to be on."[4]

Truman would years later write of this memo from "the striped pants boys," saying that they were "in effect telling me to watch my step, that I didn't really understand what was going on over there and that I ought to leave it to the experts." However, the new president was not to be intimidated. He felt that "as long as I was President, I would see to it that *I* made policy."[5] While it may seem unlikely that the memo pushed Truman to support Zionism, what it did ensure was that whatever his decision on the subject, it would be made quite independent of State Department pressure.

Another factor that would influence Truman's support of Zionism was the plight of the remainder of the Jews in Europe. As the Germans were finally defeated, so were the death camps liberated. The world was not only shocked by what had been done to these people, but over the months to follow would also be shocked about what was to be done with them in their "liberation." Death camps were replaced with DP (displaced persons) camps, and there seemed little difference between their accommodations except that one had been set up to kill them and the other was trying to save them. The DP camps were horribly sparse, since there were so few resources at the end of the war to dedicate to them. Add to this that those who had nothing to cling to for so long but the hope to survive had little idea what to do now that they were "free." There was nothing for them to return to in Europe. There was no place for them to go and no place for them to stay. Solving this problem would become a key issue for Truman throughout his considerations for the destiny of Palestine. One of his first acts was to request that Britain open its doors again for the immigration of one hundred thousand displaced Jews.

It was not long before the struggle for control of Palestine again became far out of proportion to the size of the region. Difficulties there had become too hot for the British to handle and were handed over to the new hope for peace in the world, the United Nations, which at the time was meeting in an old gyroscope factory building in Lake Success, New York, on Long Island. Britain had no cure for the violence between the descendants of Abraham's two sons; perhaps the world assembly did.

As unlikely a place as the UN seems today for the endorsement of an Israeli state in Palestine, it was just there, in the odd, post–World War II, pre–Cold War politics of the day, that the state of Israel found its first legitimate right to exist. In one of the oddest workings of opposing world politics, the United Nations Special Committee on Palestine (UNSCOP)[6] suggested that Palestine be partitioned into two states—one Jewish, one Arab—with one economy and a UN international zone around Jerusalem.

The odd thing about this is that enemies voted as blocs to bring it about, both the Arabs and the Jews alike. The Jews did not want a protectorate; they wanted their own state, while the Arabs (who felt that their only hope of smashing the possibility of a Jewish state was to eliminate any protectorate in the region) opposed continuing the control of Palestine by a protectorate. Arab countries voted unilaterally against the UNSCOP Partition Plan as well, but that their vote against a continued protectorate also made the Partition Plan the only one to which the UN could give any serious consideration. By being so firmly against everything proposed, they, in effect, left the destiny of Palestine up to everyone else.

On May 14, 1947 Soviet Ambassador Andrei Gromyko stood at the United Nations and said that the Soviet Union understood "the legitimate rights of the Jewish people" and that the Soviet Union supported the formation of an "independent, dual, democratic, homogeneous Arab-Jewish state" in Palestine. Having the U.S.S.R. give such strong support to the proposed Jewish state forced the U.S.'s hand, despite State Department pressure in the opposite direction, to try to become an even stronger supporter of the new nation or risk Israel's becoming a Soviet satellite. Thus both the United States and the Soviet Union used their influence to vote as a bloc as well, and UN Resolution 181—the Partition Plan—was accepted by a majority vote on November 29, 1947. Decades later, Gromyko would raise his hand and declare, "With this hand I created the state of Israel,"[7] referring to his historic speech that day and later vote in favor of the Partition Plan.

Despite the passage of the Partition Plan, trouble would soon emerge again as the State Department withdrew U.S. support of the UNSCOP's proposal without President Truman's consent in the early months of 1948. This created a new chaos in the infant United Nations that also opened up real trouble in Palestine. While the UN struggled with what to do in seemingly endless hours of debate, Britain declared that it would pull out of Palestine in mid-May 1948, leaving Palestine as a UN protectorate. For their part, the Jews decided that they would implement UN Resolution 181, even though the UN no longer supported it, and declare their state by May 16.

Thus it was that on May 14, 1948, as the UN struggled to come to a new consensus on what should happen in Palestine, the last British high commissioner of Palestine, General Sir Alan Cunningham, lowered the British colors in front of Government House and made his way to the HMS Euryalus, which would leave Haifa at midnight with the last units of his civil government. That afternoon, the Jewish state council convened at Museum Hall in Tel Aviv and declared the State of Israel would begin at midnight. Midnight in Israel was 6:00 PM in Washington and at Lake Success. So it was that at 6:00 PM Eastern Standard Time in the United States, the British protectorate over Palestine expired, and Israel declared itself a nation. At 6:11, President Truman signed a document to be the first nation to recognize Israel de facto without his State Department's knowledge or approval. Sometime shortly after that, the United States' recognition of Israel was announced in the General Assembly of the United Nations and pandemonium erupted. The next day, May 15, the Arab League launched an invasion of the new nation. The four million Arabs were planning to push the four hundred thousand Jews into the sea.

Abba Eban, who was at the United Nations representing Zionist interests, described the events of that day:

> So between one dawn and another, all the obscurities of the day before had been resolved. British rule had ended; Israel had proclaimed its birth; America had moved to Israel's side; the Arabs had launched their invasion, and the United Nations by its own default had enabled these streams of history to rush together in a single torrent . . .
>
> Nothing in history was similar to the resurgence of a people in a land from which so many centuries had kept it apart. For many millions in the world this was a unique and noble mystery. Israel's independence resembled neither of the conventional forms of national liberation. Here was neither an indigenous uprising against an occupying power nor a colonial migration to an unfamiliar land, but a reunion between a people and a land that had once lived together and had been separated for nineteen centuries. Yet for all the length of the separation, the restored nation still uttered the speech and upheld the faith that that same land had nourished three thousand years before. A world that had seen the death and birth of many nations now, for the first time, beheld something like a resurrection . . .
>
> At dawn the next day Egyptian aircraft bombed Tel Aviv and Arab armies moved ever closer to our centers of population.
>
> Israel held the joy of birth and the fear of death in a single taste.[8]

Despite the politics of the situation, President Truman did not miss the biblical significance of the event. A year or so after Truman recognized Israel, the chief rabbi of Israel met with him. He told Truman, "God put you in your mother's womb so you would be the instrument to bring about Israel's rebirth after two thousand years." Truman wept. Ben-Gurion recounted a similar experience when he met him in New York. "His eyes were still wet when he bade me good-bye." Ben-Gurion held the president so that Truman could collect himself before he went out to face the cameras of the press.[9]

To all of this, the State Department responded by implementing an arms embargo on Israel. The U.S. would not openly help Israel defend itself. Despite his personal endorsement of the nation, Truman would not reverse the embargo. However, mainly through Czechoslovakia, but also through less-open U.S. channels (U.S. organizations that supported Israel and did what they could clandestinely to arm Israel), Israel armed itself sufficiently to hold the day in its war for independence. That a ragtag group of Jewish refugees with secondhand weapons could hold off the entire Arab League is also no minor indication that God was ready for Israel to exist again on the earth. So it was that on January 25, 1949, a permanent government was established for Israel following democratic elections. Six days later, the United States recognized Israel not only as a nation "in fact" (*de facto*), but also as a legal and legitimate government (*de jure* recognition). It was as if, on her own, Israel first had to prove its legitimacy to the U.S. by establishing itself without U.S. help. Arab oil sheiks did everything possible to pressure America to stay out of the fight.

The boundaries of Israel by January 1949 were in the end more generous for the Jews than what the UN had suggested, though they left Jerusalem a city divided between Jews and Arabs. The Palestinians never declared the state the UN had offered them. Instead, Jordan stepped in, taking control of East Jerusalem (including the Old City and the Temple Mount) and the West Bank. Egypt would control the Gaza Strip.[10] A cease-fire soon settled these boundaries, which would remain the same until the Arab League again instigated war with Israel in 1967.

Though Truman would always have a warm place in his heart for Israel after his recognition made way for its recognition by other nations, and the U.S. supported Israel's economic growth through loans and aid, Truman would have little more to do with the Zionists after this.

For him, he had solved the key issue, and that was finding a secure place for the refugees displaced by the Nazis.

In the following four years, more than 600,000 Jews would emigrate to Israel and help in its development. The Soviet Union allowed more than two hundred thousand Jews who had fled Germany to Russia during World War II to leave for the West or Palestine. Thousands of others followed from Romania, Hungary, and Bulgaria. To show their further support, these countries were also willing to provide military training for those headed to Israel.[11] Under their diligent hands, the desert bloomed and Israel blossomed.

The eight years of Eisenhower's presidency that followed Truman's were perhaps the iciest of U.S.-Israeli relations. Eisenhower refused to meet with Jewish leaders, kept Israel at arm's length for the most part, and courted the Arabs, hoping to turn them away from the Soviets. However, U.S. aid continued to flow to the fledgling country with only one interruption. This was during the ill-advised invasion of the Sinai Peninsula in 1956, known today as the Suez Crisis. Dubbed "Operation Musketeer" by the three countries involved (Great Britain, France, and Israel), it was a ruse to allow Britain and France to retake control of the Suez Canal region. The idea was that Israel would invade the Sinai Peninsula and push through toward the canal, and in response to "help" Egypt, Great Britain and France would land troops to take control of the area and stay to be a buffer zone between the two hostile neighbors. Naturally, this "protective" zone would include controlling the canal.

With France and Britain being Israel's two largest sources of arms at the time, it is easy to see why Israel felt obliged to go along with the plan—and, of course, they would have loved a little more elbow room from an increasingly antagonistic neighbor, Gamal Abd al-Nasser's Egypt. English Prime Minister Anthony Eden always referred to him as "Colonel Nasser" in likeness to a young "Corporal Hitler"—and he was not the only one who saw similarities between the two men. Nasser's aggressive nationalism, which he desired to have under the flag of Islam, had far too many similarities in most people's eyes to Hitler's Third Reich. Nasser, however, made the traditional monarchies of

Saudi Arabia and Iraq (which was ruled by a pro-Western king at the time) nervous with his aggressiveness. He could never get their support in creating the Arab unity he sought, though he did create an Arab alliance with Syria for a time starting in 1958. Until the Suez Crisis, the Baghdad Pact, which joined Britain, Iran, Iraq, Pakistan, and Turkey into an alliance, kept the majority of the Middle East pro-Western. For them, the enemy was the Soviet Union; for Nasser, it was Israel. This difference made Israel's attention rest most uneasily on Egypt—it was the most likely place from where the next war with Ishmael would begin.

Despite the success of the military part of Operation Musketeer, the ruse failed. The U.S. and U.S.S.R. saw England's and France's true designs immediately and both stepped in to defend Egypt's right to sovereignty over its lands. Through U.S. pressure and a complete cutting off of aid to Israel until it withdrew from the territory, the three musketeers of Britain, France, and Israel retreated—somewhat chastised—from the Sinai Peninsula.

The U.S. arms embargo stayed firmly in place during these years as well, despite a small "one-time only" sale of a hundred unsophisticated antitanks in the last days of Eisenhower's term. The decade-old nation of Israel had to wonder if its old friend had turned cold while wrapped up in its own Cold War.

It was the warm personality of John F. Kennedy that would take U.S.-Israeli relations out of Eisenhower's deep freeze and into a new place of prominence in the eyes of America. "Let every nation know," Kennedy announced in his inaugural address, "whether it wishes us well or ill, that we shall pay any price, bear any burden, meet any hardship, support any friend, oppose any foe, to assure the survival and success of liberty."[12] It was Kennedy's aim to find out just who in the Middle East did wish America well or ill, who would support democratic liberty there, and solidify our friendships with those nations to further promote freedom and peace in the world.

While it was Nasser's Egypt that Kennedy aggressively pursued initially, for a number of reasons that friendship never developed, not the least being Nasser's aggression into Yemen in an attempt to join the

Arabs by force after his other coercing failed. Nasser would slide from the world stage as that struggle turned into a winless Vietnam for him. Thus when Kennedy was ready to look elsewhere in the Middle East for friends, Ben-Gurion was already knocking at the door.

Israel knew it needed the support of major powers to survive, and with the largest population of Jews being in the United States, it seemed the best friend to make, especially after the debacle of the Suez Crisis left things with England and France on a questionable footing and with the Soviet Union supplying weapons to Israel's enemies. As one Israeli diplomat once put it, "The Almighty placed massive oil deposits under Arab soil. It is our good fortune that God placed five million Jews in America."[13] Thus Ben-Gurion knocked, because it was time for Israel to take its relationship with the U.S. beyond simple economic support.

Ben-Gurion told Kennedy that there was a missile gap in Egypt's favor and that Egypt's new Soviet MiG-19s were superior to Israel's fleet of French-manufactured Super-Mystères. Thus if Egypt attacked, Israel would be at a deficit. The American-made Hawk missile—whose name was an acronym for "Homing All the Way Killer"—was a ground-to-air defensive weapon that would home in on attacking jets and knock them out of the sky. Such a weapon could balance arms technology between the two countries and discourage a possible Egyptian offensive. Since it was also strictly a defensive weapon, it could not be used for another Suez-type Israeli invasion. As Shimon Peres would one day word it, they just wanted to ask President Kennedy for a few Hawks on behalf of Israel's doves.[14] Kennedy seemed to think that this sort of help to Israel might just be a possibility.

A Hawk sale would also be a precedent, however. The Hawk had a technologically advanced system that the U.S. had not even made available to many of its allies. While the tactical necessity of Israel's acquiring this weapon was the main discussion of the day, the sale's symbolism was evident. This was much different from Eisenhower's "one time only" sale of antitank rifles. If Kennedy agreed to sell Israel the Hawk, he was letting Israel into the U.S.'s closest military confidence, throwing open the door for Israel to request anything else it wanted in the U.S. arsenal. The arms embargo would be a thing of the past.

Opinion seems to range widely on why Kennedy seriously considered, and finally agreed to, this request, despite so many reasons not to do so. His father, Joseph P. Kennedy, had been noted for his anti-Semitism and support of Hitler prior to World War II, but it did not seem to have infected his sons to the same degree. Kennedy had even once been confronted on the issue of his father's feelings for the Jews. "Jack, everybody knows the reputation of your father concerning Jews and Hitler. And everybody knows that the apple doesn't fall far from the tree." Kennedy's response was, "You know, my mother was part of that tree, too."[15]

The State Department advised against the sale because they were afraid it would start a Middle Eastern arms race, with the U.S. supplying one side and the Soviets the other. Yet on the other hand, there were the midterm elections coming up—would a sale of Hawk missiles throw Jewish votes to the Democrats? Then again, they probably already had that vote. It also appears that the documentary record doesn't support that the lifting of the arms embargo was for this political reason.[16] Kennedy knew the full ramifications of the sale, so he knew it was a major step to a new relationship with Israel. Were there other influences that may have tipped the scales in the direction of Israel?

It is well known that Robert Kennedy, John's attorney general and younger brother, was also one of the president's most trusted advisers. What isn't so well known is that it was a younger Robert Kennedy, fresh out of Harvard and reporting for the *Boston Post*, who was in Israel when it declared itself a nation and through the early days of the war for independence. The Kennedy brothers also went to Israel in 1951 on a seven-week congressional tour of the Middle East. They left with a further respect for the young country's willingness to "bear any burden" in the pursuit of its dreams. It seems likely that President Kennedy saw in the young country the friend in the Middle East he had been looking for—a friend worthy of the dreams of Camelot.

When Robert first met with Shimon Peres during the negotiations over the Hawk missile purchase, the memory of Robert's 1948 visit was the first thing they talked about. The second was Israel's desire to break America's "elegant arms embargo."[17] It seems unlikely that Robert didn't exert at least some influence on Peres's behalf to allow Israel's acquisition of the Hawk.

Others saw Robert's influence in this decision as something that Arabs of the world could do without—especially after U.S. arms helped Israel win the Six-Day War of 1967. If the young Kennedy was to be despised for helping to end the arms embargo as attorney general, how much more would he be a problem as president?

In 1968, Robert Kennedy was running for president on the Democratic ticket, and was campaigning in California. In fact, the day that he won the California primary was June 5, 1968, the anniversary of the outbreak of the Six-Day War. Kennedy's staff had requested a photo opportunity with Yitzhak Rabin, who had been the chief of staff in Israel during that war and was now Israel's ambassador to the U.S., to commemorate the day. However, that photo opportunity never took place. It was that evening Robert was shot to death by a young Jerusalem-born Jordanian named Sirhan Bishara Sirhan. Or at least Sirhan was considered a Jordanian before the 1967 war. After that war, the world began to know Jordanians born in the West Bank territories and East Jerusalem as Palestinians. As Rabin wrote in his memoirs: "The American people were so dazed by what they perceived as the senseless act of a madman that they could not begin to fathom its political significance."[18]

What was its political significance? According to a report made by a special counsel to the L.A. County district attorney's office, Sirhan shot Kennedy for his support of Israel and had been planning the assassination for months. In an outburst during his trial, he confessed, "I killed Robert Kennedy willfully, premeditatedly, and with twenty years of malice aforethought."[19] [Twenty years, of course, date back to Israel's declaration of nationhood in 1948.] In a notebook found in Sirhan's apartment, investigators found a passage written on May 18, 1968, at 9:45 AM "Robert F. Kennedy must be assassinated before 5 June 68"— the first anniversary of the beginning of the Six-Day War. Mr. and Mrs. John Weidner, who owned the health food store where Sirhan worked, testified that he had told them, "The state of Israel had taken his home, and the Jewish people were on top and directing the events in America."[20] It also came out during the trial that it had "provoked a heavy shock in Sirhan" when Senator Kennedy pledged during a speech, in late May or early June 1968, to send fifty Phantom jets to Israel.[21] On the night Sirhan was apprehended for the assassination, among other things in his pockets were two newspaper clippings, one inviting the public "to come and see and hear Senator Robert Kennedy on Sunday, June 2, 1968, at 8:00 PM, Coconut Grove, Ambassador Hotel, Los Angeles," and the other was a story by columnist David Lawrence, which noted part of Senator Kennedy's speech in which he stated "favored aid to Israel with arms if necessary."[22]

No one seemed to suspect at the time that a Palestinian terrorist had assassinated Senator Robert F. Kennedy. Sirhan had made himself into a suicide gunman in the same way many of his countrymen since that day became suicide bombers—and Sirhan chose the night of the murder to be the anniversary eve of the war that resulted in the prophetic reunification of the city of Jerusalem and returned East Jerusalem, Sirhan's birthplace, to Jewish control for the first time in nearly nineteen hundred years.

You can be sure of one thing, a young terrorist by the name of Yasser Arafat was shouting with joy! The PLO was founded in 1964 under the auspices of Egypt and other members of the Arab League, three years before the Six-Day War. At that time, Judea, Samaria, and East Jerusalem were in Arab hands. Its purpose, purely and simply, was the destruction of the Jewish state. When the Arabs attacked Israel in 1967 and were defeated, there was only one name on their minds—Kennedy! The PLO was convinced that the key to victory was a Vietnam-style terrorist war of attrition, and Sirhan Sirhan was the first PLO hero. And, while he may not have been directly connected to such groups as the PLO, it does appear they felt, at least, a kinship to him.

When Yasser Arafat's Black September terrorists stormed the Saudi embassy in Khartoum in March 1973 and took U.S. Ambassador Cleo Noel, Charge d'Affaires George Curtis Moore, and others hostage, Sirhan's release was one of their main demands. On March 2, 1973, after Nixon rejected that demand, Arafat was overheard and recorded by Israeli intelligence and the U.S. National Security Agency giving the code words for the execution of Noel, Moore, and Belgian diplomat Guy Eid, who all were shot to death. James Welsh, a Palestinian analyst for the NSA, went public with charges of a cover-up of Arafat's key role in the planning and execution of these kidnappings and murders. If Sirhan had acted independently of the PLO, why were they willing to kill Americans to try to gain his freedom?

Though it was not necessarily U.S. weapons that tipped the scales in the Six-Day War, the fact that Israel had them was significant. With the arms embargo ended because of the "missile gap," there was now no reason for the U.S. not to help Israel solve her "tank gap"—so in 1965, Israel bought 210 U.S. tanks. In 1966, Israel went on to purchase forty-eight Skyhawk bombers. Obviously, arms sales to the Israelis were no longer limited to defensive weapons, as was also evidenced by Senator Robert Kennedy's remarks about being willing to give Israel Phantom jets. Though President Lyndon Johnson would try to barter these sales for inspections of their nuclear center near Dimona, with the hope of keeping the atomic bomb out of the hands of the Israelis, U.S. inspections would fail to do so.

Johnson can hardly be faulted for this. He, as Kennedy and Eisenhower before him, probably knew quite well what Israel was doing in Dimona and couldn't blame them for developing the bomb, knowing that the United States would not risk a nuclear World War III if the Soviets attacked the small sliver of a country. During February 1968, Johnson's last year in office, the governor of New York's foreign policy adviser met privately with some academics at the home of Major General Elad Peled, the director of Israel's Defense College, where the adviser had been an instructor the year before. His message was clear, according to Shlomo Aronson, a scholar who specialized somewhat in Israeli nuclear policy:

> The United States would not "lift a finger for Israel" if the Soviets chose directly to intervene by, "say a Soviet missile attack against the Israeli Air Force bases in Sinai . . . The

main aim of any American President is to prevent World War III. Second, that no American President would risk World War III because of territories occupied by Israel. Three, the Russians know this."[23]

The man telling them this was Henry Kissinger. It also appears that this was not such a far-fetched scenario—the U.S.S.R. had already added Tel Aviv, Haifa, Beersheba, and Ashdod to its nuclear targeting list the year before. As Soviet Ambassador Anatoly Dobrynin later said, "If the Israelis threaten us, we will wipe them out within two days. I can assure you our plans are made for this eventuality." The plans for the fulfillment of what Scofield saw in Ezekiel 38 and 39 had already been drafted.

Johnson also seemed to have his moral reasons for hoping the Jews would succeed. At the end of World War II, he had gone on a congressional fact-finding tour to Dachau. His wife, Lady Bird Johnson, told a historian from Johnson's native Texas some years after his death that he had returned from the trip "just shaken, bursting with overpowering revulsion and incredulous horror at what he had seen. Hearing about it is one thing, being there is another."[24]

Though top government officials seemingly played dumb about Israel's bomb, the intelligence community had documented evidence that they could launch them.

"We had a direct line to God," a middle-level CIA technical analyst recalled. "We had everything—not only from the French but also from the Israelis. We stole some and we had spies. I was able to draw a scale model of the system. I even designed three warheads for it—nuclear, chemical, and HE [high explosive]—as a game. We were predicting what they could do." What Israel could do, the former CIA official said, was successfully target and fire a nuclear warhead. The problem arose in conveying the intelligence. "I was never able to get anything officially published" by the CIA for distribution throughout the government, he said.

"Everybody knew" about the Israeli missile, he added, "but nobody would talk about it." The official said he decided to bootleg a copy of the intelligence report—risking his job by doing so—to senior officials in the Pentagon and State Department. "I remember briefing a D.I.A. [Defense Intelligence Agency] admiral. He wasn't ready to believe it. I got him turned around, but he retired and no one else cared."[25]

Israel was also well on her way to developing nuclear strike capability, and wouldn't even let her closest ally, the United States, deter her.

Thus the U.S. became a solid source of conventional weaponry for Israel at a crucial time, for the Six-Day War also saw the Soviet Union break relations with Israel and increase Soviet support to Egypt, Syria, and Iraq. However, it would ultimately be Israel's nuclear strike capability that prompted the U.S. to pull out all the stops to save its Middle Eastern friend when she was attacked again less than a decade later.

It was at this time, on October 6, 1973, the holiest day of the Jewish year, Yom Kippur, that an Arab coalition struck Israel with a sneak attack in the hope of finally driving the Jews into the Mediterranean. Two times during that conflict, the Soviet Union armed Egypt and Syria. The U.S.S.R. was determined to unify the Arab world through the defeat of the Israelis. When the war began, Israel was tragically caught off guard. Most of Israel's citizen army was in synagogues, its national radio was off the air, and, overall, people were enjoying a restful day of reflection and prayer. Israel had no immediate response to the coordinated attacks of Egypt and Syria. Israeli intelligence had not seen the assault coming, and her military was ill-prepared for war. By the third day of fighting, Israel had lost several thousand soldiers (more Israeli casualities occurred in the first day than in the entire Six-Day War), forty-nine planes, one-third (more than five hundred) of its tank force, and a good chunk of the buffer lands gained in the Six-Day War. The Israelis were again on the brink of a holocaust.

On the fourth day of the war, in an act of desperation, Prime Minister Golda Meir opened three nuclear silos and pointed the missiles toward Egyptian and Syrian military headquarters near Cairo and Damascus. Army Chief of Staff Moshe Dayan was reported to have said, "This is the end of the Third Temple," in one of the crucial meetings. Later he told the press, "The situation is desperate. Everything is lost. We must withdraw."[26]

Earlier in his presidency, "Nixon made it clear he believed warfare was inevitable in the Middle East, a war that could spread and precipitate World War III, with the United States and the Soviet Union squaring off against each other."[27] He was now staring down the barrel of that war. So President Nixon authorized Henry Kissinger to put every American plane that could fly in the air to transport all available conventional arms to Israel. The resulting supply to defend Israel was larger than the Berlin airlift that had followed World War II, and literally turned the tide of the war, saving Israel from extermination and the world from nuclear war. Nixon carried Kennedy's agreement to militarily support Israel to the next logical level—a full military alliance.

When the Soviet Union realized what was happening, they scrambled to further assist Egypt and Syria. The Soviet threat was so real, Nixon feared direct conflict with the U.S.S.R. and elevated all military personnel worldwide to DefCon III (DefCon stands for "Defense Condition"; DefCon I—the highest level of alert—being war, DefCon II being preparation for imminent war, DefCon III being increased readiness that war is likely. DefCon IV and V were norms for all areas at the time except Southeast Asia, which was at permanent DefCon III level because of the legacy of the Vietnam War).

However, the U.S. and the U.S.S.R. finally worked out a cease-fire adopted by all parties involved, and the Yom Kippur War was ended. The pressure that brought this about was directly the Soviet Union and the United States, but indirectly it was the OPEC oil embargo. The pressure, added to the slow-burn disintegration of his presidency as the Watergate scandal began, pushed Nixon to the manic act of meeting with the Saudi ambassador and telling him, should the Arabs end the embargo, he would find a permanent solution to the Arab-Israeli disputes as quickly as possible. "The full prestige of my office is dedicated to that. You should know that that means I will catch it from some groups in this country."[28] The gesture was both misleading and meaningless. Less than a year later, Watergate would force Nixon to resign.

It was shortly after this, in 1974, that the United States finally decided to give normal military aid to Israel for the first time. The U.S. knew that if Israel were attacked yet again, we would do whatever necessary to protect it as a full ally, thus if a strong Israel could deter another possible war or defend itself if necessary, it would save the U.S. higher direct expenditures in the long run. Also, as author A. F. K. Organski stated:

> The shift in American policy in treating Israel as an important strategic asset was probably due to the fact that after twenty years U.S. leaders had become convinced that Israel could fight and that if it won, contrary to what conventional wisdom thought, expansion of Soviet influence would stop cold, and indeed, be made to recede.[29]

So Congress approved the first-aid packages to Israel, with part earmarked for defense (before this time, most aid to Israel was in the form of loans, all of which Israel repaid, or sales; in this, there were some loans for defense reasons, but no grants or gifts). Starting in 1976, however, Israel became the largest recipient of U.S. foreign assistance. Since 1974, Israel has received roughly $80 billion in aid (much of which was given as loans).

Because of all this, one historian has gone on to say that while "Harry Truman was the father of the U.S.-Israel special relationship; John Kennedy was the father of the U.S.-Israel alliance."[30] It is interesting to note that this change from friend to ally came in the same year that school prayer ended: 1962. While Israel's recognition had come at the hands of a Bible-reading president, commitment to Israel's protection came while the U.S. still had prayer as an institution. The power of such prayer, even as rote as it was, should never be underestimated. Though there had already been some rumblings of turning from our

Christian heritage before this time, it is hard to ignore the demarcation of what America was like before and after 1962. It is not hard to blame the moral morass that we are in today on the relativism that was born and nurtured in the later 1960s.

CHAPTER EIGHT

Reviving Ishmael

Oh people of the book,
do not go beyond the bounds in your religion and
do not say about Allah anything but the truth.
There is no God but Allah
He has no co-partner.
The messiah, Jesus, son of Mary,
is but a messenger of Allah and His word
which he cast upon Mary and a spirit from Him.
So believe only in Allah and of his messenger
but do not say three (trinity) and it will be better for you.
Allah is only one God
far be it from His glory that He should have a son.
Verily the religion in Allah's sight is Islam.

Translation of an inscription in Arabic
from the wall of the Dome of the Rock Mosque
The Temple Site, Jerusalem (Koran, Sura 2:193)[1]

You declare, my friends, that you do not hate the Jews, you are merely anti-Zionist. And I say, let the truth ring forth from the highest mountaintops. Let it echo through the valleys of God's green earth. When people criticize Zionism, they mean Jews. Zionism is nothing less than the dream and ideal of the Jewish people returning to live in their own land.

Martin Luther King Jr.[2]

It may seem strange that no one was very concerned about how the Arabs would react to a Jewish homeland in Palestine when the Balfour Declaration was written, but the fact of the matter was, at that point there wasn't much to be concerned about. The Turks, not the Arabs, controlled Palestine, and Britain hoped to liberate it by the end of World War I. The Arabs, on the other hand, were scattered throughout the region with no central leadership or apparent nationalistic leanings. Thus no one foresaw the war in 1917, which would erupt almost the same hour that a Jewish state was declared three decades later. The reason for this is that while Isaac was struggling to be reborn into statehood, Ishmael was finding his legs again after being knocked from the height he had reached at the dawn of the second millennium AD.

The Islamic world was at its height in the early part of the second millennium, excelling beyond all others in arts and sciences, and Islam was expanding on all fronts—into Northern Africa, Europe, and the Near East. Since all other cultures were infidels and barbarians to them at this point in history, Muslims cut themselves off from the rest of the world and basked in their own glory. Because of this isolationism, the kingdoms of Islam failed to notice when Europe emerged from its Dark Ages into the Renaissance, the Reformation, and the technological revolution of the early industrial age. In fact, until the late eighteenth century, only one Western book was ever translated into a Middle Eastern language, and that was a medical book on syphilis, which they allowed because, after all, they felt the disease had come from the West.[3] Earlier in the rise of Islam, Western Christianity had been the greatest threat to its spread, but as it seemed to be fading with the crumbling of the Roman and Byzantine Empires, Arabs had little trouble thwarting the West's Crusaders. In their view, Christians would eventually fall to the sword of Allah as did all the other religions at the time. China was too remote to be concerned with yet, Africans were easily made into slaves, and India and the Near East were in the process of being Islamized. Muslims grew content to conquer the world little by little through the wisdom of Allah. After all, they saw their eventual dominance as inevitable.

For Muslims, Judaism and Christianity are foundational religions that the revelations of the prophet Muhammad in the Qur'an brought to completion, in much the same way that Christians believe Jesus brought to fulfillment the Old Testament and its covenants with Abraham, Moses, and David. After all, these men were prophets mentioned in the Qur'an. What was true of these religions Allah had incorporated into the Qur'an; what was false was left out. And so the threat of Christianity was not a threat of conversion (for why would someone return to the old, incomplete revelations of the Bible when they had the complete revelation of the Qur'an?), but of power, technology, and conquest. Buddhism, Confucianism, and the other religions of the East had not produced these things as well as Christianity had, so they posed a much smaller threat. Muslims were not afraid of ideas at this point—for their culture was so much more advanced—but they did fear Europe's military might. Over time, most Muslims even developed a tolerance for Christians and Jews as monotheists and "People of the Book," because they were mentioned in the Qur'an.

However, the West's culture and ideas soon rose and eclipsed those of the Islamic empires as Arabs and Persians fell to fighting. Author and Islamic history expert Bernard Lewis notes that, had it not been for the Ottoman Empire's differences with Persia, Europe may well have become part of their empire in the mid-1500s.[4] However, the Ottomans fought with the East instead of the West and the struggle went on for centuries, keeping their attentions focused away from Europe. The Ottoman Turks were Sunni Muslims, and those of Persia, Egypt, and the Arabian Peninsula were Shi'ites. In response to the Shi'ites' casually converting those of the Ottoman extreme east to their "denomination" of Islam, Ottoman Sultan Selim I (and subsequent Ottoman rulers) invaded. At its height in the late 1600s, the Ottoman Empire stretched east to the Caspian Sea, engulfing the westernmost parts of Persia (which is today Iran), south to the base of the Red Sea and along the Asir Mountains (thus they controlled Lebanon, Syria, Palestine, Egypt, Iraq, Kuwait, and edges of the Arabian Peninsula), west in North Africa nearly to Morocco, and north to Hungary and the provinces on the northern shores of the Black Sea. The bulk of the center and southern edges of the Arabian Peninsula, however, vast desert at the time, remained free, and the Arabs of that region became tribal, nomadic, and divided during the centuries before World War I.

However, as Zionism was rising in the West and Britain was encouraging Jews to look to Palestine as a possible new homeland with the Balfour Declaration, men such as T. E. Lawrence (of *Lawrence of Arabia* fame) and Harry St. John Bridger Philby were organizing the Bedouin Arabs to help Britain oust the Turks from the Middle East. While the bulk of this was structured by Lawrence, with Sharif Hussein as the "documented" puppet leader of the Arab nation (in other words, he was leader on paper only for official British purposes), Philby was sent to clean up a bit of muck hampering that cause. A small group of dissident Muslims from an extremist sect were running terrorist raids on Hussein's forces. Philby was sent to dissuade their leader, a Muslim ruler of the extremist Wahhabist sect named Abdul Aziz ibn Saud, from doing this and to join the British cause. Ibn Saud, as the West came to know him, eventually went on to establish the nation of Saudi Arabia, and all of its leaders today are his direct descendants.

In the mid-1700s, Muhammad ibn Abd al-Wahhab had formed this fundamentalist sect and propagated it to the Saudis by making an alliance with Muhammad ibn Saud in 1744. It appears that Muhammad ibn Saud even married ibn Abd al-Wahhab's daughter, so the Saudi royal family of today actually has ibn Abd al-Wahhab as an ancestor. Ibn Abd al-Wahhab preached that Islam was deteriorating because it was being infected with heresy from outside religions—a form of polytheism (*shirk*). Things such as the veneration of the early Islamic disciples, worship of sacred trees, and the like were all forms of idolatry—and, again, polytheism. In his *Book of Tawhid*, ibn Abd al-Wahhab wrote, "*Shirk* is evil, no matter the object, be it king or prophet, saint or tree or tomb."[5] Since there was not a large enough Christian or Jewish populous in the Middle East to merit his attentions, he attacked other Arabs who had "apostated" from true, traditional Islam. To justify this, ibn Abd al-Wahhab reinterpreted the ideal of *jihad*. For most Muslims of his day, particularly the Shi'ites, *jihad* (which literally means "struggle") was described as the spiritual struggle toward holiness and included missionary outreach, but it no longer necessarily called for battles. However, ibn Abd al-Wahhab taught his followers that for the prophet Muhammad, *jihad* had been a "holy war upon the infidels" and it had never changed. Those who were of false faiths—including Muslims who had perverted their religion with outside influences—should either be converted or killed, and conversion was definitely the secondary goal. So polytheists, called *mushrikun*, were considered less than human, cattle to be slaughtered in sacrifice to Allah, the one true god, and women, children, the elderly, and the defenseless were no exception. The Spanish Inquisition had nothing on Wahhabism. Under ibn Abd al-Wahhab's doctrines, committing mass murder became a way of getting closer to God.

With the strength of the Saudi armies, ibn Abd al-Wahhab soon established a nationalist Arab state in the Najd (the region in the central Arabian Peninsula around Riyadh). From here they waged a war to purify Islam, and, among other things, sacked the Shi'ite holy city of Kerbala in 1802 (which was still part of the Ottoman Empire and is part of Iraq today), destroying its religious shrines and temples, and ruthlessly slaughtering the Shi'ites as infidel polytheists. He even went so far as to destroy the tombs of the first disciples of Muhammad as they were being venerated in a similar fashion to those of Christian saints. In their raids they cold-bloodedly murdered thousands: men, women, children; the young, the elderly, and the pregnant were all executed mercilessly.[6] In 1803 the Wahhabists captured Mecca and even threatened taking Damascus from 1803 to 1805. Eventually, though, they were pressed back and retreated to Riyadh, which they set up as their capital in 1824 and recaptured much of the land they had previously occupied. However, the dynasty fell into civil war after 1865 (the same year the U.S. Civil War ended), and their kingdom was divided among the Ottomans and various clans. The Saudi royal family fled into exile in Kuwait. However, they would rise again. As a young man, Abdul Aziz ibn Saud retook Riyadh in 1902, and by 1906 his forces controlled the Najd region and were establishing themselves as a force to be reckoned with, even though they were still a small force. Ibn Saud's forces showed the same brutality in their warfare that their Wahhabist predecessors had a century earlier.[7]

For ibn Saud and his predecessors, the extreme fundamentalism of Wahhabism was an incredible tool for religious and political control. Isolationistic and nostalgic by nature, Wahhabism built a longing in its followers to return Islam to its former greatness. It created a romance around the Bedouin lifestyle and the glory of the ancient Arabic royal courts.

One thing to note about this Muslim fundamentalism is that culture, government, and religion are inseparable for them. The idea of the separation of church and state was actually neither introduced by our forefathers nor modern liberals, but Jesus Himself when He said to "render to Caesar the things that are Caesar's, and to God the things that are God's."[8] Christianity was to be of a spiritual kingdom that superseded and influenced the natural through a change in the people's hearts, while Islam is a religion of natural laws of government and culture that would determine the spiritual. Therefore, Christians can deal with the heart issues of the Bible through a more literal interpretation of it and apply them to any culture, but they do not try to return to the dress and cultural practices of Jesus and the disciples. Wahhabists, however, not only return to a more literal interpretation of the Qur'an, but also to the culture and practices of when those scriptures were written; hence progress and modernization are seen with great suspicion as temptations and corruption. Ibn Abd al-Wahhab preached an ascetic and legalistic doctrine that rejected all luxury, dancing, gambling, music, and the use of tobacco among other things. Such a belief system could not exist within another, but must pervade and dominate—thus its intolerance and desire to take the whole world back to the ninth and tenth centuries. Being backward by its very essence, all that is modern is seen as perversion (except, of course, modern weapons, which could lead to the ascendancy of Wahhabism) and those that propose such are followers of "the evil one."

Government and conduct in most Muslim countries today is based on *Shari'a* law, which is derived from four principal sources: (1) the Qur'an; (2) the Sunnah, a collection of actions and sayings of the prophet Muhammad; (3) *ijma*, meaning "consensus," which refers to the consensus over the centuries of the schools of law, but can also refer to the consensus of the Muslim community; and (4) *qiyas*, reasoning by analogy, in which jurists and scholars formulate new laws based on the Qur'an or the Sunnah. Wahhabists, however, reject *ijma*—there is no room for consensus or other opinions. Law is thus handed down from the Qur'an by clerics/judges/leaders, called *ulema*; or scholars, called *mufti*; or in decrees, called *fatwa*. Such declarations are binding and not debatable. The populace needed no education besides these *fatwa,* and, as a result, more than half the population in most fundamentalist Muslim countries today cannot even read the Qur'an for themselves. Therefore, ibn Saud could rule without opposition with a religion that enforced his absolute authority.

Outsiders, especially modern Europeans, were viewed quite dogmatically as infidels, and contact with them was seen as risking contamination. Thus when European Jews reached the shores of Palestine to build homes and set up shop, they were an incredible threat to the Wahhabist way of life. And with no great love for ruling by consensus, democracy was no welcome neighbor either. The British and the Balfour Declaration were nothing ibn Saud wanted to see setting up shop next door.

Despite this, however, Philby and Saud hit it off—probably because they could be mutually beneficial to one another. It appears that Philby helped make ibn Saud king of Saudi Arabia, and Saud helped make Philby rich. Perhaps part of it was also that Philby had an equally strong contempt for the Jews. These two men formed a lasting partnership that would empower Ishmael with both the hope and the means to return Islam to greatness. What ibn Saud and Philby began in World War I led a straight and clear path to September 11 and the war we are fighting against terrorism.

During World War I, both Lawrence and Philby fell in love with the Arab cultures and ways, went "native," and felt that Britain was promising independence to Arabia if it helped defeat the Turks and Germans. They promised their Arab counterparts everything they wanted in exchange for their loyalty. As a result, each of them took it as a slight betrayal when Britain adopted the Balfour Declaration, and as full betrayal when Britain refused to move significantly on Arab independence. In the eyes of Great Britain, the Arabs were a ragtag lot that couldn't hold a government together if it were handed to them on a silver platter, and therefore weren't worth the trouble of empowering, so they refused to let go of the strings they held on its leaders. While Lawrence took this as an affront, he remained loyal to the Crown; for his part, Philby decided to turn traitor. He preferred the Arab ways and its harems to ever returning to England, though he did return home from time to time to keep up appearances. Philby was, above all, though, an excellent spy (as was his son, Kim Philby, who became the most infamous Soviet double agent in British history). Unfortunately, he turned those skills on his government and used them to help ibn Saud and to line his own pockets.

After the First World War, ibn Saud began to call for the overthrow of the British puppet leaders in the region. Philby, who had actually been fired for his outlandish attitudes and outspokenness on behalf of the Arabs, managed with the help of Lawrence to stay on in the Middle East as a chief British representative in Amman, Transjordan. Thus he was in a perfect place to feed ibn Saud the intelligence he needed to overthrow the puppets Philby was supposed to be helping. Ibn Saud took Jebel Shammar in 1921, Mecca in 1924, Medina in 1925, and Asîr in 1926 with remarkable swiftness. Ibn Saud proclaimed himself king of Al Hijâz. In 1932, after unifying the conquered territories, he declared Saudi Arabia a nation.

Saudi Arabia remained somewhat of a backwater, however, until its oil deposits were discovered in 1938. Saudi Arabia played both sides of World War II until it was obvious the Allies would win, and then declared war on Germany and Japan in March 1945. By the time Israel declared itself a nation, ibn Saud had collected a decade of oil money. U.S. companies had by that time paid $53 million in royalties, which quadrupled to $212 million by 1952.[9]

Despite all this, however, the Middle East of the 1950s became a checkerboard of the Cold War. As independence from imperial powers was found and Arabs began to adopt self-rule rather than British protectorate status, two trends began in the Middle East: one toward Arab nationalism and modernization, following the vision of Egyptian President Gamal Abd al-Nasser, and the other toward the nostalgic Wahhabian vision of the region's monarchies. Saudi Arabia, of course, was foremost among this latter group. The monarchies of Saudi Arabia, Iraq, Iran, and Kuwait also had a legitimate edge over the nationalists because they controlled the oil. The Cold War further polarized the region. Because of the influence of American oil companies, the U.S. supported the monarchies, and though Presidents Eisenhower and Kennedy had made solid efforts to court Nasser, Egypt and Syria moved to the Soviet side of the table, having received most of their military technology from them.

The checker pieces of the Cold War began jumping as East and West played their game: Britain signed the Baghdad Pact in 1955 with Iraq, Iran, Turkey, and Pakistan in an attempt to keep these nations pro-Western. In 1956, Britain moved with France and Israel to invade the Sinai Peninsula and precipitate the Suez Crisis. In response to these maneuvers, Egypt and Syria formed the United Arab Republic in 1958, which would eventually be the alliance that initiated the Six-Day War in 1967 and the Yom Kippur War in 1973. In response, Jordan and Iraq formed the Arab Union of Jordan and Iraq that same year, joining their Hashemite kingdoms, and Nuri as-Said, former premier of Iraq, was named premier of the new joint nation. Nasser responded to this by calling on the people, police, and military of Iraq to overthrow their pro-Western government. This resulted in the July 14, 1958, coup d'état that put the military in control of the country and dissolved the Arab Union. Iraq withdrew from its own Baghdad Pact in 1959.

This made for an odd trend: The U.S. favored the regressive over the progressive regimes. While both were dictatorships and repressive, America was supporting the side of Ishmael, which would produce terrorism and continue to try to push the Middle East back to the Middle Ages, not the side that would move his descendants toward modernization and a better standard of living. As America had depleted its own oil reserves in Oklahoma and Texas to win the Second World War, Middle Eastern oil, particularly that from Saudi Arabia, Iran, Iraq, and

Kuwait became of great interest, if not a necessity, to keep the U.S. economy prospering. As America paid richly to pump the crude to keep its economy thriving, it was also funding a growing underground movement against Israel and stability in the region.

Through it all, Saudi Arabia maintained the neutrality ibn Saud had exhibited during World War II and waited to see what would become of it all under ibn Saud's second son, King Saud (ibn Saud died in 1953). Though Saudi Arabia had no love for the fledgling Jewish state, at this time it was more concerned with its aggressive neighbors, particularly the Hashemite kingdoms of Jordan and Iraq on its northern border. Under King Saud, despite the continual flow of oil money into the region, Saudi Arabia plunged into financial disarray. King Saud was eventually deposed and replaced by his younger brother, Faisal bin Abdul Aziz, in 1964. The Wahhabi *ulemas* had a good deal to do with this change in leadership, and Faisal wouldn't forget it. Where Saud's government had grown soft and more open, Faisal would return the country to its ultraconservative Wahhabist roots. According to the advice of King Faisal's maternal grandfather, who raised him after Faisal's mother's death when he was six, "Saudi Arabia should lead the Arab world and the ideology of Wahhabism should be exported."[10]

Though Faisal's grandfather died not long after giving him this advice, it appears that it was never forgotten. It also appears that Faisal was more like his father, ibn Saud, than his older brother had been. But it was the clever, behind-the-scenes ibn Saud that came out in Faisal rather than the cutthroat invader who had retaken Mecca and Medina. He would use his influence and the power Wahhabism gave him, not military might, to promote Saudi interest. And so it was that, just as ibn Saud had supplied only two Saudi brigades to help fight the Jews in their war for independence in 1948–49, Faisal would supply only one for the Six-Day War in 1967, and that division would not even see action. Saudi Arabia would, however, benefit from Israel's victory in more ways than one. With Egypt embarrassed and weakened, Nasser would pull his troops from Yemen, where he had hoped to begin a *coup* that would deliver the Arabia Peninsula into Pan-Arab nationalist control. With Nasser's withdrawal, Saudi Arabia's southern borders were again secure.

However, King Faisal showed no gratitude for this and soon found another way to undermine the Israeli cause and the Arab states that might rival Saudi in the Middle East. He began to financially support an upstart organization called *Fatah* (the Movement for the National Liberation of Palestine), headed by an Egyptian named Yasser Arafat. *Fatah* and brother organizations would use Saudi money to destabilize Jordan, and eventually force Jordan to use its full military might to oust them from their country during "Black September" of 1968. However, the *Fatah* would still go on to take full control of the Nasser-created Palestine Liberation Organization (PLO) in 1969, combining several terrorist groups under one umbrella.

All the while, Saudi Arabia kept solid relations with the U.S. and oil flowed to America, American money flowed into Faisal's coffers, and from there, U.S. dollars flowed to promote and export Wahhabism— the doctrine of Ishmael's hatred for Israel and the West.

CHAPTER NINE

Exporting Hate

Saudi Arabia is the key supporter of terrorism. A suicide bomber is Islamic in nature, a social norm in struggle against the infidel. The West must be made to understand that Islamic Fundamentalism is a worldwide threat.

Dr. David Burkay
Haifa University
Jerusalem Summit
October 12–14, 2003[1]

As for Ishmael, I have heard thee: Behold, I have blessed him, and will make him fruitful, and will multiply him exceedingly; twelve princes shall he beget, and I will make him a great nation. But my covenant will I establish with Isaac.

Genesis 17:20–21

The Six-Day War of 1967 and the Yom Kippur War of 1973 not only defended Israel, but also turned the tide in the Arabic world from the progressive, pro-socialist pan-Arab nationalists to the regressive, pro-Western monarchies. As the Arab nationalists following the Nasser flag failed again and again to defeat the small sliver of a country of Israel and, in fact, ended up losing more and more control over the area in the process, Saudi Arabia sat back quietly and paid thugs to keep its interest on the rise. This money also acted as protection money to keep targets such as the TAPLINE (the Trans Arabian Pipeline that passed from Sidon in Lebanon, through the Golan Heights, and on into Saudi Arabia), off the terrorists' lists of targets (though it did eventually close down when Lebanon collapsed in 1983). As the PLO took prominence over the terrorism in the region, Saudi Arabian princes and kings became Arafat's most faithful supporters.

While King Faisal had for a short time suspended oil exports to the U.S. and Great Britain during the Six-Day War, the results were minimal, and Faisal didn't yet see that oil could be used as a weapon. However, the world changed greatly from 1967 to 1973, and by that time, both Saddam Hussein, who was vice president of the regime that had toppled the Iraqi monarchy in 1972, and Colonel Muammar Qaddafi, whose regime took power in June 1973, had nationalized all oil interests within their borders. The influence of the Organization of Oil Producing Countries (OPEC) was at its height. While Saudi Arabia was content to sit on the sidelines as the Yom Kippur War erupted on October 6, 1973, and sat on its hands through most of the struggle, King Faisal finally decided to step in when it looked like all was lost as Israeli troops under the command of Ariel Sharon crossed the Suez Canal on October 16 and were within sixty-three miles of the Egyptian capital Cairo, by October 20. So on October 20, Faisal cut off oil supplies to the U.S. and urged the rest of OPEC to do the same. They did. On the twenty-first, he cut off the oil to the U.S. sixth fleet in the Mediterranean. Suddenly, Israel's allies were urging the signing of a cease-fire.

Though the war ended with neither side conceding defeat, the only real winners were the Saudis, who had won the war without firing a shot. They had shown the other Arab nations that they had power the pan-Arab Nasserites and Syrians did not. This might have had enough of a ripple effect on its own, but the embargo would have an unexpected additional benefit: Oil prices soared. Saudi oil revenues in 1972 had been $2.7 billion; however, in 1973 they went to $4.3 billion, and in 1974 they skyrocketed to $22.6 billion.[2] Suddenly, Faisal had nearly unlimited resources with which to propagate Saudi and Wahhabist interests.

Saudi Arabia soon developed the leading economy among Muslim countries, so it became a destination for Muslims who could not find decent-paying jobs in their own countries. Wahhabist *ulemas* would put this to work for them. These immigrants would be indoctrinated with Wahhabism while they were in Saudi and, eventually, when they had made enough money, they would return to their own countries with a "renewed" mind. Wahhabism would become the cry for Islamic ascendancy to a place of dominance in the world system. Saudi Arabia became the ideal of every other Muslim nation, and Saudis preached Wahhabism as the belief system that Allah blessed so richly. The Muslim world looked to Saudi Arabia both for financial deliverance from poverty and for enlightenment. Wahhabism was introduced as the seed of revival to true Islam.

Additionally, with Saudi control over the holy cities of Mecca and Medina, to which every Muslim had to travel at least once in their life as part of the *Hajj* (which means "pilgrimage" and is one of the five pillars of Islam). This gave them another way of showing the rest of the world what "true" Islam was. Pilgrims were introduced to extreme fundamentalist Wahhabist doctrine as a return to the true Islam of Muhammad. As interest in it grew, Wahhabism spread throughout the Muslim world and became a standard curriculum in schools, mosques, and universities—Saudi grants and donations to Islamic charities made sure of this.

The West glossed this over, calling the move "Islamism." The U.S. State Department, intelligence community, and other concerned branches of the government paid it little attention. In a relativist culture of "separation of church (religion) and state," Islamism was viewed simply as a cultural movement to uplift the spirits of some of the poorest nations in the world. For them to think that a religious teaching could actually be dangerous bordered too closely on intolerance (the greatest sin of political correctness) and went against the grain of the relativistic ecumenism of the "global village." We wouldn't, in fact, begin to take notice of it until the attacks of September 11, and even then it would take more than two years before any government agency publicly announced that Wahhabism might be a threat.[3] Until that day, no one in the U.S. government was willing to suggest that someone could hate us enough to hijack a plane and commit suicide in the hope of killing thousands. They assumed anyone on such a mission would lose their resolve before carrying it through. They were wrong. They had totally underestimated the narcotic power of Wahhabism and the hatred it created.

The Yom Kippur War also brought other changes in the Islamic world and the Middle East. After Egypt and Syria's defeat in a conventional war, it became evident, especially when the U.S. began to back Israel as a military ally and bolster her military with advanced U.S. weaponry, that there was little chance of winning a direct conventional war against Israel. Despite the fact that they had only one-eighth of 1 percent of the land of the Arab states, this little country was much more than a David against their Goliath. Somehow Israel had become *the* Middle Eastern superpower, especially since it was the only country in the region with a nuclear bomb. This brought about the concern that Israel might attack Iraq with nuclear weapons if provoked during the 1991 Gulf War, again causing America to rush weaponry to defend Israel—this time the Patriot missile—in exchange for Israel's promise to stay on the sideline. As a result, Israel absorbed thirty-nine missiles without firing back once, while keeping Baghdad in its nuclear crosshairs the entire time.

As a result, in 1974 at a meeting in Rabat, Morocco, the Arab League appointed the PLO terrorist organization as the sole, legitimate representative of the Palestinian people, and the Egyptian-born Mohammed Abdel-Raouf Arafat al Qudwa al-Hussaeini as its leader. We know him today as Yasser Arafat.

Another result was also the brightest ray of hope we have seen in the Arab-Israeli conflict in the last century, the peace treaty and "normal relations" between Egypt and Israel that returned the Sinai Peninsula to Egypt on the guarantee that it remain demilitarized. Yet even here there were signs of dissension. After Egyptian President Muhammad Anwar al-Sadat made his unprecedented trip to Israel in 1977 and became the first Arab leader to address the Israeli parliament, known as the Knesset, I asked Prime Minister Menachem Begin what he thought of the Egyptian leader in an informal meeting we had some time later. He responded, "I didn't like his tie, and I didn't like his letter." I didn't know what he meant at the time, but felt it was inappropriate to pursue it at that moment. I later discovered that as Sadat addressed the Knesset, he wore a tie with a dazzling pastiche of large Nazi swastikas up and down its length. I also discovered that, as rumors spread in 1953 that Adolf Hitler may have escaped capture and was alive and well in Brazil, Egyptian weekly *Al-Musawwar* asked its leaders what they would write to the führer if they could. Sadat (who had helped in Nasser's coup to oust King Faruk) replied, "I congratulate you with all my heart, because, though you appear to have been defeated, you were the real victor. You were able to sow dissention between Churchill, the old man, and his allies on one hand and their ally, the devil, on the other . . . That you should become immortal in Germany is reason enough for pride. And we should not be surprised to see you again in Germany, or a new Hitler in your place."[4] Even prior to this, in the midst of World War II, Sadat had spent time in jail for his openly pro-Nazi stance and frank endorsement of Hitler in British-ruled Egypt. Sadat would thus sign a peace treaty with Israel, while wearing his anti-Semitism at the same time.

Despite this, Sadat was assassinated in 1981 for his efforts at bringing peace to the Middle East. "Normal relations"—the establishment of embassies and exchange of ambassadors and as opposed to "normalization," which would mean not only that but also open trade and transportation between the countries—even broke down as Egypt withdrew its ambassadors from Israel in 2001. Sadat's move, did, however set a precedent that would be followed by the Jordanians when they signed a peace treaty with Israel in 1994. To date, Egypt and Jordan are the only two Arab countries to agree to such treaties; the rest of the Arab nations have retained the right to remain openly hostile toward Israel. However, anti-Semitism is starting to take back its ground in Egypt as more and more of it appears in their media.

If direct military confrontation was not the answer to defeating Is-

rael, however, what was? Ayatollah Khomeini provided part of the answer to that question in toppling the shah, and the PLO had provided
the rest in their toppling of Lebanon. The Arabs would fight a war of
attrition against Israel, defeating the nation little by little and destroying its will to fight back. This would be accomplished through spreading the virus of rabid anti-Semitism and asymmetrical terrorism.
Khomeini showed how to unify secular, social, and religious groups in
their hatred for the shah and the U.S., and used this unified hatred as
a political and military tool to overthrow the government—and he
started it all while not even in the country. With the storming and capture of the U.S. Embassy on November 4, 1979, he showed that the
West was far from all-powerful. Islam suddenly became the David beginning to defeat the new Goliath of the "Great Satan," America, and
"the illegitimate offspring of the Great Satan," the nation of Israel.

The surprise of the revolution to Washington and Langley (CIA
headquarters in Virginia) didn't help things much. When the Mossad
reported to the Americans in 1978 that Shah Muhammad Reza
Pahlavi's position in power was shaky and would not hold, they rejected
it, giving continual forecasts that he would cling to power. When he fell
roughly a year later, it was not only shocking to the American government, but extremely embarrassing. Unfortunately, this would not be
the last event of this magnitude about which the CIA would fail to correctly warn their president.

Despite the U.S.'s surprise, the Saudis welcomed the overthrow in
more ways than one. Saudi Arabia benefited from the Iranian revolution as it cut off Iranian oil to the West. Saudi oil revenues again grew
disproportionately as a result, just as they had after the OPEC embargo
of 1973: Their royalties were $32.2 billion in 1978, $48.4 billion in
1979, and $102.1 billion in 1981.[5] As a result, between 1982 and
2002, 1,500 mosques, 210 Islamic centers, and 2,000 Muslim schools
were built in non-Muslim countries alone in order to promote Wahhabism. The Saudis also donated academic chairs for Islamic studies to
Harvard Law School and the University of California in Berkeley, as
well as grants supporting Islamic research at American University (in
Washington, D.C.), Howard University, Duke, and Johns Hopkins.[6] In

a two-year period in the 1980s, according to Muslim World League internal documents, the Saudis spent $10 million to build mosques in the United States.[7] Since 1973, Saudis have spent $87 billion to spread Wahhabism throughout the U.S. and the Western Hemisphere.[8] Thus Khomeini provided Saudis not only with an example, but also furthered their means.

The Saudis also started their arms purchases from the United States about this time. It was in February 1978 that Jimmy Carter informed Congress he wanted to sell fifty F-15 fighters to Saudi Arabia. Despite objections from Israel, pro-Israel lobbyists, and demonstrators marching in the streets with signs saying things such as "Hell No to the PLO" and "Aid to Israel! Best Investment for America," the sale was eventually approved.[9] America was now selling advanced arms to both prophetic brothers.

The PLO and Hezbollah ("Party of Allah") contributed to the rise of Islamism by creating something that eventually became known as "asymmetrical terrorist attacks." The term "asymmetrical" was used because the attacks were disproportionately one-sided: these were not battles with visible soldiers on each side wearing distinguishing uniforms shooting at each other over a no-man's-land; these were sudden, surprise kamikaze attacks that were aimed to kill as many as possible. There would be no opportunity to retaliate because there would be no one alive to shoot back. Under their careful manipulation of zealous minds, they had created a new "H"-bomb—the "Human" bomb—that could be used to zero in on any target with greater precision than any of America's smart bombs and cost millions less—unless, of course, you wanted to include that loss of the life to which the bomb was strapped, a cost that those who sent them never considered.

Using these H-bombs, the PLO and Hezbollah showed how to use asymmetrical terrorist tactics to scare an enemy into retreat. I was in Beirut in October 1983 when two truck bombs were used against the U.S. and French troops stationed there. The explosions killed 241 U.S. military personnel and fifty-eight French paratroopers. I remember the chaos and panic that rippled through the streets that day. The result was that the foreign troops withdrew, and Lebanon was turned into a terrorist incubation center where Christians were killed and where children in daycare centers and kindergartens were taught the glory of being martyred for Allah as suicide bombers against Israel. America had lost its first significant battle in the war on terrorism, and we didn't even know we were at war.

Yet while Wahhabism focused its hatred on the West, it felt no better about the communist East. Thus when the Soviets invaded Afghanistan at the end of 1979 to help protect the Soviet puppet government there from the *Mujahadeen* (from the Arabic word for "warriors") rebel uprising, the twenty-three-year-old heir of the largest construction business in Saudi Arabia, along with many others, left the Middle East to fight for the freedom of these Islamic brothers in Afghanistan against the government and the Soviets. He received Saudi, Pakistani, and U.S. support to fight a guerrilla war of nomads against sophisticated Soviet military might. The Saudis gave $4 billion in aid to the various Afghan rebel groups between 1980 and 1990, which excludes the amount they gave through various Islamic charities and the private funds of the princes.[10] This construction engineer also received special training from the CIA and created a network throughout the Muslim world to successfully recruit fighters and equipment to join the rebels' cause and push back the Soviet infidels. After nearly a decade of fighting, the Soviets finally withdrew in February 1989, showing they were no longer able to move into a region and suppress an uprising as they had throughout the Soviet bloc countries in previous decades. As a result, Soviet Republics began to declare their independence and secede from the U.S.S.R. one by one. Moscow had no resolve to fight a civil war to bring them back into the Soviet Union, and, as a result, the Berlin wall came down on November 9, 1989, and the Union of Soviet Socialist Republics finally dissolved completely in December 1991.

However, the fighting in Afghanistan did not end with the Soviet withdrawal; rebel forces continued their same drive to take over the government that had precipitated the Soviet intervention. The government held out against these forces for some time until, before its demise, the Soviet Union signed an agreement with the United States to stop giving aid to either side. Over the next few years, various groups claimed control until a Wahhabi-like movement headquartered in Herat, called the Taliban, finally won out and set up a government. This movement was organized with the help of the Saudi construction engineer, who was suddenly a George Washington to the Arab world because he had not only toppled the Soviet Union, but also made way for the first Wahhabist government outside Saudi Arabia. The name of this new Muslim folk hero was Osama bin Laden, and with the help of the Taliban and Saudi funding, Afghanistan was set up as a terrorist incubating state with its own special terrorist training camps.

Intoxicated by his success in vanquishing the Soviets, bin Laden would turn his attention to the only remaining superpower that threatened the Wahhabist worldview: the United States. The incredible network that bin Laden had formed to defeat the Soviets became *al Qaeda* ("the Base") in 1988. And so began more than a decade of violence against the U.S., which would not really be noticed until fifteen Saudis and four other Muslim al Qaeda hijacked four U.S. airliners and crashed them into the World Trade Center towers and the Pentagon on September 11, 2001.

Saudi Arabia quietly funded terrorism and coerced more and more advanced military hardware and protection from the United States in order to keep its oil flowing in our direction. In 1991, Saudis even let the U.S. launch attacks on its Muslim neighbor Iraq from their soil in defense against tyranny and terrorism, all the while hiding that their true intention was to weaken the Hashemites. They sat back as others on both fronts died for the strengthening of Saudi Arabia. The threat to them was real, however, in 1991—Saddam Hussein could easily have pushed through Kuwait to Riyadh if he had so desired because of Saudi Arabia's poor defensive ability. While they had some of the most sophisticated U.S. weapons available, their troops weren't combat-ready and could hardly be expected to operate effectively. America, for its part, pulled it off beautifully. There was no more than a bump in the U.S. economy as gas prices temporarily soared in response to the possibility that the wars might bring shortages; then it returned to normal. As was expressed by Martin Indyk, a former U.S. ambassador to Israel,

"We've struck a Faustian bargain, turning a blind eye to Saudi Arabia's domestic policies . . . and a blind eye to Saudi Arabian efforts to export Wahhabism."[11]

In roughly that same time period (1990–2001), the Saudis were the number one world customer for advanced U.S. conventional weaponry, with sales totaling more than $45 billion. Saudis have also invested about $200 billion back into the U.S. economy through the years. However, despite having the most sophisticated weaponry in the region, without mercenaries or U.S. troops to operate and maintain them, they are little more than fancy, and extremely dangerous, toys to show off. Like much else that has been done in Saudi Arabia, great sums of money have been spent to look good, but no infrastructure has been built to maintain them. Saudi Arabia's wealth is based solely on its oil reserves, but all those billions have created no lasting industry in the country and no Saudis trained to run anything. The entire country is kept going by engineers and experts from the West and cheap labor from the rest of the Muslim world. Saudi citizens have not benefited much from the reign of the House of Saud. Instead of creating more wealth and raising the standard of living in the country, Saudi riches have been wasted on the opulent lives of their government officials (almost all of which are relatives of the seven-thousand-member-strong royal family), and on exporting the hatred of Wahhabism.

Right after the Iraqi invasion of Kuwait in August 1990, Osama bin Laden offered the aid of his well-trained mujahadeen forces to protect his Saudi homeland from Saddam Hussein's continuing march through Kuwait to Riyadh. This would keep Saudi Arabia free of the possible infidel infection of letting Western troops into the country to defend it. The Saudi government did not take bin Laden's offer seriously, and soon began the U.S. troop movements into Saudi Arabia that would form the invasion force of Desert Storm. The presence of American troops in his homeland became another mark against the United States for bin Laden, and also a mark against what he must have seen as obvious Western corruption of Saudi leadership. This is further evidenced by the fact that bin Laden became more and more critical in his comments about the Saudi regime, to the point that the Saudi government revoked his citizenship in 1994. There is also good evidence that it is this sentiment that motivated al Qaeda members to carry out the four bombings in May and November of 2003 in Riyadh that murdered forty-two, mostly Muslims (only eight of the victims were Americans), and wounded hundreds in the pursuit of chasing all Westerners from Saudi soil.

In April 1991, Ishmael's rage began to become more consolidated and focused. From the twenty-fifth through the twenty-eighth of that month, radical Islamic groups that sympathized with Iraq during Desert Storm convened in Khartoum at the invitation of Hassan al-Turabi. Islamic militants called the National Islamic Front (NIF) had toppled the Sudanese government in June 1989, and Sudan moved into the Islamic world (after the Soviet withdrawal from Afghanistan, bin Laden made trips to Sudan to help organize the NIF). Many of the groups attending received Saudi financial support. Fifty-five nations were represented, including several from the Middle East as well as representatives from Hamas (an acronym for the "Islamic Resistance Movement") and Islamic Jihad, as well as Yasser Arafat and bin Laden. Bin Laden even set up residence in Khartoum from 1991 until he was expelled in 1996 (at which time he returned to Afghanistan to set up new headquarters for al Qaeda). In those few years he initiated various businesses there as money-collecting fronts for al Qaeda.

What these groups all had in common was their hatred for the United States and its Middle East protégé, Israel. From this hatred came the Popular Arab and Islamic Congress (PAIC), which met every couple of years until Sudan closed its offices in Khartoum in February 2000. In a parting shot, al-Turabi blamed the U.S. chiefly, among other nations, for the shutdown because the United States "is well known for its hostile attitudes toward Islam."[12] In that time span, PAIC became a convention where the terrorists made new relationships and alliances, shared bomb-making secrets, coordinated efforts and logistics, and encouraged one another in their hatred. Al Qaeda blossomed as a result of the connections bin Laden made there and at the next conference held in January 1993. On his own, bin Laden would coordinate efforts with Hezbollah in 1992, and Hezbollah would attend PAIC's 1995 conference. PAIC became a who's who of international terrorists.

The first attack against American interests, possibly inspired by the fledgling organization PAIC, was the 1992 attack on the Goldmore and Aden Hotels in Yemen, where U.S. Marines on their way to Somalia had been temporarily housed. This was followed in 1993 by the carefully constructed but poorly executed plan to bring down the World Trade Center with a truck bomb.

Sheik Omar Abdel-Rahman was the organizer of that devilish plot. His associate (and a disciple of Osama bin Laden) El Sayyid Nosair wrote in his notebook:

> The obligation of Allah is upon us to wage *jihād* for the sake of Allah . . . We have to thoroughly demoralize the enemies of Allah by blowing up their towers that constitute the pillars of their civilization . . . the high buildings of which they are so proud.[13]

In an uncompromising fit of moral relativistic blindness, they marked across the top of the boxes, "Irrelevant religious stuff," dismissing the very reason for the attacks and failing to connect them to the worldwide Wahhabist movement that had fueled it. They saw Abdel-Rahman's group as a fanatic splinter group much the same as Jim Jones's and the Branch Davidians of Waco, Texas, they faced only a few days after that bombing.

Abdel-Rahman, who was involved in the assassination of Egyptian President Anwar Sadat, came to America in 1990, free to set up his terrorist shop in New Jersey. A PBS special aired in 1994 documented a quiltwork of Islamic groups and terrorist sponsors that had sprung up across America since the Iranian revolution. These groups included arms of Islamic Jihad, Hamas, and Hezbollah with cells in New York, Florida, Chicago, Kansas City, and Dallas. The groups hide behind a smoke screen of small businesses and religious and charitable groups. These team members work in the U.S. to raise funds, recruit volunteers, and lay plans for terrorist missions in the ultimate battle against

"The Great Satan." Their primary objective was to succeed in the mission without being blamed, to realize widespread media coverage, and to maximize psychological and economic damage through terror.

Thus, in 1993, Ishmael's hatred for his half brother was in full bloom and intent on attacking America and Israel. This hatred was empowered by U.S-paid oil royalties, training and experience in toppling superpowers, organization and coordination by groups such as PAIC, and terrorist-harboring states, businesses, and charities in the U.S. Another piece of the puzzle leading to September 11 was the December 1994 attempt by the Algerian Groupe Islamique Armé to hijack an Air France plane with the plan to crash it into the Eiffel Tower. Most in the group were Arabs who had fought in Afghanistan. The plan failed, however, because none of the hijackers could fly the plane, so it landed in Marseilles instead, where it was stormed by French police. No direct connection was made to al Qaeda, but the attempt alone must have seeded the idea for September 11 along with the caution to make sure there were terrorists on board who could fly the airliner, even if they didn't know how to land it. If nothing else, America was now directly in the crosshairs of prophetic rage.

Yet we were also at a crossroads between the two brothers. In September 1993, I sat in the audience as President Bill Clinton held a celebration on the White House lawn for what he called "a brave gamble for peace," where he forced—standing with his thumb in the prime minister's back—Israeli Prime Minister Yitzhak Rabin to shake hands with PLO Chairman Yasser Arafat—who had probably just shaken Osama bin Laden's hand in the same way only months before—over a blank sheet of paper that represented the Declaration of Principles, or Oslo Accords, which led to Israeli concessions to the Palestinian Authority that would be answered only with more H-bombs in Jerusalem and Tel Aviv. The paper lay on the same table over which President Jimmy Carter had presided as Menachem Begin and Anwar Sadat signed the Peace Treaty between Israel and Egypt in 1979. President Clinton later described it as one of "the highest moments" of his presidency as the two "shook hands for the first time in front of a billion people on television. It was an unbelievable day."[14]

It was indeed an "unbelievable day" and a defining moment for the forty-second president of the United States, but hardly in the terms that he described. America had not only negotiated an official agreement between a democracy and a terrorist organization, but had sent a signal to terrorists worldwide that crime pays.

CHAPTER TEN

Treason

America will never be destroyed from the outside. If we falter and lose our freedoms, it will be because we destroyed ourselves.

Abraham Lincoln[1]

All nations before him are as nothing; and they are counted to him less than nothing, and vanity.

Isaiah 40:1

Almost exactly a year before the September 11 attacks, on September 8, 2000, President Bill Clinton welcomed an incredible assembly of world leaders—made up of dignitaries, ambassadors, and heads of state who were attending the United Nations Millennium Summit—to a reception held in one of the most remarkable places in New York City: the Temple of Dendur, a Nubian shrine honoring the Egyptian goddess Isis. The temple was rebuilt stone by stone in the Sackler Wing of the Metropolitan Museum of Art, which is a glass room large enough to hold a house and overlooks Central Park. The ancient relic was disassembled in the 1960s to preserve the ancient site when the Aswan Dam project would have covered it in water. It was given to the United States in 1965 as a gift of friendship from Egyptian President Gamal Abd al-

Nasser, and awarded to the Met the same year that Nasser provoked the Six-Day War.

The symbolism of the event and the location seem to speak volumes about the Clinton presidency; not only the symbolism of meeting with the UN members in a room housing a gift from a man who hated Israel, but also the symbolism of the temple itself. The temple was erected roughly fifteen years before Christ's birth as a Roman tribute to Egyptian heritage. It even depicts the Roman Emperor Caesar Augustus (the emperor responsible for Mary and Joseph's going to Bethlehem for Jesus' birth)[2] sacrificing to the Egyptian gods alongside other pharaohs, symbolizing the supremacy of such gods to even the greatest world leaders of that day. Isis, to whom the temple is dedicated, has been one of the most enduring goddesses of all time, being the great mother-goddess, maternal spirit, enchantress, goddess of magic, and protector of the dead: an archetype identified with mother earth, the earth goddess, Gaia, and similar worldly traditions—in other words, she symbolizes *Spiritus Mundi*, the "spirit of the world." If ever there was a gathering that epitomized the moral relativity of Bill Clinton's eight years in office, this was it—perhaps even going one step farther than the day he lied before a federal grand jury concerning his sexual harassment of Paula Jones.

Many liberals gloss over the issues surrounding Bill Clinton's impeachment as a right-wing Republican witch hunt to oust a progressive, educated, highly intelligent, and charismatic world leader—the man who has come closest to bringing peace to the Middle East and the president who presided over the greatest time of prosperity in American, if not world, history. "So the man had a few sexual scandals; so did President Kennedy, and look at what a great man he was!" Yet, as often happens, they have their facts confused. William Clinton wasn't impeached for having an affair with Monica Lewinsky or even using his position as governor to sexually harass Paula Jones. He was impeached for placing his hand on the Bible, promising to "tell the truth, the whole truth, and nothing but the truth," and *lying* to cover up his own indiscretions. If the man would lie to do that, what else would he be willing to lie about? If he were willing to twist the reasoning of moral judgment to justify perjury, what else would he do to achieve the goals he set for himself? And would this president's lack of moral judgment make him a danger to the citizens of the United States?

In his first year in office, Clinton worked with more different focus groups than George H. W. Bush did in his entire four-year term as president. Through this practice, he became a master of manipulating image and public opinion, keeping a high approval level through most of his presidency while selling the United States and its allies down the river.

One of President Clinton's greatest hopes was to go down in history as the man who finally solved the Arab-Israeli conflict in the Middle East. In order to do this, he used his tremendous aptitude at image transformation to change the terrorist and murderer Yasser Arafat into a "freedom fighter" and a diplomat. Arafat became the most welcomed foreign leader to the White House during the Clinton years. It also seems likely that Arafat got some coaching from Clinton and his advisers on what to say, how to speak, and what to do to help in this metamorphosis.

I remember talking with Jim Wright, a former congressman and Speaker of the House, as Arafat spoke to an audience on the lawn of the Rose Garden at the September 1993 meeting when Arafat and Rabin shook hands. In his speech, as one reporter put it, Arafat said:

> "I assure you that we share your values of freedom, justice, and human rights for which my people have been striving," . . . his reading glasses and soft tone belying his ogre status. "Our two peoples want to give peace a chance," he said to applause from a crowd of 3,000, a Who's Who of the American establishment . . .
>
> "We are relying on you, Mr. President, and all the countries who know that without peace in the Middle East, peace in the world is incomplete."[3]

Afterward, former Congressman Wright turned to me and said, "Wasn't Arafat's speech brilliant? He is a charming fellow, and I used to not like him."

Such comments leave me astounded at how well glitz can sell over substance. Yasser Arafat has left a trail of blood since he first got involved with *Fatah* in the 1960s, with some of his most recent actions being his renewed call for a million martyrs—suicide bombers—to march on Jerusalem and kill innocent men, women, and children. However, all of this magically disappeared as Arafat and his entourage marched into the White House on thirteen different occasions during the Clinton era as welcome guests to negotiate the release of "Palestine's occupied territories."

Clinton's aim was to hold the hands of both brothers—Isaac and Ishmael—as he walked each of them through the "peace" process—and he did so by legitimizing one and applying pressure on the other. One of the other things that he did to legitimize Arafat, perhaps with further aid from his focus groups, was to change the language of the discussion. The PLO would no longer be referred to as "terrorists," but as "freedom-fighters" or "militants." Somehow, the building of Israeli settlements on the West Bank became morally equivalent to suicide bombers' murdering innocent people in major Israeli cities. Each was pitched as the reason negotiations were continually failing. A clear example of the Clinton administration's moral makeover happened in 1997, when Sara Ehrman, a cofounder of *Americans for Peace Now* who became a senior adviser to Clinton, organized a conference call in New York between Secretary of State Madeleine Albright and some American Jewish leaders. Among the participants was Ken Bialkin, who noticed this tendency on the part of the Clinton administration. He asked Albright, "How can you compare building in the settlements [in the West Bank] to Arafat's terror? You are creating moral equivalence."

The conference call ended and everyone hung up. But one participant remained on the line and recorded the rest of what was said. Sara Ehrman angrily asked her friend Steven Cohen, who had been Shimon Peres's contact man with the PLO during the 1980s, "How is it that there are people here asking such embarrassing questions? Don't they realize that Arafat has no choice but to use terror?"[4]

He had no choice? The PLO and similar organizations have no choice but to send some of their most dedicated youth to murder innocent people by committing suicide? Then what are the peace talks about? Do Arafat and the other Arab nations really want peace with Israel? If so, why have they rejected it time and again? Why did they reject it in Madrid in 1981 when they were offered 95 percent of the lands won in the Six-Day War? Why did they renew their *intifada* (uprising) after they were given the Gaza Strip, Jericho, and Bethlehem, if what they really want is peace? Do they really have no option but to renew violence time and again after Israel makes concessions to them? On the other hand, the Palestinian Authority—whose strings are pulled by Arafat and the PLO—has yet to honor its word in any of these negotiations and blames the continued violence on the Islamist "splinter groups" of Islamic Jihad and Hamas—many of whose attacks were, however, coordinated with Arafat and the PLO before being carried out. Wouldn't a better choice be to follow through on what they have promised, as Israel has done, rather than breaking agreement after agreement by reinitiating the violence time and again? As Democratic Congressman Elliot Engel from New York put it:

> It's not poverty; it's fanaticism that causes terrorism. They are the product of a system that hates the Jews. Islamic Fundamentalism is against anything Western. Israel has the right to go after the terrorists everywhere. The fight against terrorism is a fight for world survival. We must speak with moral clarity—there is no equation between suicide bombers and Israeli actions.[5]

We need to realize that it is this type of moral relativism that has given birth to this mess, not "the love of truth" that provides moral clarity. It is the United States that has raised Ishmael's hopes. He thinks we will help him get it all, so he won't settle for anything less than 100 percent of what Israel won in 1967, and after that he will continue to work to get what Israel won in 1948.

As author Alan Dershowitz said in the first pages of his book *Why Terrorism Works*:

> Terrorism is often rationalized as a valid response to its "root causes"—mainly repression and desperation. But the vast majority of repressed and desperate people do not resort to the willful targeting of vulnerable civilians. The real root cause of terrorism is that it is successful—terrorists have consistently benefited from their terrorist acts. Terrorism will persist as long as it continues to work for those who use it, as long as the international community rewards it, as it has been doing for the past thirty-five years.[6]

Why does terrorism work? Because we try to appease it! We pay attention to it and make its perpetrators valid representatives of their causes, even if the people they claim to represent do not. We let their acts of violence get them more concessions or prompt intensification of negotiations. Whenever the violence increases, we go out of our way to get them more concessions. So why should they stop?

It was in doing just this—validating the PLO's acts of violence by pandering all the more earnestly to them—that Bill Clinton and his obsession with going down in history as the author of peace in the Middle East caused an unremitting erosion in Israel's negotiating positions with the Arab world in the 1990s; and when Israel was forced to fight against terror—striking back at military targets to disable terrorists, not randomly to create an equal number of innocent Palestinian victims—he did not give it his full backing. As Israel was the center of it all, it was also the main focus of Clinton's pressure to force agreements. According to Oslo, Israel would negotiate separate peace accords with Jordan, Syria, and the Palestinians, yet only one of these was ever signed, and that was with Jordan on October 26, 1994. For Syria, Israel's deportation of 415 Hamas members in December 1992 precipitated a crisis in continuing the talks, so that Syria demanded the PLO be part of their negotiations and that the PLO also be given the power of veto. The fate of the Golan Heights was also a major issue because these mountains provide a natural protective barrier from which to launch attacks, as Syria had done in the Six-Day War. Rabin himself stated during his 1992 election campaign that "to come down from the Golan Heights would be a betrayal of Israel's security." So, at least for the meantime, Rabin saw no mutual basis on which Jerusalem could negotiate with Damascus.

In the wake of the signing of the Oslo agreements, however, Clinton formulated a comprehensive peace plan for the Middle East with Syria as the main objective. So in 1994–95, he pressured contacts between Israel and Syria to go into high gear. As a result, a peace agreement appeared to be taking shape. The proposed peace settlement, which included a full Israeli withdrawal from the Golan Heights, awakened tremendous opposition within the Israeli populace. In the context of the contacts with the Syrians, Yitzhak Rabin gave President Clinton what became known as the "deposit," a paper that stated if all Israel's security needs were addressed and its demands regarding normalization and a withdrawal timetable were met, it would be willing to carry out a full withdrawal on the Golan Heights. The paper was not a diplomatic commitment, but rather was intended to serve only to inform the president as to what Israel would be willing to have as its final position in order to ultimately attain a peace agreement. According to a different version, Rabin was willing later on to explicitly mention the June 4, 1967, borders, when Syria still possessed the Golan Heights.

To this day, it is not yet clear how this "deposit" was born. It is quite possible that in the relationship between the Israeli prime minister and an American president constantly pressuring for "progress" with the Syrians, the Israeli prime minister was forced to reveal a position of this kind. Considering how Clinton later acted, it appears that Clinton's role in the "deposit" may well have been greater than Rabin's. However, the result was that the Clinton administration was willing to exploit Rabin in order to attain Israel's withdrawal from the Golan Heights and a subsequent peace agreement. Clinton betrayed Rabin and showed the Syrians the deposit that had been intended for his eyes only. But it was

Rabin, instead, who was seen as a traitor and was assassinated by an Is-raeli extremist on November 5, 1995. What Clinton had called his "brave gamble for peace" did not pay off for Rabin due to Clinton's double-dealing. I remember standing at Rabin's state funeral and watching a tiny bead of sweat roll down Bill Clinton's face as he looked on. He looked sullen and tired, but unfortunately not remorseful. The damage done to the negotiations was irreversible, and talks with the Syrians deteriorated from there until they finally ended in late 1998.

When Binyamin Netanyahu ran for prime minister in 1996, Clin-ton did not find him as malleable as Rabin had been. In fact, Ne-tanyahu posed such a barrier to Clinton's fulfilling his dreams for history that he did something unprecedented: He sent his own Demo-cratic campaign advisers to try to help Netanyahu's incumbent oppo-nent, Shimon Peres, win the election (Peres had been foreign minister and was an integral part of the peace negotiations under Rabin. After Rabin's assassination, he became leader of their Labor Party and prime minister).

Why did Clinton see Netanyahu as such a threat to his plans? Binyamin Netanyahu was a man who saw that the problems in the Arab-Israeli conflict could not be solved without moral clarity, and he also saw through Clinton's double-talk. He would not sell Israel's secu-rity down the river for repeatedly violated agreements from Arafat and the Palestinian Authority. After the violence was renewed in a series of murderous bus bombings in February and March 1996, Netanyahu was already leading Peres in the polls because the Israeli public, though they didn't know it at the time, had found that Clinton's "peace" process had an evil twin: Palestinian suicide attacks. When Netanyahu and his Likud Party spoke of security, they liked what they heard as op-posed to the Labor Party's "peace" process, which led only to more vi-olence. Clinton, for his part, viewed the Likud Party and its leader, Netanyahu, as a Middle Eastern chapter of the Republican Party. Un-fortunately, due to the Clinton administration's double-dealing and pressure, Netanyahu would not be able to deliver the security that he had promised Israeli voters.

A few weeks before the elections, Rahm Emanuel, Clinton's senior adviser on internal affairs, arrived in Israel. Emanuel, by the way, comes from an Israeli family of former Irgun (the Israeli resistance movement of the 1940s) members. He came to hear assessments as to what could be expected in the elections and to coordinate the possibility of helping Peres's campaign with his staff. The American embassy in Tel Aviv invited a number of Israeli political experts, such as Yitzhak Herzog, Yaron Ha'ezrahi, Rafi Smith, and others for a meeting with Rahm Emanuel. Only one of those invited to the meeting dared disagree with the general consensus in the room, maintaining that the question was not if Binyamin Netanyahu would win the election, but rather by how much. Everyone laughed, including Emanuel.

That same individual happened to bump into Emanuel on a plane to Washington, where they had many hours to argue. "Get used to the idea that soon there will be a new sheriff in town," he told Clinton's top adviser, telling him about the policies Netanyahu planned to introduce after the election, based on what Netanyahu wrote in his book *A Place Among the Nations*. When the two parted company in Washington, Emanuel said, "Tell your friend that if he dares to act according to what you have described—we will kick him in the —— so hard and he will be so miserable, that he won't know what hit him."[7]

Netanyahu, however, held the day and won the election. The confrontation between Clinton and Netanyahu on the personal-political level became evident immediately during Netanyahu's first state visit to Washington as prime minister in the summer of 1996. For the first time, Clinton encountered a head of state standing next to him during a press conference whose sound bites were better than his and who gave a more impressive appearance. Telling the truth makes a difference. Clinton found it virtually intolerable. Afterward, when Netanyahu spoke before Congress and received a standing ovation, especially from the Republican wing, Clinton began to treat the prime minister not as the person expressing the will of the Israeli people, but rather as if he were head of the opposition party. Ultimately, Clinton made every effort to undermine Netanyahu while he was in office.

American-Israeli relations in the mid-1990s should be viewed in the context of Clinton's overall policy, which may be defined as conciliatory toward terror and all potential aggressors. If Arafat wanted faster action or more concessions from Israel in their talks, all that had to happen was for the violence to increase. He could blame Netanyahu for moving too slowly (while he, in fact, moved backward), and Madeleine Albright and the Clinton team would start scrabbling and chastising the Israelis. Clinton didn't care about Israel's security and Palestinian violence—what he cared about was keeping the "peace" process going because it bumped up his approval ratings and acted as a diversion from his moral scandals. Clinton demonstrated laxness in the war against terror (as evidenced by his continually ignoring the growing threat of al Qaeda), and he was largely responsible for creating an environment friendly to terror and the creation of destructive trends in the world. During his term, the United States' systems and will to deter terrorism deteriorated, as did Israel's. Clinton made only a gesture (blowing up an empty Iraqi government building in the middle of the night with cruise missiles) to respond to the 1993 Iraqi assassination attempt on former President George H. W. Bush in Kuwait, and he paid virtually no attention to the first World Trade Center bombing, which took place that same year. This was followed by a series of terror attacks that peaked with the attack in Dhahran, Saudi Arabia, in which nineteen Americans were killed.

The year 1998 saw mass terror attacks in Kenya and Tanzania, in which 224 were killed and almost 5,000 were injured as the U.S. Embassies in Nairobi and Dar es Salaam (which, oddly enough, translates as "Haven of peace") were attacked with truck bombs almost simultaneously. Clinton's response—the firing of cruise missiles on insignificant targets in Sudan and an empty terrorist camp in Afghanistan (poor judgment on Clinton's part led to bin Laden's being tipped off about the attacks and escaping by minutes)—sent the message that the Clinton administration wanted to do only enough to make it look as though he were taking action, in order to keep American public support. Once Americans turned to go on with their lives, thinking he was taking care of things, Clinton went back to his agenda and forgot about the terrorist threat. Subsequently, seventeen Americans were killed and thirty-seven more injured aboard the USS *Cole* when a suicide bomber hit it on October 12, 2000, as it sat at dock refueling in Aden, Yemen. It was the deadliest attack on a U.S. warship since World War II. Clinton's continual weakness in the face of terrorists proclaimed an "open season" on Americans throughout the world.

In 1999, Clinton tried to restore American deterrence of violence and the appearance of our military strength during the war in Kosovo, but the massive air strike on the Serbians instead sent a positive message to Yasser Arafat and a negative message to Israel, without Bill Clinton's even intending to. It was a pro-Muslim war (the Kosovars were largely Muslim, while the Serbs were Orthodox Christians), and Arafat could see himself in the Kosovo Liberation Army (KLA) militants fighting to free Kosovo at a time when, for many in world opinion, Israel found itself pushed into the role of a Serbian-type aggressor.

Israel also showed Clinton raw data that proved Arafat had given the green light to the renewal of terror attacks by Hamas. Israel had monitored the talks that Arafat held with the Hamas leaders in Gaza on March 12–19, 1997. Based on that information, the then head of military intelligence, Moshe Yaalon, determined that Arafat had indeed approved and sanctioned these terror attacks on Israel. Clinton could have been expected to respond to this very harshly. However, he did nothing because he was unwilling to abandon Arafat, who was part of the Oslo legacy and "peace process" to which he was committed.

Also in 1999, Clinton made even more blatant use of his special position as president of the United States in the eyes of the Israeli public to undermine Netanyahu's standing and cause him to lose the election. Psychologically, Israel's unique relationship with the United States is one of the most important underpinnings of Israel's national security. If this relationship were to be viewed by the Israeli public as being shaken due to a particular individual, even if this had no objective basis in reality, it could result in serious public stress. Right at the start of the 1999 election campaign in Israel, Clinton sent a very clear message as to what he wanted: He sent the team that had run both of his successful election campaigns to lead Ehud Barak's campaign. This team was composed of James Carville, Stanley Greenberg, and Bob Shrum, a team worth more than a million dollars, and considering the activities for which the three were responsible, much more than that. Stanley Greenberg had already been involved in the process of figuring ways to win against Netanyahu back in 1998. He kept close contact with Barak. As the most prominent figure among the three, Greenberg did public opinion surveys and analyzed focus-group data. While the general opinion in the U.S. and Israeli press during 1998 was that Netanyahu would be in power for at least four more years, Greenberg found, and told Barak, that there was a way to beat Netanyahu. The main idea was to cross the security image threshold, and stick to the economy and social affairs—the same strategy Clinton had won with in the United States behind his sleight-of-hand slogan "It's the economy, stupid!" He kept America focused on their pocketbooks while he did whatever he wanted. That was the main input of "the Americans," said Tal Silberstein, one of Barak's top advisers for the campaign. "They structured the research, they came with the insights, and we adapted it to Israel."[8]

Some of the top donors to the Democratic Party and to Clinton's campaigns were mobilized for Barak's campaign as though this were another election the Democrats must win.

Overall, the Labor Party spent between $50 and $80 million on its anti-Netanyahu campaign, roughly ten times what Netanyahu's own Likud Party spent. In early 2000, the state comptroller of Israel produced a report that stated the Labor Party, in doing so, had grossly violated strict Israeli campaign finance laws. The government fined the campaign an unprecedented $3.2 million and is still following through on a criminal investigation of Barak's "One Israel" campaign financing.[9]

Clinton personally contributed to Ehud Barak by continuing his warm meetings with Arafat in the White House, while freezing out Prime Minister Binyamin Netanyahu and receiving Barak and Yitzhak Mordechai, both of the candidates running against Netanyahu in the election. "Clinton helped Barak more than he had to, " said one of Barak's men.[10] The fact that Arafat had become the White House's most welcome official guest (he could have also been awarded the Blair House's frequent-guest prize) was interpreted in the Israeli media to the detriment of Netanyahu rather than of the American president. The result of all those efforts was the collapse of the Israeli political center, with 6 percent of Netanyahu's voters moving over to the other side, causing a change of government in Israel.

Clinton, now with his new Israeli Labor Party partner, continued his intensive race to curry favor with the most extreme leaders in the Arab world and attain his long sought-after "peace." The timetable of the new Israeli prime minister in regard to the peace process on both fronts, the Palestinian and the Syrian, was now pinned to that of the American president, who had only one more year in office. It became evident with the Camp David initiative of July 2000. Politically, it was very risky for Barak to rush to Camp David, but the partnership with Clinton dictated a tight schedule. The results regarding both the Syrians and the Palestinians were disastrous. Syrian President Hafiz al-Asad, although he had an Israeli agreement in his pocket to return to the June 4, 1967, border, refused to sign it, and negotiations over parts of the Sea of Galilee and the northern mountainous part of the Jordan River began. Exactly the same thing happened with the Palestinians, who got everything they demanded, only to present new ultimatums backed by an onslaught of terror the likes of which had yet to be seen in the region. Of Clinton's appeasement policies, it has already been said that the road to hell is paved with good intentions. It's not enough to imagine. More than three months after the Palestinians' beginning a second *intifada* against Israel (September 2000) with an increased wave of bloody suicide bombings, Arafat was still a welcome guest in Clinton's Washington and the White House.

On January 2, 2001—when the lame-duck president was supposed to be getting ready to vacate the White House to make way for the about-to-be inaugurated President George W. Bush, and about a half a year after Israel's prime minister had presented the most far-reaching concessions ever offered the Palestinians—President Clinton came up with yet another peace initiative, this one involving even more far-reaching Israeli concessions than those Israel's Prime Minister Ehud Barak had agreed to at Camp David and Arafat had refused. The Second *Intifada* was having its desired effect.

President George W. Bush observed afterward that Clinton's final plan was the work of two "desperate people"—Clinton and Barak. One wanted to leave behind a legacy of peace in the Middle East when he completed his presidency in addition to his personal need to clear his name after the Lewinsky affair; while the other needed a peace agreement in order to survive the next elections. Arab sources show that Clinton's far-reaching offer involved an extraordinary new development: it gave Arafat almost everything he wanted, including 98 percent of the territory of Judea, Samaria, and Gaza, all of East Jerusalem except for the Jewish and Armenian quarters, Palestinian sovereignty over the Temple Mount, conceding only the right of Jews to pray there, and a compensation fund of $30 billion.

Arafat landed at Andrews Air Force Base. From there, he went to the Ritz-Carlton Hotel where he met with the ambassadors of Saudi Arabia and Egypt. They promised to back him up if he agreed to the Clinton plan, and warned him that he would receive no backing if he went back to war. When Arafat left the hotel for the White House and his meeting with Clinton, it was clear that there were only two possible answers he could give: yes or no. Arafat was late returning. Clearly, the meeting was not going as planned. Clinton told Arafat: "It's five minutes to midnight, Mr. Chairman, and you are about to lose the only opportunity that your people will ever get to solve their problem on satisfactory ground by not being able to make a decision . . . The Israelis accepted."[11]

The Saudi ambassador, Prince Bandar, knew that Arafat was responsible for causing the Clinton offer to fail and told him that missing the opportunity was not just a tragic mistake, but a crime too. Nevertheless, the next evening, a spokesperson representing Clinton said that Arafat had agreed to accept Clinton's proposals as the basis for new talks—in other words, he would not sign the agreement and expected yet more concessions to be made.

This pattern of willingness to negotiate endlessly with enemies, even when they are already shooting, was one of the trademarks of Clinton's presidency and in particular characterized his relations with Israel. On the eve of the 2001 Israeli elections, Eyal Arad, Ariel Sharon's strategic adviser, described Clinton and Barak as two children playing with a barrel of gunpowder.

Bill Clinton was a president who could not stand being disliked, even by his enemies or those he had betrayed. As Saudi Ambassador Bandar said of Clinton, "He gets excited by the possibility of talking to his enemy and converting him. If Clinton leaves office . . . and doesn't have a relationship with Cuba, North Korea, Iran, or Libya, he will feel internally that he has not accomplished his mission."[12]

In September 2003, almost three years after leaving office, Clinton visited Israel to express his continued solidarity with Israel—even if it was only with a particular part of the Jewish state. He came to celebrate Shimon Peres's eightieth birthday.

I was in Jerusalem at the King David Hotel at the time to speak at a world summit on winning the war on terrorism through moral clarity. I spent the evening with dear friends Binyamin and Sarah Netanyahu. Binyamin, now a former prime minister, and present minister of finance, was also a keynote speaker.

He said, "Mike, are you going to the party in Tel Aviv?"

I said, "No chance. How about you?"

He replied, "Are you kidding? No chance."

I asked Binyamin, "Remember when he was pressuring you to give up more land to the PLO, and the meeting was cut short because the Monica Lewinsky scandal had broken?"

I added, "It just hit me! The date that the report was submitted to Congress was September 11, 1998. Very interesting! By the way, I heard a rumor that Monica is in the air and on her way to Jerusalem. Is that true?"

Binyamin responded, "Yes, it is. President Clinton had better not stay too long."

However, that same evening we were speaking, across town there was another telling moment occurring that further revealed Bill Clinton's relativism and worldview. At a certain point in the celebrations for Peres's party, which was in the midst of a renewed onslaught of mass terrorist attacks and murders in Israel, Bill Clinton, dressed to kill, got up on the stage and burst into song, crooning John Lennon's 1971 hit

"Imagine," which could be considered a theme song for moral relativists. Can you imagine the president of the United States in the Bible land (where more suicide bombers have blown up Jews than in any spot on earth)? This is the same president who treated the Godfather of Terrorism (Yasser Arafat) as a hero. Now, picture the former president singing about no heaven, no hell, no religion, and from this distorted New Age view comes the deduction that the world will live as one!

CHAPTER ELEVEN

Lunatics, Liberals, and Liars

America will never be destroyed from the outside. If we falter and lose our freedoms, it will be because we destroyed ourselves.

Abraham Lincoln[1]

He who says to the wicked, "You are righteous,"
Him the people will curse;
Nations will abhor him.

Proverbs 24:24 NKJV

Thus as the nation that helped the Jews find a state of refuge in the land that had been theirs two millennia before, and as the nation that had raised Ishmael's princes from obscurity with the power of the petrodollar, America stepped out of the eye of the prophetic storm on September 11, 2001, and into the fury of the hurricane. It was also the day that the beautiful economic house of cards the Clinton administration took credit for began to topple. The nation went from a time of unprecedented hope and economic confidence to despair in a matter of an hour.

The elections of 2000 were filled with debate about what America should do about its incredible budget surplus—pay down the national debt? Save Social Security? Give tax cuts back to the taxpayers? The government's budget surpluses of 1997 and 1998 were the first in back-to-back years since 1957. January 2001 estimates projected that by the year 2010, the U.S. government could have as much as $5.6 trillion to work with in surplus income. However, by March 2002, that forecast dropped to $1.6 trillion. In 2000, the United States budget had a surplus of $237 billion, which fell by almost half to $127 billion in 2001, even though the attack hit us three-quarters of the way through the year. The budget was $158 billion in the red in 2002, and will likely hit a record deficit of roughly $374.2 billion in 2003 in the wake of the Iraqi war. In early 2003, national forecasts for 2010 were cut from the $1.6 trillion surplus to a deficit of $4 trillion, a drop of $9.6 trillion from the 2001 estimate.

When the stock market reopened on Monday, September 17, after the attacks, it saw record losses in the first few hours of trading. Not only did the U.S. economy take a dive, but also those of countries around the world that depend largely on the U.S. consumer market. In the weeks following it rebounded, only to be hit again and again as the consumer confidence of the 1990s had apparently been misplaced. Tech stocks corrected themselves from being grossly overvalued. Corporate accounting scandals hit companies like Enron, WorldCom, and Tyco. America had been robbed by the inflated economic optimism preached in the 1990s and by corrupt corporate leaders. At the same time, the airline industry took a hit as a result of the attacks, and United Airlines was knocked into filing for Chapter 11 bankruptcy.

However, one industry did boom—the security industry. Americans have spent more trying to stay safe in recent years than ever before. The new Department of Homeland Security (DHS) created by the Bush administration was allotted $37.70 billion for its 2003 budget—an increase from $19.5 billion in 2002. This was, of course, a department that didn't even exist as Bill Clinton finished his second term and created a yet greater expense to be covered by U.S. taxpayers.

Yet, eclipsed by all that were the lives changed forever that day—the children who lost mothers or fathers, those who lost a spouse, a friend, a son or daughter. I can remember driving home a few days after the attacks and listening to the account of a father, such as myself, only with younger children, calling his sister in the minutes before the second tower fell and giving her a final message to pass along to his wife and children. My eyes welled with tears for the first time since the tragedy had struck because I finally felt the real loss and madness of those attacks. Innocent lives were scarred in an instant because of jealousy and a murderous doctrine of hatred. I am not sure there has been a moment that better defined the senselessness and horror of terrorism. Unfortunately, that has not been the only time I have experienced such moments.

The moral clarity that could have prevented the September 11 attacks also could have saved us tremendous amounts of money in the long run, though it might have slowed the economic growth that had been based on deception during the 1990s. Unfortunately, and despite the increased awareness of our real needs brought about by September 11, our deep ties to Ishmael still cloud our vision. It appears that warning signs continue to be ignored.

One example of this is that a group of Americans on a federal commission tried to sound a warning twice: in September 1999 and in January 2001, just eleven days after the Bush inauguration. The first was a preliminary report by former Senators Gary Hart and Warren Rudman, cochairs of the United States Commission on National Security, given to then-President Bill Clinton. It stated: "Americans will likely die on American soil, possibly in large numbers" as the result of terrorist attacks.[2] This warning was virtually ignored by top officials and the news media. The commission continued its work, however, and on January 31, 2001, seven months before the attacks on the World Trade Center and the Pentagon, Hart and Rudman presented the commission's final report of 150 pages to newly elected President Bush. It was called "Road Map for National Security: Imperative for Change." In it the commissioners reissued their warning, along with a detailed plan of action to make America safer from terrorism. Again, the report was ignored—until after the September 11 attacks.

Yet this relativity continued. On April 24, 2002, some seven and a half months later, an eight-plane Saudi delegation set down at Ellington Air Force Base in Houston, Texas, on its way to meet with President George W. Bush at his "Western White House" in Crawford. It propagated what should have been an international incident, but instead turned into a State Department cover-up. Why? Because among the passengers in Crown Prince Abdullah's entourage was one person on the FBI's most-wanted list and two others on the terrorist watch list. The FBI was ready to storm the plane in the interest of national security and arrest the three; however, the State Department had other priorities—after all, it had been the State Department who issued them visas in the first place. Following the State Department's intervention, the planes left without incident, though, thanks to the FBI and the Secret Service, they got nowhere near Crawford, Texas. With the planes also left the three terrorists who had easily been within U.S. grasp.[3] Moral relativity had won the day again—economics and oil carried more weight than national security.

Even worse than this, perhaps, was the Visa Express program that gave Saudis U.S. visas through travel agents rather than through a trip to the embassy, as is the system everywhere else in the world. At least three of the fifteen Saudi terrorists of September 11 entered the U.S. via Visa Express, yet the program continued to run uninterrupted through September 11, 2001. It took another ten months and extreme media pressure to finally shut it down.

In the wake of September 11, the Saudis hired several public relations firms to clean up their image in the eyes of the U.S. public. They spent some $17 million on this, according to Justice Department filings. The firms they hired included one of Washington's most prominent, Patton Boggs, which reportedly received some $200,000 a month for their services. Patton Boggs is especially known for its contacts among Democrats. Thomas Hale Boggs Jr., a well-connected Democratic lobbyist, founded it. His father, Representative Hale Boggs, was majority leader.[4]

The *New York Times* reports that the Saudi government has also hired Akin, Gump, Strauss, Hauer & Feld, a firm founded by Robert W. Strauss, the former head of the Democratic National Committee, and payed them $161,799 in the first half of 2002. Frederick Dutton, a former special assistant to President John F. Kennedy and a long-time adviser to the Saudis, received $536,000 to help manage the Saudis' handling of the aftermath of September 11 and has an ongoing contract with them.[5]

The Saudi government has run hundreds of television and radio commercials in virtually every major American media market and placed advertisements in publications like *People* magazine and *Stars & Stripes*, presumably for the U.S. troops in Iraq. The latter is apparently an effort to make up for Saudi reluctance to respond to President George W. Bush's call for support on Iraq—and the Saudi memory lapse regarding how the U.S. saved the kingdom from extinction at the hands of Saddam in the 1991 Gulf War.

The Saudis also hired three well-connected Washington lobbying and law firms to advance their cause. One firm, which was paid more than $420,000 in 2003, is headed by former Representative Thomas Loeffler, a top contributor to President Bush when he was governor of Texas and a major fund-raiser in Bush's presidential campaigns.

Ex-Washington officials have also been paid handsomely from the kingdom's coffers. This list includes such figures as Spiro T. Agnew, Jimmy Carter, Clark Clifford, John B. Connally, and William E. Simon.[6] The *Washington Post* lists other former officials, including George H. W. Bush, who have found the Saudi connection "lucrative." It also quotes a Saudi source as saying the Saudis have contributed to every presidential library in recent decades.[7]

Amnesty International, however, reports 123 executions in 2000 in Saudi Arabia, some on charges of sodomy and "sorcery." The body of one of those put to death, an Egyptian national, was reportedly crucified following his execution. There were thirty-four reported cases of amputation last year, seven of which were cross amputations (of the right hand and left foot). Another Egyptian national had his left eye surgically removed as a punishment handed down by a court in Medina. Flogging continues to be a punishment widely imposed. Two teachers, arrested following demonstrations in Najran, were reportedly sentenced to fifteen thousand lashes each, with the sentence carried out in front of their families, students, and other teachers. Torture of prisoners, including the use of electroshock, is common.[8]

We have got to emerge from our slumber. All is not well. We cannot be taken in by appearances any longer. Obviously it wasn't enough to find out that fifteen of the nineteen September 11 terrorists were Saudis nor that Saudi Arabia was the largest supporter of al Qaeda. These considerations have been overlooked to keep the oil that lubricates our national economy flowing. We have accepted the cultural unconsciousness of the last decade that has said repeatedly, "Everything will be all right. The economy will recover. Go back to sleep."

The ebbs and back currents of prophecy are starting to disappear as the various currents come together and flow more and more quickly toward the rapids ahead. As we proceed toward the next key events of prophecy, it is easy to look at the present world stage and see the players slipping into position:

Israel

As we have seen, against all odds and vast opposition, the Jews were pulled from obscurity and Israel reborn. In that, Israel had much for which to thank America. It now also stands on the world stage as a nuclear power and one that has on more than one occasion brandished that power in the wake of invasion and possible defeat (the Yom Kippur War of 1973 is the most blatant example of this). Israel seems to stand ready today to take on the world if need be—and she soon may have to.

The European Union (EU)

As the nations occupying the same lands that the Roman Empire did, these have traditionally been seen as the "ten toes" of Nebuchadnezzar's dream as revealed in Daniel 2:31–45. However, this mixture of iron and clay, representing the alliance of two things that cannot truly mix together—like oil and water—may more likely be the alliance of two forms of government that are so different they do not easily mix: Middle Eastern monarchies and European democracies, whose leadership is based in the lands of ancient Rome. Whatever this alliance is, however, it seems likely the EU will be at the center. As a member of the quartet (the U.S., EU, UN, and Russia) that tried to force the Road

Map (a peace plan for the Middle East) down Israel's throat, it can easily be seen as part of the end-time government that will ratify a false seven-year peace agreement with Israel.

The United Nations

This second member of the quartet has become a major proponent of the Arab League and anti-Semitic thought in the past decades. While it has done everything to fester the Palestinian refugees' plight since the War for Independence of 1948, it has also spoken with one voice time and again against Israel. Of all the nations cited for human rights violations, Israel stood unique under their scrutiny—not North Korea, China, *Shari'a* law nations, or any other. This masquerade extended even farther when terrorist-supporting states such as Syria became the head of the Security Council, and countries such as Libya became the head of the Human Rights Commission. No wonder the UN Human Rights Commission proclaims that the Palestinians can use "all available means, including armed struggle" to regain their "occupied territories"—a clever endorsement of suicide bombings.

At the 2001 Anti-Racism Conference in Durban, South Africa, the entire gathering banded together to condemn one nation as blatantly racist—Israel. The only democracy in the Middle East committed to civil rights, the rule of law, and Arab participation in democratic government was accused of genocide, ethnic cleansing, and apartheid.[9] Israel and the United States walked out on September 4, exactly one week before the attacks on the World Trade Center and the Pentagon— the only two nations willing to acknowledge the lunacy and prejudice of the entire proceedings. During the conference, the streets were filled with banners reading, "The blood of the martyrs irrigates the tree of revolution in Palestine" and "George W. Bush: Palestinian blood is on your hands." It is too easy to see that this organization has changed greatly from its original intent and will be a puppet of Ishmael's vengeful whims in the earth's latter days.

Russia

Since the fall of communism in Russia, we have been content to no longer view this superpower as a threat. The Cold War (which some have called World War III) may have ended, but if the world edges toward a World War IV to be fought over control of the world's oil supplies, this former superpower will be a key player (especially considering it may be harboring oil reserves to rival those of Saudi Arabia, Iraq, Iran, and Kuwait, which were at one time considered to be as much as two-thirds of the world's remaining oil reserves). As a third member of the quartet, the once leader of the communist world, a nuclear power, and the probable coalition leader of the Gog and Magog in biblical prophecy that will sweep down from the North to attack Israel, Russia's side in the final conflict also seems evident.

China and the East

These nations can also be seen easily fitting into an anti-Israel coalition because of their links to the former Soviet Union and utter dependence on outside sources of oil. We also know from Revelation 16 that the "kings of the east" will join with those of the river Euphrates (Babylonia) in the final battle.

The Terrorists

Their most vocal plea has been for the destruction of Israel and the return of the third holiest site in Islam, Jerusalem (and in particular the Temple Mount), to Arab control. Most experts agree that the war the terrorists began with the U.S. on September 11 will never truly end. As they have lumped us together with Israel in the fight, it is easy to see them and their anti-Semitism (which is again infesting Europe and Russia as it did at the dawn of the twentieth century) as the glue that binds the anti-Israel coalition together in the last battle.

The United States

In the midst of the gathering clouds of this storm stands our nation. We were the only member of the quartet who really had the voice to urge Israel's acceptance of the Road Map; however, our strategic alliance with Israel also makes us its greatest defender. Our position in the last days will be determined by our choice of allegiance: Will the growing liberal tendencies of our nation pull us to join the EU, UN, and Russia in a globalization move that will, in the end, force a false peace on Israel and begin the Tribulation? Or will we, with our moral clarity, large Jewish populace, and Christian consciousness, align ourselves so closely in the final conflict that the U.S. and Israel are literally indistinguishable in the final chapter of biblical prophecy?

As you should be able to tell from this brief summary of the players, such a decision will be made ourselves, not imposed by outside nations. While outside forces will influence us, either through negotiations or terrorist attacks, the final decision is up to us. What will we do? Will we trade our freedom for cheap oil, globalization, and moral relativism, or will we stay the course our forefathers began and hold to the Bible as our guide? Will our nation be on God's side in the final conflict? Will we give in to the lunatics, liberals, and liars in weakness? Or will we stand strong and seek a revival of moral clarity in our land?

CHAPTER TWELVE

The Battle Lines Are Drawn
Through the Heart of Jerusalem

Arabs may have the oil, but we have the matches.

> Ariel Sharon, to a colleague while touring Dimona, Israel's
> nuclear facility[1]

*Jerusalem represents the earthly point where God came into contact
with man and where eternity crossed history.*

> Archbishop of Krakow Karol Wojtyla (later Pope John Paul II)
> Jerusalem, 1964[2]

*But I have chosen Jerusalem, that my name might be there; and have
chosen David to be over my people Israel.*

> 2 Chronicles 6:6

Thus the lines for the future Battle of Armageddon have already been
drawn by UN resolutions, terrorist demands and intents, and U.S. acquiescence along the Israeli boundaries of June 4, 1967, declaring the
Golan Heights, the Gaza Strip, the West Bank, and East Jerusalem and
the Temple Mount "Occupied Territories." To this point, on three different occasions from 1991 to 2001, the PLO has been offered basically

all of that, minus control of East Jerusalem. Each time they have refused and escalated their violence. The conclusion is only too obvious: The PLO will not sign any "final" agreement with Israel until that agreement includes their control of East Jerusalem. The battle line is indeed drawn through the heart of Jerusalem: the Old City and the Temple Mount.

Both Israel and the Palestinians declare Jerusalem their capital, yet countries such as the United States have their embassies in Tel Aviv, not Jerusalem. The reason for this is our hesitancy to back one side or the other. If the United States were to set up the embassy in Jerusalem, we would be symbolically recognizing Israel's declaration of it as theirs. For the PLO and Palestinian Authority, who claim it as the capital of a state that is yet to exist, this would signal the end of our possible recognition of it as their potential capital. Such a move would send a strong message to Ishmael that we, as of yet, have been hesitant to make.

I met with Mayor Giuliani in New York to discuss Jerusalem, and asked him what were the most important things Jerusalem and New York have in common. He answered:

> The most important thing we share is that we both live in freedom. We are both blessed with freedom and democracy. Much of the world doesn't have freedom and democracy. Because we share the same principles on which government and society are based, than all of the other friendships become even stronger.
>
> The relationship of blood also exists between New York and Jerusalem. There are so many who have family in both places.
>
> We have the relationship of religious significance for Jews, Christians, and Muslims—the historical significance and the reality that we are two of the world's great cities. Jerusalem is older than New York. A good deal of the world passes through both places. We share great bonds.

New York and America indeed hold a great bond with Jerusalem—the city that will be the center of the whole earth's attention in the final days.

Even after more than three decades of visiting Israel and studying the conflicts and prophecies surrounding the country, I still don't fully comprehend why this is. While the Temple Mount is the holiest place in Judaism, and perhaps second only to Golgotha (which is just across from it) to Christians, it is considered the third holiest place in the world to Muslims, though neither Palestine (*Filistin*) or Jerusalem (*al-Quds*) are mentioned in the Qur'an (the holiest being Mecca, and the second holiest, Medina). For the Jews, it is the place of which God said, "In this house [the temple], and in Jerusalem, which I have chosen before all the tribes of Israel, will I put my name for ever."[3]

Why has Jerusalem been a bone in the throat of the world? Why is such a tiny city world news? It is because of an ancient prophecy whose fulfillment Yahweh Himself will guarantee!

Every nation that has come against Jerusalem has been cursed, the latest being Babylon. In 586 BC, the Babylonian army besieged Jerusalem, and the temple was ransacked. On Friday, April 11, 2003, the Iraqi National Museum in Baghdad was plundered by a lawless society. More than 170,000 ancient and priceless artifacts were stolen. These relics covered the entire seven thousand years of Babylonian history.

Saddam Hussein, who claimed to be Nebuchadnezzar incarnate, ended up cursed just as the first Nebuchadnezzar was cursed. Saddam should have read his Bible. Who would ever have believed that the man who caused nations to tremble would end up with matted hair, a nasty, unkempt beard, and with a diet of rotten food in a dirty hole in the ground? Bums living under bridges look better than Hussein did when captured.

For decades, I have challenged leaders in America not to touch Jerusalem. I remember standing up to Robert McFarland, the national security adviser to Ronald Reagan. McFarland had said, "The status of Jerusalem must be determined by negotiations."

I said, "Excuse me; I have the book on Jerusalem. God is not negotiating with you or anyone else."

In Madrid, I was the first to challenge then-Secretary of State James Baker over Jerusalem. I asked, "Why can't America recognize Jerusalem as Israel's capital?" Baker was hot at my remarks and said he refused to be entangled in a fruitless debate; the status of Jerusalem should be determined by negotiations.

Why have I been so concerned? There is no city in the world for which God pronounces a blessing on those who bless it, and a curse on those who curse it. The nations that divided Jerusalem will be cursed beyond their ability to comprehend. If that happens, no amount of prayer or repentance will reverse the curse on that nation. Once prophecy is touched, the Lord's anger will boil over.

The revelation is amazing. Presidents have placed their hands on the prophecy of King Solomon[4] as they were sworn into office. They trusted that God would bless America and their term in office. It is unlikely, however, that any have read another prophecy by the same king found in 2 Chronicles 6:6: "But I have chosen [(*bachar*) *Yaruwshalaim*], that my name [*shem*] might be there." This amazing prophecy denotes that Jerusalem is the only city in the world in which the Lord has chosen to place His name.

Is it important that Jerusalem not be touched? Yes, one thousand times, yes! Heaven and earth met in Jerusalem (the coming of Jesus Christ), and will meet again (His return). The prophecies say that Jerusalem will be united—not divided—when the Messiah returns. He is not coming back to a Muslim city.

At the end of the age, Jerusalem will be the center of all prophecy.

> I saw the Holy City, the new Jerusalem, coming down out
> of heaven from God, prepared as a bride beautifully dressed
> for her husband. (Revelation 21:2 NIV)

As the prophet Joel proclaims,

> The LORD also shall roar out of Zion, and utter his voice
> from Jerusalem. (Joel 3:16)

And from the prophet Zechariah:

> This is what the LORD says: "I will return to Zion and dwell
> in Jerusalem." (Zechariah 8:3NIV)

It is no coincidence that the first words of the New Testament are:

> A record of the genealogy of Jesus Christ the son of David,
> the son of Abraham. (Matthew 1:1NIV)

David was the first king of Jerusalem, a forerunner of the true King of Jerusalem, Jesus Christ.

The final battle of the ages will be over Jerusalem. If America chooses to line up against the Scriptures, America will find itself fighting against Yahweh, and will definitely lose!

Satan's challenge to God Almighty can be found in Isaiah 14:12–15:

> How you have fallen from heaven, O morning star, son of
> the dawn! You have been cast down to the earth, you who
> once laid low the nations! You said in your heart, "I will as-
> cend to heaven; I will raise my throne above the stars of
> God; I will sit enthroned on the mount of assembly, on the
> utmost heights of the sacred mountain. I will ascend above
> the tops of the clouds; I will make myself like the Most
> High." But you are brought down to the grave, to the
> depths of the pit.

Notice he says he will sit on the Temple Mount in Jerusalem, on the north side. Yet God Himself says, "You will be cursed and brought down to the lowest pit of hell."

Most wars have been fought over disputes of land and property ownership. Personal battles have raged over someone's illegally using the name of another person to write a check or buy goods. It is called "fraud." The person who commits fraud can be punished severely. America even has laws that grant a citizen the right to bear arms to protect his property. Jerusalem's title deed does not belong to anyone; it belongs exclusively to the Lord. He placed His name there!

A brilliant and respected scholar whom I have known for decades told me: "If you look at a satellite image of the city of Jerusalem, you will see the tetragrammaton YHWH. It is clearly visible in the photo. What does YHWH mean? It is the Hebrew for Yahweh—the (unspoken) name of God! Yes, mystically inscribed in the very city of Jerusalem is God's name."

The prophets also declare that

> Then shall the LORD go forth, and fight against those nations, as when he fought in the day of battle. And his feet shall stand in that day upon the mount of Olives, which is before Jerusalem on the east, and the mount of Olives shall cleave in the midst thereof toward the east and toward the west, and there shall be a very great valley; and half of the mountain shall remove toward the north, and half of it toward the south. (Zechariah 14:3–4)

It's amazing that the U.S., supposedly a Christian nation, wants to divide Jerusalem, and give East Jerusalem over to a terrorist regime, the PLO, to become an Islamic state.

The same scholar that told me about his discovery in the satellite image of the city of Jerusalem also told me: "The geological formation created by the Kidron Valley between the Mount of Olives and the Treble Mounts, the Tyropaean Valley and the Hinnom Valley (Gehenna) which lies at the bottom of the Temple Mount and sweeps northward, forms the Hebrew letter for *shem*, which looks like a warped *W*." God's name is buried in the very geological foundations of Jerusalem—and cannot be removed. If my friend is correct, this is another fascinating and prophetic sign concerning ancient Jerusalem and man's futile battle over it.

There is, indeed, in ancient prophecy, a curse that God will place on the nation that divides Jerusalem:

> Behold, I will make Jerusalem a cup of trembling unto all the people round about, when they shall be in the siege

both against Judah and against Jerusalem. And in that day will I make Jerusalem a burdensome stone for all people: all that burden themselves with it shall be cut in pieces, though all the people of the earth be gathered together against it . . . In that day will I make the governors of Judah like an hearth of fire among the wood, and like a torch of fire in a sheaf; and they shall devour all the people round about, on the right hand and on the left: and Jerusalem shall be inhabited again in her own place, even in Jerusalem . . . In that day shall the LORD defend the inhabitants of Jerusalem; and he that is feeble among them at that day shall be as David; and the house of David shall be as God, as the angel of the LORD before them. (Zechariah 12:2–3, 6, 8 NIV)

And this shall be the plague wherewith the LORD will smite all the people that have fought against Jerusalem; Their flesh shall consume away while they stand upon their feet, and their eyes shall consume away in their holes, and their tongue shall consume away in their mouth . . . And Judah also shall fight at Jerusalem; and the wealth of all the heathen round about shall be gathered together, gold, and silver, and apparel, in great abundance. (Zechariah 14:12,14 NIV)

According to Genesis 22, this is the location where Isaac was to be offered to God as a sacrifice before the angel stayed Abraham's hand. In Muslim tradition—echoing the jealousy of Ishmael, the eldest but not favored son—it was Ishmael, not Isaac, who was offered here. It is also said to be the place from which Muhammad ascended one night into heaven for a special visit. Muslims do not refer to the area as the Temple Mount, but as the Noble Sanctuary.

The Mosque of Omar, more commonly known as the "Dome of the Rock," is built over the rock upon which Abraham reportedly laid Ishmael to sacrifice him (some believe that this is also the location of the

altar of the first two Hebrew temples—though this may be more because of the Crusaders confusion of it with the temple of Solomon than
actual archaeological evidence). It was built sometime around AD 700.
Caliph Omar I, the successor to the prophet Muhammad, took
Jerusalem in AD 637. This is the Golden Dome, which you see in all
modern photographs of Jerusalem that include the Temple Mount.
Though it is the more famous of the two mosques of the Noble Sanctuary because of its brilliant dome, it is not considered the holiest.

That attribute rests with the second mosque on the Mount, called
the *al-Aqsa* Mosque (which means "the farthest place of worship of the
One God," referring to its distance from Mecca when it was built); it
is just to the south of the Dome of the Rock. It is the largest mosque
in Jerusalem. This mosque was built soon after the Dome of the Rock
and is dedicated to Muhammad's "night visit" to heaven and supposedly rests on the place from which he took that journey.

It was also this location that became the focal point for the beginning of the Second *Intifada,* which is also called the *al-Aqsa Intifada* because it began when Ariel Sharon visited this holy site. Though the
violence had already started in smaller outbreaks some days before this,
on September 28, 2000, it reached new heights after Sharon stood at
the door of the *al-Aqsa* Mosque. Though Sharon entered none of the
mosque buildings on the Temple Mount, his mere presence on the
Noble Sanctuary (all of which Arabs actually consider a mosque)
caused an eruption of shouting and rock throwing that resulted in
twenty-eight Israeli policemen being injured, three of whom had to be
hospitalized. There were no reported Palestinian injuries on the day of
Sharon's visit. The next day, however, significant orchestrated violence
erupted after the Muslims' Friday prayers, resulting in deaths and casualties on both sides. It began the worst period of Palestinian violence in
Israeli history. From September 29, 2000, to September 11, 2002, Israel saw 427 civilians and 185 members of Israeli security forces killed,
and 3,202 civilians and 1,307 security members injured.

Though the violence had probably already been set to start because
Arafat had just walked out on Camp David talks with Israel in July, the
fact that Sharon's visit to the Noble Sanctuary was used to catalyze the

violence in earnest is a testament to how close to the heart of the conflict control of the Temple Mount really is. It has also been the site of other outbreaks of tension between Palestinians and Jews, such as that on September 24, 1996, which led to four days of fighting, with tanks and attack helicopters being brought in for support, and ended with more than seventy dead and hundreds wounded. The pretext of that fighting was the opening of a new exit to the Hasmonean Tunnel, an archaeological site that runs along the Western Wall and under part of the Old City of Jerusalem, because at the time visitors had to enter and exit by the same opening.

It has traditionally been believed that the Dome of the Rock will have to be removed before the third, and last temple can be built—a prophecy well known to the Arabs and a reason for their further distrust of Jewish custody of the Mount. However, some believe that the original site of the temple may have been on the northern part of the Temple Mount, which is open, not in the south where the Dome of the Rock sits today. If this is the case, it is possible that the temple could be rebuilt without harming the two mosques, which would be more peaceable considering the importance of each to the Jews and the Muslims. One way or the other, it seems likely that the rebuilding of the temple will be one of the bargaining chips used by the Antichrist to draw Israel into the seven-year peace pact.

Thus Jerusalem is edging its way back to being the center of world attention, even as it is already the center of Jewish and Muslim attention. As it does, the fate of Jerusalem will become the greatest reason for hope in the world as the seven-year peace pact is signed and the Tribulation begins. It will also be the site of the final breakdown of hope when the Antichrist enters the rebuilt temple and desecrates it, marking the beginning of the Great Tribulation. If the spirit of antichrist truly is behind the actions of the PLO and other terrorist groups, and I firmly believe it is, that adds a spiritual dimension to why Jerusalem is so key to the Palestinian Authority's acceptance of a treaty with Israel, and why it is such a sticking point for anyone proposing peace in the region. It is about much more than how many have died in suicide bombings or Israeli police actions, it is about who controls the center of the world and the rock on which God first cut a covenant with humanity.

Not only has the line been firmly drawn, but both sides also know what they are willing to sacrifice to get what they want: the Palestinians to chase Israel from their land and the Jews to protect their place there. Though America and the U.S.S.R. wanted to avoid an arms race in the Middle East, they could not and at the same time keep their loyalties, so the Soviets armed Nasser's Pan-Arabists, and the United States eventually promised to keep Israel one step ahead of her neighbors after the Yom Kippur War. This proved more difficult as America also agreed to supply weapons to Saudi Arabia, Egypt (after Sadat signed a treaty with Israel in 1978), and the United Arab Emirates: Kuwait, Bahrain, Jordan, Oman, Lebanon, Qatar, and Yemen (in that order according to sales from 1990 to 2001).[5] If any one of these got an advanced weapons system (missiles, planes, ships, tanks, etc.), the U.S. was obliged to offer the same or better to Israel. From 1990 to 2001, the U.S. sold $79.4 billion in arms to these Arab nations. This easily rivals the $81.3 billion the U.S. has granted Israel between 1976 and 2001, much of which was in economic aid and loans, not arms sales. In roughly the same time period, since 1991, the U.S. has specifically given Israel $18.1 billion in weapons and military aid. Thanks to us, those on both sides of the line running through Jerusalem are well prepared to wage conventional warfare in order to control it.

So far, the edge has been to the Israelis, not only because we have promised to keep them one step ahead in this race to obtain U.S. arms, but also because of Israel's nuclear strike potential. Almost from Israel's rebirth, which was only three years after the bombing of Hiroshima and Nagasaki, Prime Minister David Ben-Gurion saw that nuclear power could be useful in making the Negev Desert bloom by supplying it with electricity and powering desalinization plants to provide with drinking water. However, as author Seymour Hersh put it, "Nuclear power was not Ben-Gurion's first priority; the desert would glow before it bloomed."[6] Ben-Gurion had his eyes set on Israel's becoming a nuclear power.

Throughout his contacts with the United States, Ben-Gurion continued to push for but could never get the U.S.'s promise that Israel would find sanctuary under the umbrella of America's nuclear weapons. Thus Israel began a cat-and-mouse game with her most sought-after ally as, on one hand, she tried to get the U.S. to promise its protection, and, on the other, she developed protection of her own.

By 1953, Israel's Weizmann Institute had developed an improved ion-exchange mechanism for producing heavy water and a more efficient method for mining uranium, which it bartered with the French for a formal agreement to cooperate in nuclear research. By 1958, Israel had begun construction of its own nuclear facility near the Negev Desert town of Dimona, which they based on their visits to the French nuclear research facility at Marcoule. Perhaps by then Ben-Gurion had realized that the U.S. was not as interested in Israeli security as he had hoped after Eisenhower's reaction to the Suez Crisis. Israel would continue her research for a decade before the first nuclear bombs began rolling out of Dimona in 1968. The facility went into full-scale production at that point, turning out four or five bombs a year. During this time, through every means possible, the U.S. tried to figure out just what was going on at Dimona while Israel tried to hide it. However, evidence seems to suggest that the U.S. had a pretty good idea of what Dimona was for but just looked the other way, knowing that Israel didn't have much choice. Some members of Congress even supported Israel's actions. A few days before meeting with President Kennedy to further discuss the Hawk missile purchases, Shimon Peres met with Senator Stuart Symington, a Kennedy supporter and ranking member of the Senate Armed Services Committee. As Peres told his biographer, Symington said, "Don't be a bunch of fools. Don't stop making atomic bombs. And don't listen to the administration. Do whatever you think best."[7]

However, this struggle didn't come without its political casualties. In the spring of 1962, President Kennedy was pushing Prime Minister Ben-Gurion hard for some solid answers about Dimona, or at least solid promises that its research was not for military purposes. Ben-Gurion held his ground. According to Yuval Neeman, a physicist and defense ministry intelligence officer who was involved in Israel's nuclear weapons program, "It was not a friendly exchange. Kennedy was writing like a bully. It was brutal."[8]

As a result, Kennedy shut Ben-Gurion out in the midst of a growing threat. That April, Iraq joined Egypt and Syria in the short-lived Arab Federation, making the threat of another Arab invasion such as that of the War of Independence much more likely. Author Seymour Hersh described the situation:

> He instinctively turned to Washington, and proposed in a letter to the President that the United States and Soviet Union join forces to publicly declare the territorial integrity and security of every Middle Eastern state. "If you can spare an hour or two for a discussion with me on the situation and possible solutions," Ben-Gurion asked, "I am prepared to fly to Washington at your convenience and without any publicity." Kennedy rejected Ben-Gurion's offer of a state visit and expressed "real reservations," according to Ben-Gurion's biography, about any joint statement on the issue with the Soviets. Five days later, a disappointed Ben-Gurion sent a second note to Kennedy: "Mr. President, my people have the right to exist . . . and this existence is in danger." He requested that the United States sign a security treaty with Israel. Again the answer was no, and it was clear to the Mapai Party that Ben-Gurion's leadership and his intractability about Dimona were serious liabilities in Washington. Golda Meir acknowledged to Ben-Gurion's biographer, "We knew about these approaches . . . We said nothing, even though we wondered."
>
> A few weeks later, on June 16, 1963, Ben-Gurion abruptly resigned as prime minister and defense minister, ending his fifteen-year reign as Israel's most influential public official.[9]

By 1973, Israel had about twenty-five nuclear warheads, with three or four missile launchers in place and operational at Hirbat Zachariah.

Israel also had a number of mobile Jericho I missile launchers at its disposal and possessed the capability of launching nuclear weapons and hitting targets as far away as Tbilisi and Baku in southern Russia. Damascus and Cairo were within easy range.

When the Yom Kippur War broke out, the United States was slow to respond as the attacks began. Several sources suggest that Nixon and Kissinger planned to let Israel get a severe bloody nose before the U.S. responded in order to teach a lesson. However, it was at this point that Israel developed what became known as "the Samson Option." Once the United States discovered this, it pulled out all stops to help Israel win a conventional war that would prevent the possibility of a nuclear proliferation starting in the Middle East.

The Samson Option emerged from Israel's determination that there would never be another Holocaust at the hands of a foreign power. As the Jews had done at Masada, it was better to die at their own hands rather than be captured by an oppressing force, whether that should be the Romans, the Germans, or the Arabs. However, it was not Masada, but Samson, from whom they took their example. In his last hour, a blinded and weakened Samson was marched into the temple of Dagon as a display to the Philistines of their preeminence over the Jews. As the mocking catcalls fell on him, Samson prayed, "O Lord GOD, remember me, I pray thee, and strengthen me, I pray thee, only this once, O God, that I may be at once avenged of the Philistines for my two eyes."[10] Then, placing his hands firmly on two pillars supporting the roof of the temple, he prayed again, "Let me die with the Philistines,"[11] and with all of his might pushed the columns over, bringing the roof down on himself and all the Philistines who had ridiculed him. The Bible tells us that in this final act, he killed more Philistines than he previously had in his entire life.

The Samson Option thus illustrated Israel's willingness to bring the world into a nuclear war and destroy much of it, rather than allowing another Holocaust at the hands of an anti-Semitic nation. Israel knew the consequences of attacking Egypt and Syria—the Soviet Union would launch an all-out nuclear attack on Israel. Armageddon would come early.

Thus Israel armed and aimed her nuclear missiles at Egyptian and

Syrian military headquarters near Cairo and Damascus just a few days into the war. Israel didn't know what else to do and was fast losing confidence. Leaders were already willing to seriously consider using their weapons of last resort a few days into the war. However, to prevent that, the United States came dramatically to Israel's aid to keep the war conventional.

By 1979, Israel was routinely gathering U.S. satellite intelligence to target cities in the Soviet Union. Israel had learned a key fact that the United States and Soviet Union also learned in the Cold War: In a nuclear war, it doesn't matter how many times you can blow up your enemies, only that you can blow them up. Israel had entered the world of nuclear superpowers.

Therefore, in essence, what victory Israel realized in the Yom Kippur War was won staring down the barrel of a nuclear missile launcher. Since Israel had nuclear weapons and its neighbors did not, this further bolstered its position as a nation that could not be defeated in open warfare. If the Arabs developed nuclear weapons, however, this distinct advantage would be lost. So it was that on June 7, 1981, Israel used U.S. F-15s and F-16s that had been purchased "for defensive purposes only" to take out the Osirak nuclear reactor, which was twelve miles southwest of Baghdad, before it became operational. Israel did not want a Samson vs. Goliath scenario.

Israel knew the seriousness of the strike and was ready for possible retaliation. Before the bombing, Dimona was shut down in case of a counterstrike and left down for roughly a year.

While the world fumed, the U.S. gave Israel only a mild reprimand for this pre-preemptive strike. According to Richard V. Allen, Reagan's national security adviser, when President Ronald Reagan was informed of the attack, the conversation went like this:

> "Mr. President, the Israelis just took out a nuclear reactor in
> Iraq with F-16s. . . ."
>> "What do you know about it?"
>> "Nothing, sir. I'm waiting for a report."
>> "Why do you suppose they did it?"

The President let his rhetorical question hang for a moment, Allen recalled, and added:

"Well. Boys will be boys."[12]

The White House announced that the next installment of a 1975 sale of seventy-five F-16s would be suspended because of the attack. However, two months later the suspension was lifted with little attention drawn to the fact, and the shipment of four new F-16s was delivered to Israel without incident.

It also appears Israel found a way to get around restrictions it had been given on the use of America's extremely advanced and secret KH-11 spy satellite system. President Jimmy Carter had agreed the Israelis could receive satellite pictures of areas within one hundred miles of their borders so they could watch for troop movements in neighboring countries that might alert them of a new invasion by Arab forces—thus, again, for "defensive purposes only." However, somehow they received in addition enough images of Osirak—which is roughly 550 miles from Jerusalem—that they could also launch this surgical strike against Iraq without being detected until they were already on their target.

Later in the 1980s, Israel planted nuclear land mines along the Golan Heights. Israel now also has impregnable submarines—each one carrying four nuclear cruise missiles. In June 2000, an Israeli submarine launched a cruise missile that hit a target 600 kilometers away, making Israel the third nation, after the U.S. and Russia, with that capacity. However, in the spring of 2002, Iran launched a missile that covered a similar distance. When asked about Iran's nuclear capabilities on May 24 of that same year during the Bush-Putin summit in Moscow, Russian General Yuri Baluyevshy, deputy chief of the general staff, said, "Iran does have nuclear weapons. Of course they are non-strategic nuclear weapons. I mean these are not ICBMs with a range of more than 5,500 kilometers and more."[13] They may not have the range to reach Moscow or Washington, but they could certainly reach Tel Aviv and Jerusalem. Goliath is quickly closing in on Samson's military edge.

Again, it doesn't matter how many times you can blow someone up, just that you can.

In November 1999, I was in the U.S.S.R. and met with a former head of the KGB. I said to him, "It is wonderful how the world is now a much safer place to live." He grinned at me and responded, "Listen, the world is not a safer place to live. Our republics are cash-poor and crime-rich. We have thousands of nuclear bombs. Last month in the Ukraine, two bombs were found to be missing. Only the casings were left. When I asked where they were, I was told, 'Russian entrepreneurs.' While your country was celebrating the end of the Cold War, we were panicking over the beginning of the hot war."

I asked him about Israel. He smiled again and said, "Listen, we have been targeting their cities, and they have had their big bomb trained on us for years. So, what else is new?" I knew he was telling me the truth, for I had heard this from a key adviser to two of Israel's prime ministers years before.

The *Washington Post* reported:

> In the ethnic conflicts that surrounded the collapse of the Soviet Union, fighters in several countries seized upon an unlikely new weapon: a small, thin rocket known as the Alazan. Originally built for weather experiments, the Alazan was transformed into a terror weapon, packed with explosives and lobbed into cities. Military records show that at least thirty-eight Alazan warheads were modified to carry radioactive material, effectively creating the world's first surface-to-surface "dirty bomb." Now, according to experts and officials, the warheads have disappeared.[14]

The Samson Option again came into play in the 1991 Gulf War. Reuben Hecht, a senior adviser to Israel's prime ministers, lived in Haifa, the target of a SCUD missile attack during the Persian Gulf War. He said to me, "We have picked up intelligence that Saddam has given the order to put chemical and biological weapons on SCUDs. I need to get into a sealed room quickly. I can assure you, however, that if they hit our cities, Baghdad will be a radioactive dustbowl. Israel has mobile missile launchers armed with nuclear weapons. They are facing Baghdad even as I speak, and are ready to launch on command. We are on full-scale nuclear alert." He added, "You know, Mike, this is not to be repeated."

Today, Dimona, the Samson Option, Project 700, the Zechariah Project, the Temple Weapons, and Z-Division are all names for parts of one of the most massive nuclear arsenals in the world in Israel. Now new names are being heard: Pumped X-ray Lasers, Hydrodynamics, and Radiation Transport—the new Armageddon generation of weapons. Israel has more than three hundred tactical and strategic weapons, including more than one hundred nuclear artillery shells, nuclear land mines, and neutron bombs that will destroy biological life without creating an explosion. They also have lasers for their planes and tanks and electromagnetic weapons that shut down radar. As of November 14, 2003, Israel took her first order of U.S. F-16I fighter jets, of which she will receive 102 by 2008, making it the largest arms deal in Israeli history. The new jet could reach nations as far away as Iran and Libya, and has AMRAAM air-to-air missiles and Northrop Grumman APG-68 radar, providing the capability of shooting down other jets from thirty-plus miles away.

At least nine nations currently have the capability of attacking an enemy with a thermonuclear bomb: Russia, the United States, China, Israel, France, Great Britain, India, Pakistan, and, it appears, Iran. This gives them all the possibility to unleash a plague of nuclear or neutron bombs that would be very much like what is described in Zechariah 14:12 NKJV:

> This shall be the plague with which the LORD will strike all
> the people who fought against Jerusalem:
>> Their flesh shall dissolve while they stand on their feet,
>> Their eyes shall dissolve in their sockets,
>> And their tongues shall dissolve in their mouths.

Others, such as North Korea, seem to be closing in on acquiring this capability. In the last battle, Russia, the European countries (Great Britain and France), and the Eastern countries (Iran, Pakistan, India, China, and North Korea) will be on the other side of the line from Israel. But where will the United States be?

As the terrorist network stands poised against us, it seems only a matter of time and money before one of the missing Soviet suitcase nukes finds its way into their hands. If we don't handle the next steps in the war on terrorism correctly, those Soviet nukes or some of Saddam's weapons of mass destruction that liberals claim "don't exist" will very likely assist in this goal.

Thus far, the war on terrorism has taken us from the attacks of September 11 to victory in Iraq. But if we are ultimately to win this war and prevent these weapons of mass destruction from striking our cities, where do we need to go from here?

We must fall on our faces in prayer and repentance. America has no idea what we could face if the nation sleeps. George Santayana said, "Those who cannot remember the past are doomed to repeat it."[15]

CHAPTER THIRTEEN

Our Nation's Issue of the Twenty-first Century: Winning the War on Terror

If changes are not made now, by the year 2000, there is doubt as to whether we will survive. By that time, there will be seven billion people in the world, and five billion of them will be starving, uneducated, and totally desperate.

Dr. Albert Sabin

Blessed is the nation whose God is the LORD,
The people He has chosen as His own inheritance.

Psalm 33:12 NKJV

George Washington, first president of the United States, took the oath of office in 1789 with his hand resting on a Bible opened to Genesis 49:13–14:

> Zebulun shall dwell at the haven of the sea; and he shall be for an haven of ships; and his border shall be unto Zidon. Issachar is a strong ass couching down between two burdens.

What an amazing prophecy Jacob (whose name was changed to Israel) pronounced over his son. The prophecy came to pass exactly as he said. Washington placed his hand over a prophecy that defined in detail the future nation of Israel. The future of his own infant nation would also be defined—ironically—by its faithfulness to this same nation of Israel.

As our nation stands on the brink of a new millennium, we truly face the greatest threat ever to America's existence and way of life. While atheistic communism once held the greatest potential of a new imperialistic culture, this threat significantly decreased with the disintegration of the Soviet Union and the end of the Cold War. The current struggle that we face in the war on terrorism is no longer just a fight for the supremacy of a political ideology through military might, but a battle for hearts and minds through a twisting of truth that turns our enemies into zealous sociopaths willing to give their lives to murder others. This is not a religion like Christianity, which can transform most cultures to righteousness through love, but a tyrannical system that takes over cultures and governments and dictates truth for its own interests. The repressive Taliban government is perhaps the best example of what bin Laden and the Wahhabists want the world to look like. In a world where Islamism is becoming the force empowering impoverished nations against their economic superiors, the greatest threat to our nation today is a foreign policy that denies truth for the sake of Clintonian-style house-of-cards prosperity and a lack of resolve to win the war on terror.

Many seem to believe that the United States needs to return to a more isolationistic stance as we had at the beginning of the twentieth century and look after our own, letting the rest of the world take care of itself. I don't believe this is possible any longer in a world that can send the same television broadcast live all over the world and where journeys that used to take months now take hours. We have come a long way from Jules Verne's fantastic idea of going *Around the World in Eighty Days* to a time when satellites can circle the globe in about ninety minutes. Besides, since most of our consumer products are made abroad today, we are irreversibly tied to the rest of the world as never before.

Because of this, I believe that the areas of foreign policy and national security will dominate the debate for the elections of the next few decades, as will the question "How do we win the war against terrorism?" As I write this, I see winning the war on terror as one of the greatest ways of securing a peaceful future for our nation. For the first time in history, we must fight a war against a deadly religious ideal, Wahhabism, rather than a political ideal or a madman bent on taking over the world. We can no longer tolerate every belief in the hope it will lead to our all getting along—some beliefs in the world are indeed damningly deadly.

When Wahhabists such as Osama bin Laden call us "polytheists" and "crusaders," they are not just demonizing our point of view or misunderstanding who we are. When we hear that pamphlets are circulated claiming that American Christians are polytheists because of our belief in the Trinity, we just shake our heads and want to mark their materials as "irrelevant religious stuff." However, when Wahhabists call us "polytheists," they are marking us as targets of *jihad*, animals for the slaughter. Brutally murdering *mushrikun* ("polytheists") is an act of worship and devotion for Wahhabists today, just as it was for the original followers of Muhammad ibn Abd al-Wahhab in the mid-1700s. While we often think of Crusaders as a mistake of the church of the Middle Ages or the name of the local Christian school's basketball team, when Wahhabists speak of Crusaders they think of the forces that wrested Jerusalem and the Noble Sanctuary from them—forces they saw as gathered to wipe out Islam as a whole in the same way that *jihad* hopes to extinguish Judaism and Christianity. It also dropped the Crusaders to a status less than human, as was exemplified by Sallah al-Din's breaking of his peace treaty with them to recapture Jerusalem. There is no need to keep one's word to "apes and pigs."[1]

Though many wars of the past have been across religious lines, bringing those wars to a point of cease-fire never before meant wiping their ideology from the face of the earth. This brings a spiritual dimension to the war on terrorism. A war against people hoping to die—

be "martyred"—will have no cease-fires. Such a war cannot be won without a tremendous dedication to truth and people praying and acting to win this battle for hearts and minds in the spiritual realm. We must support righteousness, not relativity, as the basis for rule of law and our relationships to other nations. The Bible tells us that the "love of money is the root of all evil" (1 Timothy 6:10). This has never been so evident as it is today, when we watch much of what is good and holy in our nation traded away for economic gain. While money is nice to have, we need to realize it is not more valuable than God's blessings of freedom and security.

We cannot win the war on terrorism, however, by vowing to defeat the terrorists on one hand and trying to appease them on the other. You can't fight the terrorists on one front and ignore them on another so that they can push in unhindered. We need to realize that a major front in the war on terrorism is the battle line drawn through the heart of Jerusalem.

Though liberals in the United States have painted the struggle of the Palestinians as a political revolution for freedom from oppression, no nation in the world before has aimed strictly at civilians in order to overthrow their enemies. The war the terrorists fight is a war on innocence—they don't care who their victims are as long as they get headlines, even if that means killing children or babies in strollers, as has happened all too often. The truth must be recognized: Arafat and those aligned with him are not "freedom fighters," but terrorists. Israel's struggle against the PLO, Hamas, Islamic Jihad, and other such organizations is their own war on terror. How can we ignore an ally's fight against terrorists—in fact, trying to force them to appease the terrorists—and expect to win our own?

We cannot win the war on terrorism by calling Palestinian terrorists "good terrorists" and bin Laden's terrorists "bad terrorists." Terrorists are terrorists, and if we hope to win the battle against them, we have to treat them all as criminals, none of them as diplomats. If a man breaks into your house to steal something or harm your family, you don't negotiate with him about which rooms in your home he can live in, you have him arrested! We can no longer afford to legitimize terrorism as a negotiating technique to win more concessions from sovereign governments. As we have seen, there will be no appeasing these thugs until they have it all.

As I mentioned earlier, during October 12–14, 2003, I attended the first annual Jerusalem Summit—a forum to discuss establishing peace in the Middle East. I had the honor of being the keynote speaker on the first evening of the conference. World leaders and media celebrities who also spoke during those three days included such men as former Israeli Prime Minister Binyamin Netanyahu, Vice Prime Minister Ehud Olmert, Middle East Forum Director Daniel Pipes, Israeli Minister of Tourism Benny Elon, the Honorable Richard Perle, FOX News host and syndicated columnist Cal Thomas, and Ambassador Dr. Alan Keyes. Interestingly enough, the theme of this first summit was "Winning the War on Terrorism Through Moral Clarity," with the Scripture of Zechariah 8:19 printed on the program cover: ". . . so love truth and peace."

As he addressed the conference, former Prime Minister Netanyahu had this to say:

> Conscience is a moral compass. Conscience is absent in some societies and they endorse terrorism. Terrorism is deliberate and systematic action to kill innocent civilians. Israel is fighting terrorism. But the U.N. doesn't make the distinction between these two kinds of "violence," because that would say some of the U.N. members are perpetuators of war crimes or terrorism . . .
>
> The U.N. will not stop the terrorists; only an alliance of free states led by the U.S., geared to bring down regimes that fuel and propagate terrorism, can do that. We must implant values and morality in civilizations. Salvation will not come from the U.N. . . .
>
> The Israeli Defense Forces must continue to fight terrorism, for Israel's survival as a nation, and to uphold justice and morality.

The minister of Strategic Cooperation between the U.S. and Israel, Uzi Landau, added this:

> No cause justifies terror . . . Israel is a small target; America is the big one. But we are on the front line. If terror is not defeated here, it will move to the U.S. and to Europe. Our war is a war of free societies against terror.

And, as Ambassador Keyes put it:

> In the wake of September 11 we should have taken a stand clearly and unequivocally, that if you practice terrorism you lose your claim to legitimate participation in all and any international processes whatsoever . . .
>
> The hope and heritage of righteousness and faith . . . says, "Come what may, do evil what it will, God is God and I shall stand for Him." This, I believe, is the moral heritage that transcends any struggle for evil . . . We shall fight the fight as it is necessary in the world but we shall win it first in our own souls and spirit. So that at the end of the day we shall stand—not as people who have defeated evil, but as people who have once again vindicated the truth that—come what may—you cannot crush out that faith which holds on forever to the righteous will of God.[2]

The war on terrorism cannot be won without resolve for victory, without a conviction to call terrorism evil (whoever may be instigating it), and without the resolve to win the battle first in the spirit realm through prayer. Natural insight is not enough to win this fight; we need God's guidance. When you begin weakening that resolve and conviction, you begin developing a tolerance to look at children with no legs and allow those who maimed them to walk free. I'm not talking about being hateful or mean-spirited, nor am I preaching a racist hatred of Arabs and Muslims—what I'm talking about is values. We cannot violate our rules of law and evidence to go after such men, but we can't let terrorists and murderers walk free for political reasons, either, when we have the evidence to convict them in our hands. What I am talking about is real love—God's love—which includes justice, but not vengeance. If we are to win the overall battle against terrorism, we must win it first in Israel.

I believe in order to do that, we must also take some clear and concise steps toward that end. Many of the things America needs to do, in fact, are already in place. Here is how we can start to win this war in Israel and send a clear message to the terrorists that their reign of terror is over:

1. Allow Israel to finish her security fence in order to save both Palestinian and Israeli lives.

Media outlets reported that the Bush administration demanded that Prime Minister Sharon's government stop expanding settlements, and stop construction on the security fence in the West Bank. This message was delivered at a 2003 meeting in Rome between Sharon and the White House top Middle East adviser, Elliott Abrams.[3]

Israel has exhausted every means to provide security for Israeli citizens. The last resort is to build a security fence to deter the terrorists who slip across into Israel from the West Bank. This decision by the Israeli government is not an ill-conceived plan. There are now similar barriers along the borders with Lebanon, Syria, Jordan, and the Gaza Strip. Would you believe that not a single suicide bomber has infiltrated Israel where those barriers are in place?

In places where no security barrier exists, terrorists have only to walk across an invisible line to get from the West Bank into Israel. The U.S., in fact, ended up capturing Saddam Hussein because they built a security fence around Saddam's hometown of Tikrit, in order to control traffic in and out. This limiting of access eventually enabled our military to capture him. A fence, no matter how limited, will make it more difficult to cross this impossible-to-patrol area and save hundreds of lives. We need to let Israel do what we ourselves would do in their place.

2. Recognize Jerusalem as Israel's capital and ratify the Jerusalem Embassy Act.

The Jerusalem Embassy Act of 1995 echoes other such legislation supporting Israel that Congress passed, but our executive branch has time and again held up on national security waivers. This act called for the U.S. to recognize Jerusalem as the Israeli capital and move our embassy from Tel Aviv to Jerusalem by 1999. However, no action has been taken because the act has continually been held up on a national security waiver. Here are a few of the basic tenets of the Jerusalem Embassy Relocation Act:

- The United States maintains its embassy in the functioning capital of every country except in the case of our democratic friend and strategic ally, the state of Israel.
- The United States conducts official meetings and other business in the city of Jerusalem in *de facto* recognition of its status as the capital of Israel.
- Jerusalem should remain an undivided city in which the rights of every ethnic and religious group are protected.
- Jerusalem should be recognized as the capital of the state of Israel.
- The United States Embassy in Israel should be established in Jerusalem no later than May 31, 1999.[4]

As Republican Senator Sam Brownback of Kansas said to the Jerusalem Summit audience via satellite:

> This point is essential. Jerusalem has been the capital of the Jewish people for three thousand years. Jerusalem has never been the capital for any other state other than for the Jewish people.
>
> The United States must have a more explicit position regarding the status of Jerusalem. Our Embassy cannot remain in Tel Aviv while we claim to support and defend Israel's right to exist.

One of the first positive steps we can take to show that we are solidly behind Israel—and at the same time send an unequivocal message to the terrorists that continued violence will only diminish their negotiating power—is to refuse to renew the national security waiver for this act and recognize Jerusalem as the Israeli capital and correspondingly move our embassy there. This would not tie our hands in later negotiations with a legitimate Palestinian representation once one arises. However, removing this act from being on national security waiver sends a clear message to the terrorists: "No longer will we let your violence be used as a negotiating chip."

3. Ratify the 1987 Anti-Terrorism Act.

The 1987 Anti-Terrorism Act is also being held up on a national security waiver, perhaps mainly because of one thing: The act names the Palestine Liberation Organization as a terrorist group, and accepting it would end our ability to negotiate with them as did the elder President Bush and President Clinton. This would also prompt the closing of the PLO's offices in New York, where the terrorist organization enjoys observer status at the United Nations.

While the younger President Bush has done everything he can to move ahead with the Oslo Accords by working with the Palestinian Authority as a separate entity from the PLO, the fact has become unavoidably clear that he will have to physically sever that tie to avoid dealing with the PLO. Though Arafat is no longer PA prime minister, he still holds its strings. The U.S. refused to negotiate with the terrorist-supporting Taliban government; why should we support negotiating with the terrorism-instigating PLO? Arafat has repeatedly thwarted efforts by other leaders to step forward and make the Palestine Authority legitimate. He has continued the violence as they have called for it to stop, to the point that the first PA prime minister other than Arafat, Mahmoud Abbas, resigned because of his inability to deliver on his promise to end the violence.

If we would step forward to declare the PLO a terrorist organization and remove them once and for all from being valid representatives to negotiate for the Palestinians, it would first of all send a clear message that terrorism no longer pays, and second of all clear the way for a legitimate representative group to arise from the indigenous Palestinians through municipal and rural council elections, as Israel and Jordan had first planned in the late 1980s. This would be a tremendously positive move toward peace in the region. The Palestinian people can never have peace, nor can Israel, as long as a terrorist organization presides over their destinies.

Further than that, once the PLO is back on the list as a terrorist organization, we should go after eliminating it in the same way we are trying to eliminate al Qaeda. We should freeze its billions of dollars in assets and imprison, or at least allow Israel to imprison, its leaders. Such actions would be a tremendously easy next step to take in winning the war on terrorism and trying terrorists for their crimes. Then the billions of dollars that Arafat has tucked away to support his schemes can be released and used instead to build the schools and establish a Palestinian economy and democracy, something that Arafat and his cronies have never done since certain territories were handed over to their jurisdiction.

4. Require the Arabs to end the Palestinian Refugee problem by taking the refugees into their nations just as Israel, Germany, the United States, Jordan, and other nations have done with other refugee groups.

The Palestinian refugee camps are the longest-standing camps of their kind in the world and the *only* ones where the children and grandchildren of those in the camps have ever been considered refugees as well. Jordan has been the only nation willing to give citizenship to those within its borders. Neither Lebanon, Syria, nor any other Arab nation has offered to do the same, nor allowed those in the camps to resettle elsewhere. The camps keep these people boxed in and growing, prisoners held by their own Arab brothers, with the blame laid squarely on Israel and the war it won in 1949. After three generations, the refugees continue to be pawns in the Arab states' game to delegitimize the state of Israel in any way possible.[5] As Israeli Minister of Tourism Benny Elon has stated:

> We have to be clear, and only then can we ask for help. We must uproot the terrorists; we must have victory. I appeal to the grassroots Christians in America to put these ideas "on the table." . . . We should give up U.S. foreign aid and give it to resettle the refugees. The problem of the refugees is our problem. The refugee camps are incubators for terrorists.

Perhaps in the light of the violence they breed, the refugee camps are Israel's problem, but they cannot truly be considered her responsibility. The number of refugees has grown from seven hundred thousand to more than four million under the UN and Arab League's watchful eye—a vast disgraced and disgruntled horde with no hope of a home or a homeland. No wonder they become suicide bombers!

Many other nations of the world have dealt with refugees that were not even of their own making, but the Arab states have refused to take in those they call "brothers" and whose refugee status came not because the Israeli's dispelled them, but because the Arab nations fighting Israel told them to "get out so that we can get in."[6] After agreeing to a cease-fire with Israel in 1949, the Arab states forcibly expelled nine hundred thousand Jews from their lands, all of which Israel absorbed, not to mention the continual flow of European "displaced persons" that they already had. The United States has absorbed refugees from Vietnam, Cuba, and even the Iran-Iraq war, to the point that there are about 5.5 million Arab U.S. citizens today—a number that rivals the number of Jews in the U.S. West Germany took in their deprived Eastern cousins with little fanfare and a great deal of hardship, yet they saw no choice but to help their former countrymen. The Arab states need to do the same with the Palestinian refugees, and the question of "right of return" will vanish from negotiations for a Palestinian state, greatly simplifying the issue.

Yet, as Gamal Abd al-Nasser said, "The return of the refugees will mean the end of Israel."[7] The Arabs need to discard this trump card in favor of doing the humanitarian thing of helping their fellow Arabs. They must dismantle these terrorist incubation centers and give these people real homes.

5. Land for peace is not an option until a true representative of the Palestinian people can be raised out of their villages.

The current Palestinian populace is a tainted and brainwashed people. These are the people who danced in the streets when they heard about the attacks of September 11, and who would probably be glad to elect Yasser Arafat or Osama bin Laden as their president the moment they could have democratic elections. These are the people who raise their children to be suicide bombers, dressing their sons as guerrilla fighters with automatic weapons and having their daughters dip their hands in liquid symbolizing Israeli blood.[8] These are the people who, because of suicide attacks, celebrated Israeli deaths in the hospitals as Jewish doctors treated the Arab casualties of those same attacks right next to them. We must reverse the cycle of this rabid anti-Semitism in the Palestinian territories.

Until a legitimate, non-terrorism-tainted Palestinian leadership can emerge, there is no one with whom Israel can negotiate. Intervention is needed to develop such a group and reverse the propagation of hatred in Palestinian-controlled areas. This is a very unlikely role for Israel to play, or even the United States. Instead, it should be handled in cooperation with an Arab partner such as Jordan—basically the same plan Israel and Jordan were working on in the late 1980s.

6. We need to fight the racism of anti-Semitism as fervently as we fight other racism in our nation.

Anti-Zionism and anti-Semitism need to be squelched as the racisms that they are. This hatred is the fuel that feeds and spreads terrorism and suicide bombers. The United States cannot financially boost, nor should we supply weapons to, nations that regularly air anti-Semitic television programming or endorse anti-Semitic literature.

The war on terrorism is a battle for hearts and minds, and only God can touch a person's heart to change it. While taking these steps politically would be a tremendous move toward a return to truth as a governing principle in the U.S., such steps will never be taken without an almost incredible step back toward God in our nation. Presently, though, our nation is still contaminated with relativism and humanism—thinking that money, education, or charm will suffice.

In the Great Commission, Jesus told the disciples, "You shall be witnesses to Me in Jerusalem, and in all Judea and Samaria, and to the end of the earth."[9] Well, this Great Commission has become the Great Omission—Christ's love is no longer taught in Judea and Samaria (the area of the West Bank) as God hopes. If we are to reverse the hatred that fuels Palestinian terrorism, we need to get back to God's first instructions to the church.

Is America headed for a great awakening and a revival? Or are we headed for the rude awakening of discovering our confidence in our position in the world is misplaced? Prophecy also indicates that we are ultimately heading toward an event that will dwarf the impact of September 11 a thousand times over—will that event be the end of our nation, or its salvation? In order to answer that question, we must first come to grips with what was the greatest moral issue of the twentieth century and promises to be even more significant in the twenty-first.

CHAPTER FOURTEEN

The "New" Anti-Semitism

Today, I believe that I am acting in accordance with the will of the Almighty Creator: by defending myself against the Jew, I am fighting for the work of the Lord.

> Adolf Hitler
> *Mein Kampf*

As our recent history teaches, what begins as a threat to the Jews is soon a menace to the entire world. It is but a short step between a knifing in Jerusalem and a bombing of the World Trade Center in New York.

> Yitzhak Rabin
> *The Rabin Memoirs*
> 1979 (reprinted in 1994)

The voice of thy brother's blood crieth unto me from the ground.

> Genesis 4:10

As the ink was drying on the newly penned Constitution of the United States, many of those who had taken part in crafting it saw that the silver lining of its promise for America's future contained a dark cloud. An issue had been sorely fought through the proceedings that at points looked to burst the young country at the seams before it was even knit together. However, rather than break the new union back into colonies that the British could easily return to conquer one by one, the delegates struck compromises such as the "Three-Fifths Clause." The black cloud that our forefathers saw was the issue of slavery, and the hatred and racism that allowed it. It was an issue they felt could have eternal ramifications. Thomas Jefferson described it this way:

> The whole commerce between master and slave is a perpetual exercise of the most boisterous passions, the most unremitting despotism on the one part, and degrading submission on the other. Our children see this and learn to imitate it; for man is an imitative animal. This quality is the germ of all education in him. From his cradle to his grave he is learning to do what he sees others do . . . The parent storms, the child looks on, catches the lineaments of his wrath, puts on the same airs in the circle of smaller slaves, gives a loose rein to the worst of passions and thus nursed, educated and daily exercised in tyranny . . .
>
> Can the liberties of a nation be thought secure, when we have removed their only firm basis, *a conviction in the minds of the people that these liberties are of the gift of God? That they are not to be violated but with his wrath? Indeed I tremble for my country when I reflect that God is just: that his justice can not sleep forever*: that considering numbers, nature and natural means only, a revolution of the wheel of fortune, an exchange of situation is among possible events: *that it may become probable by supernatural interference!*
>
> *The Almighty has no attributes, which can take side with us in such a contest.* [1]

Jefferson obviously felt that America's racism, despite whatever Christian principles our nation was founded on, could well bring our nation's destruction, and worse than that a destruction at the hands of a just and moral God. In fact, in the midst of the Civil War, Abraham

Lincoln included this thought in his second inauguration address of 1865:

> If we shall suppose that American Slavery is one of those offenses which, in the providence of God, must needs come, but which, having continued through His appointed time, He now wills to remove, and that He gives to both North and South, this terrible war, as the woe due to those by whom the offense came, shall we discern therein any departure from those divine attributes which the believers in a Living God always ascribe to Him? Fondly do we hope—fervently do we pray—that this mighty scourge of war may speedily pass away. Yet, if God wills that it continue, until all the wealth piled by the bondmen's two hundred and fifty years of unrequited toil shall be sunk, and until every drop of blood drawn with the lash, shall be paid by another drawn with the sword, as was said three thousand years ago, so still it must be said, "The judgments of the Lord are true and righteous altogether."
>
> With malice toward none, with charity for all, with firmness in the right as God gives us to see the right, let us strive on to finish the work we are in, to bind up the nation's wounds, to care for him who shall have borne the battle and for his widow and his orphan, to do all which may achieve and cherish a just and lasting peace among ourselves and with all nations.[2]

However, racism lingered into the civil rights movement of the 1960s and still has its foothold in America today, though it has receded somewhat into the shadows.

If God's hedge of protection was removed from the Christian nation of the 1860s to the point it allowed the Civil War, what can we expect to happen to us if we tolerate the racism of anti-Semitism that is arising today in our world just as it did in Germany in the 1920s and 1930s?

Tolerance of European fascism was common in political circles of the 1920s and 1930s. Major American business leaders maintained rich financial ties to Hitler's Third Reich. Among these prominent Americans were Republicans Allen and John Foster Dulles. The Dulles brothers reflected the country-club anti-Semitism prevalent in upper-crust society at that time.

John Foster and Allen Dulles's connections with Germany between the World Wars helped to fund the Nazi Party; their connections with the oil companies delivered power to Saudi Arabia's wresting Middle Eastern oil rights from the British in order to give them to U.S. companies; and their political careers blossomed under President Eisenhower as one became secretary of state and the other director of Central Intelligence. The Washington Dulles International Airport was named in honor of John Foster Dulles, the one who became secretary of state because of his strong stand against communism—and despite his and his brother's connections with and support of the Nazis that lasted all through World War II. Simply put, according to Supreme Court Justice Arthur Goldberg, who served in U.S. intelligence during the Second World War, "The Dulles brothers were traitors," because they had given aid and comfort to U.S. enemies before and after World War II.[3]

John Foster Dulles saw Hitler's aggression as a legitimate German reaction to World War I's punitive peace terms. Historian Robert E. Herzstein wrote that Dulles believed "the Axis powers were trying to redress an awkward balance" in international relations. "Hitler's attacks on the Jews and his growing propensity for territorial expansion seem to have left Dulles unmoved," Herzstein reported.[4]

The Dulles brothers built investment ties between their U.S. clients and major German firms, such as I. G. Farben, a principal supporter of the Third Reich.[5] During the 1920s, one of Hitler's ploys was to attack the industrial corporate structure of Germany as part of the Jewish international conspiracy to destroy the country. Dulles's client I. G. Farben, one of the largest chemical companies in the world, was at the top of the list. At one point, Hitler threatened to dismantle the company. In 1933, when Hitler needed additional votes to assume power, a meeting was held with Hitler, Goring, and a number of German industrialists. The purpose was to persuade Hitler to cease his propaganda attacks against the corporate structure, particularly I. G. Farben. A deal was finally made. The industrialists donated three million marks to the Nazi Party in return for cessation of harassment. Of course, included in the deal was the eventual dismissal of all Jews.

Foster Dulles in 1934 drafted an agreement between Standard Oil of New Jersey and I. G. Farben to provide the Nazi war machine with synthetic oil and rubber patents. Farben later manufactured the products using slave labor at Auschwitz, the notorious death camp. So while John Foster Dulles sat on the board of directors of I. G. Farben, the company contributed to the genocidal policies of the German government by working slave laborers to death for profit.

This is one of John Foster Dulles's infamous quotes:

> I am aware how almost impossible it is in this country to carry out a foreign policy [in the Middle East] not approved by the Jews. Former Secretary of State George Marshall and former Defense Secretary James Forrestral learned that . . . terrific control the Jews have over the news media and the barrage the Jews have built up on congressmen . . . I am very much concerned over the fact that the Jewish influence here is completely dominating the scene and making it almost impossible to get congress to do anything they don't approve of. The Israeli Embassy is practically dictating to the congress through influential Jewish people in the country."[6]

John Foster died in 1959. Allen was eventually forced to resign as director of the CIA by President Kennedy because of the Bay of Pigs debacle, but was eventually appointed by President Johnson as a member of the presidential commission that investigated Kennedy's assassination.

The Jew-hatred of Germany between the World Wars has found a new home in the Arab nations of today. In fact, as we have seen from Herzl's experiences in France, Germany was not the only European nation that disliked the Jews, and while that anti-Semitism was buried under the guilt of the Holocaust, it was not extinguished. Nearly seven decades after the Holocaust, it is beginning to reemerge. Yet, today, hatred of the Jews has turned to hatred of the nation of Israel, which is seen as their representative, and hating Jews now hides behind the politics of opposing Israel.

This anti-Zionism is spread "democratically" by fanatics across the ideological spectrum, from the extreme left to the extreme right. Recent comments by Malaysian Prime Minister Mahathir Mohamad at the Organization of the Islamic Conference summit in October 2003 are typical:

> I will not enumerate the instances of our humiliation and oppression, nor will I once again condemn our detractors and oppressors. It would be an exercise in futility because they are not going to change their attitudes just because we condemn them. If we are to recover our dignity and that of Islam, our religion, it is we who must decide, it is we who must act . . .
>
> We [Muslims] are actually very strong. 1.3 billion people cannot be simply wiped out. The Europeans killed 6 million Jews out of 12 million. But today the Jews rule this world by proxy. They get others to fight and die for them.[7]

Mohamad is a respected national leader who has turned his country into the world's seventeenth-ranked trading nation during his twenty-two years in power and was the host of the conference. Yet his comments didn't stop there. He continued with the statement that the Jews "invented socialism, communism, human rights and democracy" to avoid persecution and gain control of the most powerful countries of the world.

While National Security Adviser Condoleezza Rice said of Mohamad's comments, "I don't think they are emblematic of the Muslim world," it seems unlikely that the delegates of more than fifty-seven nations to whom he spoke would agree with her comments, as they all stood when he finished and clapped loudly, shouting their approval.

Newspapers around the world are noting the rise and new openness of the anti-Semitism exemplified by remarks of men such as Prime Minister Mohamad. How different are such remarks from those of Hitler's propaganda secretary Paul Joseph Goebbels on, of all dates, September 11—but in 1937, not 2001:

> Who are those responsible for this catastrophe? Without fear, we want to point the finger at the Jew as the inspirer, the author, and the beneficiary of this terrible catastrophe: look, this is the enemy of the world, the destroyer of cultures, the parasite among the nations, the son of chaos, the incarnation of evil, the ferment of decomposition, the visible demon of the decay of humanity.[8]

Early in 1937, Goebbels documented a meeting on church affairs, where Hitler freely expressed his world-historical vision. In his diary, Goebbels wrote:

> The Fuhrer explains Christianity and Christ. He [Christ] wanted to act against Jewish world domination. Jewry had him crucified.[9]

This common doctrine of accusing the Jews of responsibility for virtually all the world's ills is resurfacing today in very similar language in the halls of European government, academia, and the media, and with worldwide distribution over the Internet. Of course, if all these ills are because of the Jews, the next logical step is to begin shutting them out of positions of power, taking away what they own, and boycotting their businesses—the first steps Hitler took in 1933. How far is the world, especially those Arab countries that won't even let Jews within their borders, from Hitler's gospel of "redemptive anti-Semitism" as he expressed it in 1922?

> My first and foremost task will be the annihilation of the
> Jews . . . until all Germany has been cleansed.[10]

Just as this traditional anti-Semitism sought to deny Jews their rights as individuals in society, anti-Zionism today attacks the collective Jewish people as a nation. Just as Jews were exploited as scapegoats for their host countries' problems, Israel is being singled out today as the root of all the world's evil—thus what happened at the UN's international Conference on Racism in Durban, South Africa, in August 2001. As far as the delegates there seemed to be concerned, racism would be a thing of the past if the nation of Israel could be eliminated. The most recent example of this was Israel's November 2003 General Assembly draft resolution calling for the protection of Israeli children from Palestinian terrorist attacks—the first resolution introduced by Israel to the UN since 1976—which was rejected by the assembly's Social, Humanitarian, and Cultural Committee, even though a similar resolution to protect Palestinian children passed just weeks before.

So-called political opposition to Israel's policies and simple Jew-hatred have become implicitly indistinguishable. Both the opponents of globalization and U.S. intervention in Iraq blame Israel—by attributing these policies to Jewish "control" over Washington, as part of the historically anti-Semitic canard that the Jews aim to take over the world.

Of what are the Jews usually accused? How is it that they have curried "control of the world by proxy"? What are their greatest sins? Don't be surprised if you can answer this yourself—you have probably been more exposed to such anti-Semitic propaganda than you have realized. The big three always seem to be: (1) The Jews control the media, (2) the Jews control the money, and (3) the Jews killed Jesus.

Is this true, though? Among the wealthiest people in the world, only 6 percent are Jewish. Who does control the money? Well, according to a BBC report, seven of the ten wealthiest heads of state in the world are Arabs, and none are Jewish. Nor are Jews CEOs of any of the world's ten largest companies.

Do they control the media? Of the ten largest media companies in the world, only one has been run in recent years by a Jew—the Walt Disney Company—hardly a pro-Israel propaganda machine. Of all the major newspapers in the U.S., only two are controlled by Jews—the *New York Times* and the *Boston Globe* (whose owners think of themselves more as Americans than Jews and regularly run anti-Zionist articles). In Europe, much of the media is government-run, and none of the government officials directing them are Jewish.

Did the Jews kill Jesus? Read your Bible. The Sanhedrin had to go to the Romans to have Jesus killed. It was the Romans who nailed Jesus to the cross and a Roman spear that pierced His side. What of the angry mob that called for his death? I have stood in the courtyard where that happened, and you could fit no more than a hundred people in it. The Sanhedrin would have probably rallied at least half that number. That is a pretty small sample for which to blame an entire race.[11] Plus, that was an awfully long time ago. No one holds the young Germans of today responsible for the Holocaust, and that was less than a century ago. How can we still hold the Jews of today responsible for the act of two thousand years ago? You might as well hold the Italians responsible for the destruction of Jerusalem because Titus was a Roman. Besides, it was the sin of all humankind that hung Jesus on the cross, not just that of the Jews.

While anti-Semitism is on the rise again in Europe, nowhere is it more vehemently expressed today than in the Arab world and, of all places, in Egypt, Israel's first Arab peace partner. A recent miniseries on Egyptian state television that was based on the notorious forgery *The Protocols of the Elders of Zion* is only one example. Egyptian schoolbooks also fill the minds of impressionable youngsters with hate propaganda against Jews, while state-controlled newspapers publish Nazi caricatures of Jews, and a vast array of anti-Semitic "literature" in original Arabic and in translation is readily available in bookstores. The fraudulent *Protocols*, in fact, is a runaway best seller in all Arab states today, as is Hitler's *Mein Kampf*. The books are illustrated, as are the daily newspapers, with depictions of grotesque hook-nosed, bearded, thick-lipped Jews and Israelis. These illustrations are indistinguishable from those in

Der Sturmer, which was published during the Holocaust by Nazi propaganda chief Joseph Goebbels.

Just before the visit of Shimon Peres to Cairo on April 29, 2001, the Nasserist newspaper *Al-Arabi* printed a swastika and a photomontage of Peres in a Nazi uniform on the front page. On April 18, Ahmad Regev, a journalist, wrote in the official Egyptian newspaper *Al-Akhbar:* "Our thanks go to the late Hitler who wrought, in advance, the vengeance of the Palestinians upon the most despicable villains on the face of the earth. However, we rebuke Hitler for the fact that the vengeance was insufficient."

Syrian Defense Minister Mustafa Tlas's 1983 book, *The Matza of Zion*—an Arab variation on the medieval Christian blood libel that also caused the Damascus incident of 1840—accuses Jews of baking Passover matza with the blood of Muslim children. It has just been reprinted. "Sucking the blood of Arabs" has been aired repeatedly in the Arab media, for example by Palestine Liberation Army Col. Nadir al-Tamimi on al-Jazeera television on October 24, 2000, and by Egyptian columnist Adil Hammuda, "A Jewish Matza Made from Arab Blood," in the government daily *Al-Ahram.* The Egyptian weekly *October* has informed its readers about "the loathsome qualities of the Jewish race throughout its long history." Meanwhile, the official Syrian daily *Tishrin* frequently accuses Israel of fabricating the Holocaust. It should also be recalled that Adolf Eichmann's sadistic deputy, Alois Brunner, found safe haven in Syria.

Holocaust denial is a frequent theme in the Arab media, with *The Palestine Times* writing of "God's lying people" who are "the Holocaust worshipers,"[12] and the Palestinian Authority's TV channel: "No Chelmno, no Dachau, no Auschwitz, only disinfecting sites . . . the lie of extermination." The PA mufti of Jerusalem, Sheikh Sabri Ikrama, explains the Holocaust, stating: "It is not my fault that Hitler hated the Jews. Anyway, they hate them just about everywhere."[13] Other Muslim clerics call on the worshipers in the mosques to "have no mercy on the Jews, no matter where they are, in any country . . . wherever you meet them, kill them."[14]

For their part, Palestinian terrorists practice a form of anti-Semitism that combines the Nazi dehumanization of Jews with glorifying in their murder—supposedly for the sake of peace and a Palestinian state. While most European countries have come a long way toward facing their past and ensuring that anti-Semitism will never again become official policy, the Arab world has done nothing to douse the flames of Jew-hatred within its borders.

The official Palestinian Authority TV station broadcasts movies in which children kill Israeli soldiers. Reports broadcast from PA summer camps show children training with weapons and singing songs filled with hatred for Jews and songs of praise for the *shahids* ("suicide bombers"). The studio map of "Greater Palestine" covers the area of the entire state of Israel—but the name "Israel" is not mentioned, and all Israeli cities are presented as the cities of Palestine.

In another obscene denial of the Holocaust, Palestinian Authority spokesmen describe Israel as a "racist country that uses the same method of ethnic cleansing that Nazi Germany used against the Jews." The Jews are presented as the enemies of Islam, "wild animals," "locusts," "swindlers," "traitors," "aggressive," "war-mongers," "robbers," "sly," "avaricious," "disloyal," and "thieves"—whose end will come as the will of Allah.[15] A typical caricature in one of the official PA newspapers shows a dwarf with a Star of David, his face copied from the face of the Jew in the Nazi *Der Sturmer*, with the caption: "The disease of the century." Another cartoon shows an Israeli soldier barbecuing Arabs, taking them off the grill, and eating them one by one with relish.[16]

Esti Vebman, an expert on anti-Semitism from the Institute for the Study of Anti-Semitism and Racism at Tel Aviv University, has been following anti-Semitism in the Palestinian Authority and Arab world for the past eight years. "Back in the Middle Ages," says Vebman, "the Christians used this motif of poisoning wells. The Arabs are now adopting the Christian anti-Semitism of the Middle Ages and Nazi anti-Semitism; they are adding Islamic motifs and integrating it into their anti-Israel propaganda."[17] Hitler is one of the heroes of Palestinian youth, according to researchers at the University of Hamburg, who conducted an international study on the perceptions of democracy among young people around the world. Booksellers in the territories report that the Arabic translation of Hitler's book *Mein Kampf* is a best seller in Palestine as well as Egypt and other Arab nations. The official Palestine Authority media are in the habit of comparing Israel's actions in the territories with those of the Nazis. Binyamin Netanyahu, while serving as prime minister, was portrayed as a Nazi and described as "a Zionist terrorist who is worse than Hitler."[18]

"It was a good day for the Jews, when the Nazi Hitler began his campaign of persecution against them," writes Sif Ali Algeruan of *Al-Hayat al-Jedida*.

> They began to disseminate, in a terrifying manner, pictures of mass shootings directed at them, and to invent the shocking story about the gas ovens in which, according to them, Hitler used to burn them. The newspapers are filled with pictures of Jews who were mowed down by Hitler's machine guns, and of Jews being led to the gas ovens. In these pictures they concentrated on women, babies, and old people, and they took advantage of it, in order to elicit sympathy toward them, when they demand financial reparations, contributions and grants from all over the world. The truth is that the persecution of the Jews is a myth, that the Jews dubbed "the tragedy of the Holocaust" and took advantage of, in order to elicit sympathy toward them.[19]

Since the beginning of the Second *Intifada* in September 2000, Israel has been subjected to a worldwide campaign of delegitimization in the media and international forums by political leaders and intellectuals. Extremists of the left and right have joined together in their hatred of the Jewish state, resulting in a dramatic increase in anti-Semitic incidents including physical attacks on Jews. These attacks on Israel's legitimacy have been accompanied by attacks on Jewish targets throughout the world, but particularly in Europe. Anti-Semitic incidents have included bombings of synagogues and Jewish schools, vandalism and desecration of Jewish cemeteries, death threats and unprovoked violence against Jews, including murder. These hate crimes against Jewish individuals and institutions are often disguised as "anti-Zionist" actions.

One of the consequences of Palestinian anti-Semitism has been an increase in attacks on Jewish targets in the Arab world, such as the April 2002 terrorist attack on the ancient synagogue in Djerba, Tunisia, during which twelve European tourists, four local Arabs, and a Jew were murdered. In Istanbul in November 2003, twenty-three persons were murdered, six of them Jews, and hundreds wounded in suicide bombing attacks on two synagogues.

The following are excerpts from a 2002 report on anti-Semitism in Europe by the European Union's European Monitoring Center on Racism and Xenophobia:

> Physical attacks on Jews and the desecration and destruction of synagogues were acts often committed by young Muslim perpetrators . . . Many of these attacks occurred either during or after pro-Palestinian demonstrations, which were also used by radical Islamists for hurling verbal abuse. In addition, radical Islamist circles were responsible for placing anti-Semitic propaganda on the Internet and in Arab-language media . . . In the extreme left-wing scene anti-Semitic remarks were to be found mainly in the context of pro-Palestinian and anti-globalization rallies and in newspaper articles using anti-Semitic stereotypes in their criticism of Israel . . .
>
> In the heated public debate on Israeli politics and the boundary between criticism of Israel and anti-Semitism, individuals who are not politically active and do not belong to one of the ideological camps mentioned above become motivated to voice their latent anti-Semitic attitudes (mostly in the form of telephone calls and insulting letters). Opinion polls prove that in some European countries a large percentage of the population harbors anti-Semitic attitudes and views, but that these usually remain latent . . .

> Observers point to an "increasingly blatant anti-Semitic Arab and Muslim media," including audiotapes and sermons, in which the call is not only made to join the struggle against Israel but also against Jews across the world. Although leading Muslim organizations express their opposition to this propaganda, observers assume that calling for the use of violence may influence readers and listeners . . . We recommend that the EUMC request state authorities to acknowledge at the highest level the extraordinary dangers posed by anti-Semitic violence in the European context.[20]

France, with its large Muslim minority, stands out as the country in which the greatest number and most serious of anti-Semitic incidents occurred in comparison with other countries in the world. These included: the physical attack and harassment of Jews all over the country, the torching of synagogues, the desecration of cemeteries, and threats and dissemination of radical anti-Semitic and anti-Israel propaganda. The perpetrators came mainly from among young North African Muslim immigrants.

It should be noted that a number of attacks were the result of organized action, rather than spontaneous mob activity or vandalism, which targeted Jews in reaction to events in Israel and were part of efforts to delegitimize Israel and Zionism. These attacks were not limited to a focus on Israel, however, but were blatant manifestations of anti-Semitism involving incitement to attack Jews everywhere—incitement in mosques and in other concentrations of Muslims to attack Jews "because they are responsible for everything 'evil' in the world."

In other European countries, especially those with large Muslim populations, there have been serious physical attacks on Jews, in addition to verbal harassment, graffiti, and cemetery desecrations. Jews have been physically attacked in Belgium, in addition to Jewish community facilities. Universities throughout Europe have become active centers of anti-Semitic and anti-Israel propaganda and threats. In Britain, Jews have been attacked, and synagogues and other community facilities have been desecrated.

Numerous anti-Semitic incidents have occurred in the Scandinavian countries, especially Denmark and Sweden, whose governments have been extremely critical of Israel. In Germany in 2002, there were a large number of anti-Semitic incidents, including physical attacks on Jews and the desecration of cemeteries by neo-Nazi and Islamic elements.

In Eastern Europe and Russia, anti-Semitic activities have mostly taken the form of propaganda and demonstrations. In Russia, a number of Jews were injured and synagogues and other Jewish facilities were damaged. One Russian innovation was the placing along highways of booby-trapped signs with anti-Semitic slurs, which exploded when anyone tried to take them down. These signs caused one fatality and a number of injuries in Russia and led to several copycat incidents in the Ukraine.

As an analysis that appeared in the London *Spectator* regarding the attitude of the British clergy acknowledged: "Animosity toward Israel has its roots in a deep hatred of the Jews."[21] This was echoed by the prominent Italian journalist Oriana Falacci, who strongly denounced the double standard practiced in Europe today: "One standard for the Jews and another for Christians and Muslims, one *vis-à-vis* Jewish blood that has been spilled and another *vis-à-vis* other blood. And there is the lack of proportion between attacks on Israel, which are not political criticism but saturated with anti-Semitic terms, and what Israel actually does."[22]

There is an ironic Jewish joke that defines anti-Semitism as a disease suffered by Gentiles that is often fatal to Jews. As such, there is not much that is new about the so-called "new anti-Semitism" at the beginning of the twenty-first century. One difference, as noted by Israeli Parliamentarian Michael Melchior, is the strange coalitions of the new anti-Semitism. "In the U.S., for example, there is striking cooperation, especially through anti-Semitic websites, between neo-Nazis and Islamic fundamentalists," he wrote. "After 9/11, both groups claimed Jews were behind the attacks. That's not a new phenomenon. A few years ago, it was discovered that the Iraqi Embassy in Sweden had financed neo-Nazi activities, even though neo-Nazis hate the Muslims."[23]

Israeli historian Robert Wistrich has noted that it is radical Muslims and not necessarily white Europeans who are leading the present wave of anti-Semitism. The Islamic world imported anti-Semitism from Europe, "converted it to Islam" as part of the Israeli-Palestinian conflict, and exported it back to Europe and the West in general by means of the Muslim *Diaspora* and anti-West and anti-globalization elements.

Regarding the new blood libels of the new century, Wistrich concluded:

> Arab governments are doing nothing against these fabrications, and in essence legitimize them in order to protect themselves from the wrath of their own embittered citizens, deprived of democracy, freedom of speech and basic human rights. Against this background it is clear how millions of Muslims are prepared to believe every falsehood, including the blowing up of the World Trade Center by the Mossad . . .
>
> This "Semitic" anti-Semitism is especially threatening when it is on a mission from Allah, and the 1979 revolution in Iran against the "Great Devil" (America and the "Crusader" West) and the "Jewish-Zionist Devil" bears witness to this. This is total war, because it is mainly a religious war. Anti-Semitism of this kind has diverted the Jihad from its original objective and turned into a death cult.[24]

This growing trend is gradually becoming not an echo but an amplification of what happened in pre–World War II Germany. While the cries against the Jews grew louder in Germany, the rest of the world simply shrugged it off with comments such as "Oh, I don't think that is emblematic of all the Germans." However, it didn't matter if it was or not—their silence made them accomplices in the murders by such "nonrepresentative" Germans. Are we any less guilty if we stand by quietly and let the cry to kill Jews grow among Arabs and in Europe? How far do we need to let such blatant hatred go before we should do something about it? My feeling is that it has already gone too far.

There is perhaps no better sign that the spirit of antichrist is again on the rise than this reemergence of rabid anti-Semitism. Satan will, of course, hate Jews first, and then Christians, because they were the first to cut a covenant with God. And we can be no less guilty as a nation for being silent about racism toward Jews than we have been because of our acquiescence to racism toward African-Americans as our Constitution was being written. We realize with Thomas Jefferson that God's "justice cannot sleep forever," and with Isser Harel, "Hitler first killed Jews, then he killed Christians. Our culture and our democracies are the root of the rage. If we're right, they are wrong."

The Jerusalem Prayer Team

This is why I started the Jerusalem Prayer Team. September 11, 2001, was a tragic day in American history. America had, as Dietrich Bonhoeffer said, "learned to see the great events of world history from below, from the perspective of the outcast, the suspects, the maltreated, the powerless, the oppressed, the reviled—in short, from the perspective of those who suffer."[25] The attack was a physical manifestation of a battle that had been lost weeks, months, and possibly years before because of a lack of prayer. Osama bin Laden had been verbally attacking America for years, but the church was asleep. The demonic powers that were influencing him needed to be violently confronted by holy angels on assignment through the power of prayer—as in the time of Daniel.

Praying for the peace of Jerusalem is not praying for stones or dirt. They don't weep or bleed. It is praying for God's protection over the lives of the citizens of Jerusalem. It is praying for revival. It is praying for God's grace to be poured out on the Bible land and all over the Middle East—prayer that demonic powers will be defeated by holy angels in a battle that cannot be seen with the natural eye. Mother Teresa was one of the first people who told me she prayed daily for the peace of Jerusalem according to Psalm 122:6. She told me, "Love is not something you say, it's something you do." I believe that with all my heart.

The pastor of Corrie ten Boom's grandfather went to him and told him that his church was going to pray for the peace of Jerusalem. It inspired the ten Boom family to begin praying weekly. As chairman of the board of Corrie ten Boom House in Haarlem, Holland, I have made the decision to revive this hundred-year-old prayer tradition. That is a big part of why we are asking for one million Christians to join the Jerusalem Prayer Team, and why we are asking one hundred thousand churches to begin praying weekly during their Sunday services for the peace of Jerusalem. The vision of the Jerusalem Prayer Team is to have one million intercessors praying daily for national revival according to 2 Chronicles 7:14, and also to pray the prayer of King David for the peace of Jerusalem.[26]

Would you like to become a member of the Jerusalem Prayer Team, or would you like to encourage others to do so? You can e-mail us at jpteam@sbcglobal.net, or write to: The Jerusalem Prayer Team, P.O. Box 210489, Bedford, TX 76095.

The House of Israel is in a state of terror as are all the children of the Bible land. They need the Lord to answer them in their day of terror. They need the God of Jacob to defend them. They need help from the sanctuary and strength out of Zion. Now you know my personal prayer, and when it began. I believe one million intercessors praying daily and one hundred thousand churches praying weekly for the peace of Jerusalem will move heaven and earth.

It is time for us to wake up, but will that awakening be a great or rude awakening? According to Genesis 12:3, God told Abraham that He would "bless those who bless you, and . . . curse him who curses you" (NKJV). Which have we been as a nation: a blessing or a cursing to Israel?

Is it possible that America might have been spared the Great Depression if it had not ignored the plight of the Jews? Is it possible that tens of thousands of Americans would not have died in World War II if America had not closed its doors to the house of Israel (divine intervention)? If so, God-fearing Americans must stand up now before it is too late. "I will bless them that bless thee, and curse him that curseth thee: and in thee shall all families of the earth be blessed" (Genesis 12:3).

CHAPTER FIFTEEN

Blessings and Cursings

Be strong and of good courage.

> President Bill Clinton
> quoting from Joshua 1:6 (NKJV) at the funeral of Yitzhak
> Rabin.
> He skipped the rest of the verse, which says:
> "for to this people you shall divide as an inheritance
> the land which I swore to their fathers to give them."
> (The Gaza-Jericho Palestinian peace accords of the Wye River
> Conference between Bill Clinton, Yitzhak Rabin, and Yasser
> Arafat gave Jericho to the PLO.)

> *I will make you a great nation;*
> *I will bless you*
> *And make your name great;*
> *And you shall be a blessing.*
> *I will bless those who bless you,*
> *And I will curse him who curses you;*
> *And in you all the families of the earth shall be blessed.*
>
> Genesis 12:2–3 NKJV

Can America be blessed by God Almighty if it rejects His Word? America has both blessed and cursed the people of the Book. America's alliance with ancient Ishmael was indeed one of convenience. We received oil, and Ishmael received weapons and concessions. It appeared reasonable at first glance. America knew that Ishmael was a mortal enemy of Isaac, but Isaac's lack of peace would not affect America—or would it?

When one wishes to remain an ally to two brothers that hate each other, someone has to be appeased, either through bombs or bribes. Like the man in the crowd shouting, "It's the economy, stupid," America is trying to balance the checkbook with moral clarity on the same scales. Someone will, ultimately, have to pay. As the ancient Word says: "Yea, hath God said, Ye shall not . . ."[1] The ancient prophetic warning has been rejected, and America has promised something to Ishmael that it does not own—Israel's Bible land, including East Jerusalem.

The first curse in the Bible came from God Almighty because of disobedience. Has God changed, or is America shaking its fist in the face of a holy God? Within moments of judgment, and blind as a bat, is America convinced that Israel gets all the curses, and so-called Christian America gets all the blessings—no matter what?

The truth is this: America has sold Israel out for oil, an act of betrayal at best. It has demanded that Israel feed their terrorists, all the while claiming the God-given right to fight its own. America is playing a very dangerous game with its future! Carter cut a Land for Peace deal with terrorists, and Clinton made good on it. The deal was simple. America was to get peace, and Israel was to give up land. Every intelligence expert in the Middle East knows this was the deal, plain and simple. The terrorists did keep their part of the bargain, more or less, for a few decades, as long as America kept promising them more and more of Israel's land, and East Jerusalem as their capital. No, America was not an honest broker, but a dishonest broker, playing Russian roulette with Jewish souls and ultimately, with American souls (September 11, 2001).

Would September 11 have happened had America maintained moral clarity? No, I do not believe it would have. American presidents could have signed the Anti-Terrorism Act, sending a signal to would-be terrorists that their acts would not be tolerated, and that Israel would not be used as a poker chip to appease terrorist regimes. President Jimmy Carter would not have interfered in Iran; the U.S. would not have supported Saddam Hussein in his war against Iran; the Soviets would not have invaded Afghanistan in response to our actions; the U.S. would not have trained and armed thousands of terrorists to fight the U.S.S.R. in Afghanistan.

Jimmy Carter, who claims to be a born-again Christian, betrayed Israel and destabilized the entire Middle East. Clinton, who also claimed the label of born-again Christian, finished the job by holding a land-for-appeasement auction. The question: Will America repent, or continue down this dark, apocalyptic path?

Blessings Under President Jimmy Carter

As Carter put it himself:

> The United States . . . has a warm and a unique relationship of friendship with Israel that is morally right. It is compatible with our deepest religious convictions, and it is right in terms of America's own strategic interests. We are committed to Israel's security, prosperity, and future as a land that has so much to offer the world.
>
> The survival of Israel is not just a political issue, it is a moral imperative. That is my deeply held belief and it is the belief shared by the vast majority of the American people . . . A strong secure Israel is not just in Israel's interest. It's in the interest of the United States and in the interest of the entire free world.[2]

So we see that Jimmy Carter definitely supported Israel in his intents, but what about his actions?

Curses Under President Jimmy Carter

A surprising development, and arguably the linchpin in forging the fundamentalist Christian-Zionist alliance, occurred in March 1977, when Carter inserted the clause "Palestinians deserve a right to their homeland" into a policy address. Immediately, the pro-Israel lobby and the Christian right responded with full-page ads in major U.S. newspapers. Their text stated: "The time has come for evangelical Christians to affirm their belief in biblical prophecy and Israel's divine right to the land." The text concluded with a line that took direct aim at Carter's statement: "We affirm as evangelicals our belief in the promised land to the Jewish people . . . We would view with grave concern any effort to carve out of the Jewish homeland another nation or political entity."

The advertising campaign was one of the first significant signs of the Likud Party's and the pro-Israel lobby's alliance with the Christian right. It redirected conservative Christian support from Carter, a Democrat, to the Republican right. Jerry Strober, a former employee of the American Jewish Committee, coordinated the campaign and told *Newsweek* magazine: "The evangelicals are Carter's constituency and he [had] better listen to them . . . The real source of strength the Jews have in this country is from the evangelicals."[3]

However, Carter continued to side with the Palestinians and was the first U.S. president to suggest that Israeli settlements in the West Bank were hindering peace in the area as much as Palestinian violence was. In his own words:

> An underlying reason that years of US diplomacy have failed and violence in the Middle East persists is that some Israeli leaders continue to "create facts" by building settlements in occupied territory.[4]

Has time changed this opinion? It appears the answer is no. In December 2003, he had this to add:

> No matter what leaders Palestinians might choose, no matter how fervent American interests might be or how great the hatred and bloodshed might become, there is one basic choice for the Israelis: Do you want peace with their neighbors or do you want to retain settlements throughout the occupied territories?[5]

President Carter was also the first president to try to turn the PLO into diplomats. Carter would not let Israel help with the Iranian hostages, but asked the PLO and Egypt, saying that this was for Israel's sake—he couldn't involve Israel in an operation against a Muslim country because he felt it could lead to further hostilities in the area.

During his presidency, it was also Carter who opened the door to sell arms to the Arabs. During his administration, Carter approved the following arms sales to the Arab states (1977–80):

Saudi Arabia	$16.9 billion
Egypt	$3.6 billion
Jordan	$427 million[6]

By the 1980 elections, the political landscape had shifted, both in the Middle East and in the U.S. The Iranian hostage crisis helped ensure Carter's defeat against his Republican rival, Ronald Reagan. However, it was not the only factor: An estimated twenty million fundamentalist and evangelical Christians voted for Reagan and against Carter's brand of evangelical Christianity that failed the test of unconditional support for Israel.[7]

Blessings Under President Ronald Reagan

In President Reagan's own words from 1982:

> Only by full appreciation of the critical role the State of Israel plays in our strategic calculus can we build the foundation for thwarting Moscow's designs on territories and resources vital to our security and our national well-being.
>
> Since the rebirth of the State of Israel, there has been an ironclad bond between that democracy and this one.
>
> In Israel, free men and women are every day demonstrating the power of courage and faith. Back in 1948 when Israel was founded, pundits claimed the new country could never survive. Today, no one questions that Israel is a land of stability and democracy in a region of tyranny and unrest.

> America has never flinched from its commitment to the State of Israel—a commitment that remains unshakable.[8]

And again from later that year:

> Israel exists; it has a right to exist in peace behind secure and defensible borders; and it has a right to demand of its neighbors that they recognize those facts. I have personally followed and supported Israel's heroic struggle for survival, ever since the founding of the State of Israel 34 years ago. In the pre-1967 borders Israel was barely 10 miles wide at its narrowest point. The bulk of Israel's population lived within artillery range of hostile Arab armies. I am not about to ask Israel to live that way again.[9]

And again from early 1983:

> Since the foundation of the State of Israel, the United States has stood by her and helped her to pursue security, peace, and economic growth. Our friendship is based on historic moral and strategic ties, as well as our shared dedication to democracy.[10]

In 1987, near the end of his presidency, Reagan had this to say at a ceremony welcoming Chaim Herzog:

> For the people of Israel and America are historic partners in the global quest for human dignity and freedom. We will always remain at each other's side.[11]

These are beautifully chosen words from the most well-spoken Republican president of our generation, but did his actions back up his words?

Curses Under President Ronald Reagan

Regan approved the sale of AWACS to Saudi Arabia after the Israeli attack on Osirak because the Saudis found out that our AWACS planes in the region watched as the Israeli fighters arched across Saudi Arabia into Iraq and back without saying a word. They then used this bit of information to force the U.S. to sell them the planes to protect themselves from possible future preemptive strikes by the Israelis. In fact, this is the incident that precipitated my trip to the White House that I shared in chapter one. Despite my arguments, the planes were sold to Saudi Arabia anyway. Here is how President Reagan justified this sale to the American people in October 1981:

> The sale of AWACS and other air defense equipment to Saudi Arabia would make a substantial contribution to the national security interests of the United States in a vital part of the world. The rejection of this sale would damage the ability of the United States to conduct a credible and effective foreign policy, not only in the Gulf region, but across a broad range of issues.[12]

And again later that same month:

> We see this as very definitely a part of our ability to help in the peacemaking process over there in the Middle East; that the Saudi Arabians are very key to this. And we've had their help already, and so on, in things that lead us to believe that going forward at this and establishing this kind of a relationship with them will bear fruit . . . if we go forward with this AWACS deal, that we will have further strengthened our credibility with them and our peacemaking ability in the Middle East. If we don't, I believe we could lose all credibility.[13]

It was also under President Reagan that the U.S. sent troops to fight in the 1982 Lebanese War, and pulled them out after the suicide bombings on the U.S. Embassy in Beirut and our military headquarters there. President Reagan had this to say about sending in the troops:

> The war in Lebanon has demonstrated . . . [that] first the military losses of the PLO have not diminished the yearning of the Palestinian people for a just solution of their claims; and second, while Israel's military successes in Lebanon have demonstrated that its armed forces are second to none in the region, they alone cannot bring just and lasting peace to Israel and her neighbors.[14]

He later said this in support of the cause there:

> All people of decency must share our outrage and revulsion of the murders, which included women and children . . . We [had been] assured that Israeli forces would not enter west Beirut. We also understood that following withdrawal, Lebanese Army units would establish control over that city. We were thwarted in this effort by the Israeli occupation that took place beginning Wednesday . . . We strongly opposed Israel's move into west Beirut . . . for fear it would provoke further fighting.[15]

At the same time, many believe that Reagan wouldn't let Begin finish off the PLO in Lebanon—a step that would have greatly simplified things in coming years—and let them go to Tunis. However, it was never Israel's intention to "finish off the PLO." As Begin told the Knesset on June 29, 1982:

> We want the terrorists to leave Beirut and Lebanon. And I want to tell the Knesset Members—they will leave Beirut and Lebanon. Nothing can help them; they'll leave.
> Now I would like to explain what we are willing [to do].

Let it be known that we don't want to humiliate the terrorists. In fact they deserve neither compassion nor respectful
treatment; there's no doubt about it, they are base murderers. Especially the one with the hairy face: he's base, a child-
murderer. But they're human beings too. Even criminals are
human beings; and a human being, every human being,
must be respected. So we don't want to humiliate them, and
therefore we haven't said they must surrender to us. We propose that the Lebanese army go into west Beirut. Why not?
It is, after all, the army of Lebanon. Lebanon is a country
that everyone thinks should be independent. It has a capital that everyone agrees is Beirut. Part of Beirut is occupied
by a foreign force. So the Lebanese army should go into
west Beirut. The terrorists will hand over their arms to
them, and then we'll let them go, via one of three routes: either the Beirut-Damascus highway—and in the 20 km.
strip that we control we will let them pass peacefully, without injury, we will see to that—or they can go north toward
Lebanese Tripoli, and from there to Syria; or they can leave
by sea. Let them choose which way.[16]

However, though this cooperation seems a blessing on the surface,
the eventual withdrawal of U.S. forces because of terrorist aggression
sent such a solid message of "terrorism pays" to the world that, in the
end, it must be seen more of a curse. It was the U.S.'s first loss in the
war on terrorism, a war we didn't even know we were in for two more
decades, and the greatest travesty in the Middle East in my lifetime.

The Anti-Terrorism Act was also passed into law on President Reagan's watch—on December 22, 1987. This also began as a blessing. It
states:

Therefore, the Congress determines that the PLO and its
affiliates are a terrorist organization and a threat to the interests of the United States, its allies, and to international

> law and should not benefit from operating in the United
> States . . .
>
> It shall be unlawful, if the purpose be to further the in-
> terests of the Palestine Liberation Organization or any of its
> constituent groups, any successor to any of those, or any
> agents thereof, on or after the effective date of this chap-
> ter.[17]

Thus Reagan was also the first president to postpone its implementation on a national security waiver. Following the passage of the law
and waiving its execution, Reagan—in the last days of his presidency
and, some say, at the request of incoming president Bush—recognized
the PLO, despite Israel's indignation and its fears of increasing terrorism.

On December 16, 1988, U.S. officials went even further to open a
dialogue with the PLO in Tunis. In a December 22 letter intended to
reassure Israeli Prime Minister Yitzhak Shamir, Reagan wrote:

> Nothing in this decision should be construed as weakening
> the United States' commitment to Israel's security, dimin-
> ishing our fight against terrorism in all its forms, or indi-
> cating our acceptance of an independent Palestinian state.
>
> I am under no illusions about the PLO. Their words will
> have to be supported by actions, namely a continuing re-
> nunciation of terrorism everywhere and disassociation from
> those who perpetrate it. Nevertheless, I believe that our di-
> alogue with the PLO potentially can encourage realism and
> pragmatism within the Palestinian leadership and thus con-
> tribute to a comprehensive resolution of the Arab-Israeli
> conflict, in which the long-term security of Israel can be
> achieved.[18]

America also continued its arms sales in the Middle East under President Reagan. From 1981 to 1988, arms sales to Arab states had the following totals:

Saudi Arabia	$26.3 billion
Egypt	$4.1 billion
Jordan	$2.5 billion

Blessings Under President George H. W. Bush

In an address to the United Nations in 1991, President George Herbert Walker Bush had this to say about the United States' relationship with Israel:

> The friendship, the alliance between the United States and Israel is strong and solid, built upon a foundation of shared democratic values, of shared history and heritage that sustains the life of our two countries. The emotional bond of our people transcends politics. Our strategic cooperation—and I renew today our determination that that go forward—is a source of mutual security. And the United States' commitment to the security of Israel remains unshakable. We may differ over some policies from time to time, individual policies, but never over the principle.
>
> For more than 40 years, the United States and Israel have enjoyed a friendship built on mutual respect and commitment to democratic principles. Our continuing search for peace in the Middle East begins with a recognition that the ties uniting our two countries can never be broken.
>
> Zionism . . . is the idea that led to the creation of a home for the Jewish people . . . And to equate Zionism with the intolerable sin of racism is to twist history and forget the terrible plight of Jews in World War II and indeed throughout history."[19]

Again, beautiful words, but what actions did the U.S. take under the first President Bush?

Curses Under President George H. W. Bush

The term of the senior President Bush was a sensitive time in U.S. relations with Israel. Israel was asking for $10 billion in loan guarantees, mainly to help them with the huge influx of Soviet immigrants. However, Israel's insistence on continuing the settlement of the West Bank was an ongoing sore point in peace negotiations with the Arabs. Bush made a tough decision to delay the loan guarantees until Israel agreed to stop building settlements in the disputed territories, because the money, either directly or indirectly, would support those settlements. This is how President Bush described his actions in a letter to George Klein, a Republican activist in the Jewish community:

> Whatever happens, it is essential that this issue not be allowed to weaken, much less cast doubt upon, the core relationship between the US and Israel.
>
> I have come to believe that the measure of a good relationship is not the ability to agree, but rather the ability to disagree on specifics without placing fundamentals at risk. We do this all the time with Britain: we should manage to do it with Israel.[20]

Following the Madrid Conference in October 1991, at the end of November the United States issued invitations to Israel, Syria, Lebanon, and the Jordanian-Palestinian delegations to come to Washington for the next phase of the talks starting December 4. Israel reacted sharply and accused the United States of setting a dangerous precedent by sending the invitation without consulting Israel; which could set a pattern for indirect talks through the United States. It would encourage the Arabs to think that the United States would play a central role in the talks. Finally, Israel wanted the talks held in the region for psychological reasons. The Arab people must know that their governments are negotiating with Israel. The statement mentioned the fact that Syria did not tell its people that it was talking with Israel in Madrid. The issue of venue again strained Israel-American relations.

The prime minister's office summed up the Israeli opinion in these words:

> The American decision to intervene in order to break an impasse on the venue question sets a dangerous precedent. The Arab negotiators now realize that by stonewalling and threatening they will persuade the United States to assume the role of arbitrator, and substitute itself for the direct talks.
>
> The United States government has consistently held the position that the Arabs and Israelis must negotiate directly. President Bush said in Madrid: "Peace will only come as the result of direct negotiations, compromise, give and take. Peace cannot be imposed from the outside." Yet, in the United States invitation to the December 4th meeting in Washington, the United States included detailed proposals and suggestions on the talks relating to every one of the three groups. Even before the agenda had begun to be discussed between the sides, the United States bypassed the issue and injected its views on the substance of the negotiations. This will only serve to strengthen the Arab resolve to talk substance only through the United States and meet with the Israelis only for imagery.
>
> A telling example for Israel's concerns is a statement by the head of the Syrian delegation to the peace talks, in an interview on Damascus television. Referring constantly to Israel as "the enemy," the Syrian Ambassador said that the negotiations with Israel were "a continuation of the war in a different form." The only way to test the Arab attitude to the peace talks is to enable Israel to conduct the negotiations directly, face-to-face, without any outside intervention on any aspect. Clearly, this is not the direction the peace process is taking today.[21]

American arms continued to flow to the Middle East. From 1990 to 1992, the U.S. sold weapons totaling these amounts to each of these countries:

Saudi Arabia	$19.6 billion
Egypt	$3.5 billion
Jordan	$60.2 million

Blessings Under President William Clinton

President William Jefferson Clinton professed to genuinely love and admire Israel. He and his wife, Hillary, saw social advancement and community models in Israel that they had hoped to apply in some of their social programs in the United States. Many in Israel returned Clinton's love. He knew how to charm Israelis, as he did the American public, and give them the feeling that they had a *haver*—a friend—they could count on. Many quipped that if Clinton ever decided to run for prime minister of Israel, he had a very good chance of winning.

In a letter to Binyamin Netanyahu commemorating the fiftieth anniversary of Israel's statehood, he wrote:

> Our relationship would never vary from its allegiance to the shared values, the shared religious heritage, the shared democratic politics which have made the relationship between the United States and Israel a special—even on occasion a wonderful—relationship.
>
> The United States admires Israel for all that it has overcome and for all that it has accomplished. We are proud of the strong bond we have forged with Israel, based on our shared values and ideals. That unique relationship will endure just as Israel has endured.[22]

Later that same year, he had this to say in a reply to the Israeli ambassador:

America and Israel share a special bond. Our relations are unique among all nations. Like America, Israel is a strong democracy, a symbol of freedom, and an oasis of liberty, a home to the oppressed and persecuted.

The relationship between our two countries is built on shared understandings and values. Our peoples continue to enjoy the fruits of our excellent economic and cultural cooperation as we prepare to enter the twenty-first century.[23]

Once again, these are beautiful words from the man who was probably the most eloquent president of our generation. But, actions speak louder than words.

Curses Under President William Clinton

Though we have already discussed much of what Bill Clinton did to Israel and America in his terms in office, I want to sum up the most significant here for the sake of this discussion. Clinton sent a signal to the terrorists of the world that crime pays. When he reached out in love to Arafat, and pressured Israel into taking "a brave gamble for peace," Clinton redefined "Islamic fanatics and terrorists" as "freedom fighters," and sent the signal to the Osamas of this world that America was weak and willing to compromise.

Clinton's refusal to meet with Prime Minister Binyamin Netanyahu during his November 1997 visit to the U.S., as well as during the period immediately preceding the Israeli elections of May 1999, was quite definitely the most direct action taken by an American president to influence the elections of another nation. Arafat received the keys to the White House while Israel was nailed to the cross.

This action also included Secretary of State Madeleine Albright's statement of November 14, 1997, in which she directly linked the U.S.'s inability to form a regional coalition against Iraq for a second further redeployment to the continued stalemate in the Israeli-Palestinian negotiations. In January 1999, Albright also refused to meet Foreign Minister Ariel Sharon during his trip to the U.S. Albright also repeatedly threatened "to reevaluate the whole U.S. approach to the peace process," accompanied by similar threats from a host of named and unnamed administration officials. Albright also reprimanded the Netanyahu government for resorting to "unilateral action" that threatened the peace process.

"It just stands to reason that anything that preempts the outcome of something that both parties have agreed should be part of the final negotiations, cannot be helpful in making peace," Clinton said, referring to the Likud government's settlement policy. Settlements are "absolutely" an obstacle to peace, Clinton added.[24]

In July 1999, Clinton had this to say of the continuing "peace" process:

> I think our position on the settlements has been clear. We don't believe that unilateral actions by any parties, including other interested parties like the United States, which compromise the capacity of the parties to the Oslo Accord to reach agreement on final status issues, should be taken. And that includes provocative settlement actions. We have made that clear and unambiguous . . . I would like it if the Palestinian people felt free and were free to live wherever they liked, wherever they want to live.[25]

During the Clinton administration, a significant breakthrough was achieved in the peace process: the Declaration of Principles (September 1993) signed by Israel and the PLO (as the representative of the Palestinian people), outlining arrangements for the Palestinians in the West Bank and Gaza. According to the declaration, Israel gave up 460 towns and villages, including Bethlehem, Hebron, Jericho, and Gaza. Consequently, Palestinian government was implemented in Gaza and Jericho in 1994 and, with the signing of the Interim Agreement in 1995, was extended to additional areas in the West Bank. These agreements were reached and carried out willingly by Israel, only to have the PLO reinitiate violence in the area and renew its *intifada* in 2000.

Also, throughout his presidency, as with the first President Bush, the

1987 Anti-Terrorism Act remained on national security waivers—something Clinton had to renew every six months for the full eight years of his two terms in office.

And the arms to Arabs states also continued to flow. Here are the totals of sales approved between 1993 and 2000:

Saudi Arabia	$23.5 billion
Egypt	$10.7 billion
Jordan	$650.7 million
Lebanon	$157.8 million

Blessings Under President George W. Bush

In an address of the American Jewish Committee in May 2001, President George W. Bush had these words to offer:

> We will speak up for our principles and we will stand up for our friends in the world. And one of our most important friends is the State of Israel . . .
>
> Israel is a small country that has lived under threat throughout its existence. At the first meeting of my National Security Council, I told them a top foreign policy priority is the safety and security of Israel. My Administration will be steadfast in supporting Israel against terrorism and violence, and in seeking the peace for which all Israelis pray.[26]

He also had this to say just the month before:

> Through centuries of struggle, Jews across the world have been witnesses not only against the crimes of men, but for faith in God, and God alone. Theirs is a story of defiance in oppression and patience in tribulation—reaching back to the exodus and their exile into the Diaspora. That story continued in the founding of the State of Israel. The story continues in the defense of the State of Israel.[27]

In regard to these sentiments, how has the younger President Bush treated the nation that he pledged his administration would "steadfastly support"? President Bush has refused to meet with Yasser Arafat, and has demanded that the PLO stop the terrorism.

Curses Under President George W. Bush

President Bush had this to offer in "support" of Israel in November 2003:

> Israel should freeze settlement construction, dismantle unauthorized outposts, end the daily humiliation of the Palestinian people and not prejudice final negotiations with the placements of walls and fences.[28]

This was followed up with the decision to rescind $289.5 million in U.S.-backed loan guarantees for Israel as punishment for illegal construction activities in the West Bank.[29]

Though Bush has tried to avoid dealing with Arafat as the leader of the Palestinian Authority, he also refuses to hold the PLO accountable for its crimes. The 1987 Anti-Terrorist Act as well as the 1995 Embassy Relocation Act remain held up on national security waivers. In addition to this, U.S. aid continues to flow to the PLO as part of the package Congress approved in 2000—a three-year package of $400 million in aid for the Palestinian Authority.

Meanwhile, arms sales to Arab countries have continued as well. The year 2001 yielded these totals:

> Egypt has been equipped with satellite-guided Harpoon anti-ship missiles. Since Sept. 11, Kuwait, the United Arab Emirates and Oman have all been slated to acquire sophisticated US weapons systems worth more than $8.5 billion. Egypt is also expected to acquire self-propelled 155mm artillery and upgrades for its fleet of 35 Boeing Apache combat helicopters in deals worth around $330 million. US military links with Jordan, Egypt, also includes four Am-

bassador III–class fast-attack missile boats. At the same time, the Saudis, a long-standing American customer, are back in the market for at least two advanced weapons systems, according to published reports. Among the weapons on the Saudis' purchase list: A new main battle tank and upward of 120 fighters to replace the kingdom's aging, US-built F-5 interceptor aircraft. The US-manufactured M-1 tank and either the F-16 or F-18 jet fighter would satisfy the Saudis' needs, according to industry officials. In the already unstable Middle East, the United Arab Emirates, is getting 80 Lockheed F-16s for $7 billion.[30]

America, what are we doing? In the last quarter century we have cursed again and again that which God wants us to bless, and we are ready to bless—with an $87 billion rebuilding package—the nation of Babylonia (biblical Iraq), which God has declared to be cursed for all times. Are we calling on God's blessings or curses? President Bush wants East Jerusalem to be the capital of an Islamic Palestine (a Jew-free state). If this happens, prayer will not prevent the wrath of Almighty God from falling on America for touching prophecy and dividing Jerusalem.

If you are not sure, consider this for a moment. Deuteronomy 28 is perhaps the most widely quoted chapter of the Bible concerning the blessings and cursings of God. I don't know how many times I have heard a minister read verses 1–14 of that chapter listing the blessings of God available to believers, but how often have we ever read the curses? Let me leave you with one of the last curses in this chapter: Read it very prayerfully.

> The LORD will bring a nation against you from far away, from the ends of the earth, like an eagle swooping down, a nation whose language you will not understand, a fierce-looking nation without respect for the old or pity for the young. They will devour the young of your livestock and the crops of your land until you are destroyed. They will leave you no grain, new wine or oil, nor any calves of your

herds or lambs of your flocks until you are ruined. They will lay siege to all the cities throughout your land until the high fortified walls in which you trust fall down. They will besiege all the cities throughout the land the LORD your God is giving you. (Deuteronomy 28:49–52 NIV)

My Christian brother or sister, it is time to decide: Are we going to live in God's blessings or incur His curses? Is America going to realize the great awakening revival, or the rude awakening of being rejected by God? It is time to answer the trumpet call, and to correct our nation's course to the right direction.

CHAPTER SIXTEEN

Our Nation's Future:
A Rude Awakening or a Great Awakening?

While the troops of Mahomet II surrounded Constantinople in 1493 and it had to be decided if the Balkans would be under Christian or Mohammedan dominion for centuries, a local church council in the besieged city discussed the following problems: What color had the eyes of the virgin Mary? What gender do the angels have? If a fly falls in sanctified water, is the fly sanctified or the water defiled?

Richard Wurmbrand[1]

If God does not judge America, He will have to apologize to Sodom and Gomorrah.

Billy Graham

Richard M. Nixon's family Bibles were both opened to the following Scripture as he took the oath of office in both 1969 and 1973:

He will judge between the nations and will settle disputes for many peoples. They will beat their swords into plowshares and their spears into pruning hooks. Nation will not take up sword against nation, nor will they train for war anymore.

Isaiah 2:4 NIV

I love America! As a veteran, I have proudly served my country. I buried my best friend, who died defending our freedom. For that reason, I cannot keep silent. For more than two decades, I have seen Islamic terrorism heading, like a whirlwind, toward our shores.

Friends have said, "Don't be negative; people want good news. Tell them good stuff. They will not hear doom and gloom." Well, my friends, they were wrong; and they could be dead wrong! America is plunging headfirst into a lake of fire and doesn't even know it. The hour is too late to tiptoe through the tulips. After September 11, I knew it was time to shout this message from the housetops. If America is to be saved, saintly, moral, God-fearing Americans have to wake up, and wake up now!

The prophet Jeremiah said,

> I appointed watchmen over you and said, "Listen to the sound of the trumpet!" But you said, "We will not listen." (Jeremiah 6:17 NIV)

The ancient prophet Ezekiel prophesied:

> The word of the LORD came to me: "Son of man, speak to your countrymen and say to them: 'When I bring the sword against a land, and the people of the land choose one of their men and make him their watchman, and he sees the sword coming against the land and blows the trumpet to warn the people, then if anyone hears the trumpet but does not take warning and the sword comes and takes his life, his blood will be on his own head. Since he heard the sound of the trumpet but did not take warning, his blood will be on his own head. If he had taken warning, he would have saved himself. But if the watchman sees the sword coming and does not blow the trumpet to warn the people and the sword comes and takes the life of one of them, that man will be

taken away because of his sin, but I will hold the watchman accountable for his blood.'" (Ezekiel 33:1–6 NIV)

I am one of the Lord's watchmen, and I cannot hold my peace!

As I write this, Saddam Hussein has been captured, and the stock market is surging to new highs not seen since before September 11. The sad news is that preachers in America by the thousands are not crying out. I hear secular, hardened commentators, ungodly politicians, and abrasive talk show hosts crying out, but Christians are complacent and silent. A statement by the head of the Gestapo in his annual report in the summer of 1938 might well characterize the church today: "The situation in the churches is characterized by weariness with the struggle, by uncertainty of purpose and by lack of courage."[2]

There is no question in my mind that America is receiving its final call to repentance. God is going to judge this nation in the same way He has judged every nation that has rejected His work challenged His prophetic plan.

Jesus prophesied:

> Just as it was in the days of Noah, so also will it be in the days of the Son of Man. People were eating, drinking, marrying and being given in marriage up to the day Noah entered the ark. Then the flood came and destroyed them all. It was the same in the days of Lot. People were eating and drinking, buying and selling, planting and building. (Luke 17:26–28 NIV)

Sodom and Gomorrah enjoyed the same prosperity as Noah's society. Ezekiel writes,

> This was the iniquity of thy sister Sodom, pride, fullness of bread, and abundance of idleness. (Ezekiel 16:49)

Sodom had no idea that the good times (like the Roaring Twenties before the Great Depression) were God's final mercy call before destruction. God judged Sodom, yet Sodom had no Bible. America is the Bible capital of the world, with an abundance of churches. If anyone should know what is going on, we should.

I am no prophet, but I say with Amos:

> I was neither a prophet nor a prophet's son, but I was a shepherd, and I also took care of sycamore-fig trees. But the LORD took me from tending the flock and said to me, "Go, prophesy to my people." (Amos 7:14–15 NIV)

I challenge you to search the ancient Scriptures, and to look up the words "judgment," "nations," and "curses." You will surely see that God is not a respecter of nations, and that mighty America is in big trouble.

King Josiah was only eighteen years old when God stirred his heart over something he read in the Scriptures. Suddenly, the young king saw that the nation had offended Almighty God and was heading toward destruction. He cried out, "God's wrath is being stored up against us."[3] Josiah truly repented and led the nation back to God.

For those who say, "America is immune; it will not happen here. There are too many godly people in America," I say, "Remember Israel!" God destroyed Jerusalem and the temple again and again. There is a prophetic line over which a nation can cross, and a point at which God says, "That's enough!"

Many think that what happened on September 11 was not a curse. I can assure you, every family that experienced the pain of September 11 felt cursed as they lost loved ones. That day of infamy was not a blessing! The fanatics who carried out the attack were very religious, but I can assure you, there is nothing peaceful about their religion.

Where are those who weep for America, who grieve for its sins of arrogance? Millions of Christians have closed their eyes to what is happening in the land of the Bible. Even preachers are telling jokes in the pulpit, and mocking those who are weeping over America's attempt to stick its finger in the apple of God's eye.

Read the words of Zechariah concerning the nations that touch Jerusalem:

On that day, when all the nations of the earth are gathered against her, I will make Jerusalem an immovable rock for all the nations. All who try to move it will injure themselves . . .

Then the leaders of Judah will say in their hearts, "The people of Jerusalem are strong, because the LORD Almighty is their God." On that day I will make the leaders of Judah like a firepot in a woodpile, like a flaming torch among sheaves. They will consume right and left all the surrounding peoples, but Jerusalem will remain intact in her place . . .

On that day I will set out to destroy all the nations that attack Jerusalem. And I will pour out on the house of David and the inhabitants of Jerusalem a spirit of grace and supplication. They will look on me, the one they have pierced, and they will mourn for him as one mourns for an only child, and grieve bitterly for him as one grieves for a first-born son. (Zechariah 12:3, 5–6, 9–10 NIV)

On that day his feet will stand on the Mount of Olives, east of Jerusalem, and the Mount of Olives will be split in two from east to west, forming a great valley, with half of the mountain moving north and half moving south . . .

This is the plague with which the LORD will strike all the nations that fought against Jerusalem: Their flesh will rot while they are still standing on their feet, their eyes will rot in their sockets, and their tongues will rot in their mouths. (Zechariah 14:4, 12 NIV)

What happens when a nation is cursed? God's hand of protection is lifted, and the powers of hell have free reign. That happened on September 11. God forgive anyone who does not see the warning signs.

That is why I mentioned 2 Chronicles 7:14 in the first chapter of this book. It is an extremely hope-giving Scripture, but its context is in the midst of a warning for Solomon. Look for a moment at the whole passage:

Thus Solomon finished the house of the LORD and the king's house; and Solomon successfully accomplished all that came into his heart to make in the house of the LORD and in his own house.

Then the LORD appeared to Solomon by night, and said to him: "I have heard your prayer, and have chosen this place for Myself as a house of sacrifice. When I shut up heaven and there is no rain, or command the locusts to devour the land, or send pestilence among My people, if My people who are called by My name will humble themselves, and pray and seek My face, and turn from their wicked ways, then I will hear from heaven, and will forgive their sin and heal their land . . .

"But if you turn away and forsake My statutes and My commandments which I have set before you, and go and serve other gods, and worship them, then I will uproot them from My land which I have given them; and this house which I have sanctified for My name I will cast out of My sight, and will make it a proverb and a byword among all peoples.

"And as for this house, which is exalted, everyone who passes by it will be astonished and say, 'Why has the LORD done thus to this land and this house?' Then they will answer, 'Because they forsook the LORD God of their fathers, who brought them out of the land of Egypt, and embraced other gods, and worshiped them and served them; therefore He has brought all this calamity on them.'" (2 Chronicles 7: 11–14, 19–22 NKJV)

Solomon was being warned: "Now that you have built your home and your temple, don't fall into pride and think you no longer need Me. If you begin to fall away, the remedy is simple: Humbly repent, seek My face, and turn from the wickedness you are doing. I will hear your prayers and respond—forgiving your sins, and healing your land. But if you continue to defy Me, regardless of establishing your throne in wisdom on My name, I will turn from you as you have turned from Me, and instead of being a symbol of My goodness, you will become a symbol of what happens to those who forsake Me."

Given our context today, this is valuable advice. America has idols worse than any Solomon could have set up: relativism and greed. With them we have made the laws and compassion of God void and meaningless. We have turned our backs on Him by adopting abominations such as abortion and homosexuality as normal. God said if we did that we would be given over to the reprobate minds that perform such acts.[4] If that is the case, how far are we from acquiescing into a New World Order?

September 11 was a warning shot across our bow of what could come. God was trying to wake up Christian America by letting the brother we have left to Allah strike back at us with his hatred. Certainly September 11 happened because of our relationship with Isaac, but it also happened because of our relationship with Ishmael. We have fed the latter on our greed, but offered him none of the truth and love that we know because of Christ. We have waved God's blessings in His face, and He hates us for it.

God sent us men like William Blackstone to help us save Isaac from the spirit of antichrist's hatred for him, but president after president ignored him. He sent us the prosperity of the 1920s to show He loved us, but we still didn't listen, so He sent us the depression as a final attempt to inspire us to "call on His Name, humbling ourselves and praying, seeking his face, and turning from our wicked ways." But we did not. Thus it was that the world, with the United States leading the way, turned its back on the Jews, and Hitler's genocidal extermination machine closed in on them. No one acted to help them until it was too late. A third of the world's Jewish population was lost with little hope of salvation. Hitler took full responsibility for the mass murders and told the Reichstag: "If anyone reproaches me and asks why I did not resort to the regular courts of justice, then all I can say is this: in this hour I was responsible for the fate of the German people. I became the Supreme Judge of the German people."[5]

Hitler, like so many demagogues before him, was beginning to ascribe godlike attributes to himself. On one occasion he displayed the whip he often carried to demonstrate that "in driving out the Jews I remind myself of Jesus in the temple." He declared, "Just like Christ, I have duty to my own people." He even boasted that just as Christ's birth had changed the calendar, so his victory over the Jews would be the beginning of a new age. "What Christ began," he said, "I will complete." In a speech just days after becoming chancellor, he parodied the Lord's Prayer, promising that under him a new kingdom would come on earth and that his would be "the power and the glory. Amen." He added that if he did not fulfill his mission, "you should then crucify me."[6]

Hitler's growing messiah complex was fed by his own egotism. As early as 1933, Hitler's cross, the swastika, surrounded the altar of the Magdeburg Cathedral. Dr. Martin, the dean, avowed: "Whoever reviles this symbol of ours is reviling Germany . . . the swastika flags . . . radiate hope."[7] Hitler's egotism took expression in such statements as: "I am founding an order . . . the Man-God, that splendid being will be an object of worship";[8] and, "Creation is not yet at an end. Man is becoming God . . . Man is God in the making."[9] His ideology was unfortunately reinforced from the pulpits of Germany. On August 30, 1933, Pastor Julius Leutherser gushed, "Christ has come to us through Hitler . . . through his honesty, his faith and his idealism, the Redeemer found us . . . We know today that Savior has come . . . we have only one task, be German, not Christian."[10] Pastor Siegfried Leffler proclaimed, "In the pitch black night of church history, Hitler became, as it were, the wonderful transparency of our time, the window of our age, through which light fell on the history of Christianity. Through him we were able to see the Savior in the history of the Germans."[11] It seems that the masses accepted the assessment of Alfred Rosenberg: "Let it happen as it will and must, but I believe in Hitler; above him there hovers a star."[12]

In 1936, after the persecution of the Jews became rampart in Germany, Oswald J. Smith wrote that Germany "had awakened." He drew this conclusion:

What, you ask, is the real attitude of the German people toward Hitler? There is but one answer. They love him. Yes, from the highest to the lowest, children and parents, old and young alike—they love their new leader. Their confidence in him cannot be shaken. They trust him to a man. "What about your elections?" I asked. "You have no choice. It is Hitler or no one. There is no opponent." "We don't want another party." They replied with indignation, "We have had enough of parties. We want a true leader, a man who loves us, and works for our good. We are satisfied with Hitler." And that feeling exists everywhere. Every true Christian is for Hitler. I know for it was from the Christians I got most of my information, and right or wrong they endorse Adolf Hitler.[13]

Hitler's contempt for the very churches that supported him knew no bounds. Hitler confided to Herman Rauschning that neither the Catholic nor the Protestant denomination had a future in Germany. He vowed to stamp out "Christianity in Germany, root and branch." "One," he said, "is either a Christian or a German. You can't be both."[14] Hitler determined that he could do anything he wanted with the Protestants: "They will submit . . . they are insignificant little people, submissive as dogs."[15]

Like others who had gone before, and those who have followed him, Hitler had great admiration for those who sought to conform biblical history to their own distorted views. He greatly admired Richard Wagner, a rabid anti-Semite. Wagner claimed to have had a revelation that Jesus Christ had been born of Aryan (German) stock. According to Hitler, "This was not the Jewish Christ of the New Testament, but a Christ who shed Aryan blood and would lead Germany back to the greatness that was her right."[16]

How can it be that so many who professed the name of Christ followed Hitler? "Many," wrote Gerald Suster, "welcome the abolition of individual responsibility for one's actions; for some it is easier to obey than to accept the dangers of freedom. Workers now had job security, a health service . . . if freedom meant starvation, then slavery was preferable."[17] Hitler was convinced that, if forced to choose between the cross of Hitler (the swastika) and the Cross of Christ, both Protestants and Catholics would betray their Savior: "Do you really believe the masses will be Christian again? Nonsense! Never again! That take is finished. No one will listen to it again. But we can hasten matters. The parsons will dig their own graves. They will betray their God to us. They will betray anything for the sake of their miserable jobs and incomes."[18] Perhaps Rousas Rushdoony stated the obvious when he wrote: "Behind every system of law there is a god . . . When you choose your authority, you choose your god, and where you look for your law, there is your god."[19]

Look around. We are going through the same cycle today.

The prosperity of the 1990s did little but make us even more selfish than we were in the decades before. September 11 hit us as something far worse than the crashing of the stock market on Black Tuesday in 1929. What was one of the main causes of the Great Depression? A new thing that had been introduced at that time called "buying on credit." The entire nation had borrowed to buy things, the economy soared because of increased consumer spending, and when the debts were called in too few had the cash to pay. America lapsed into the depression, and then a World War.

America had prosperity in the 1990s, terrorists hit on September 11, and then a recession. Now we face a time of war that has no logical end, and U.S. citizens are again borrowing like never before—and again the Jews hang on the edge of a precipice as anti-Zionism arises the world over. As Great Britain and we have been the only nations with enough moral backbone to stand up to terrorism, so we are also the only nations that can stand up and defend Israel—but will we do it? We didn't in the 1920s and 1930s—why should we do it today?

Isaiah 24:6 declares: "Therefore a curse consumes the earth; its people must bear their guilt. Therefore earth's inhabitants are burned up, and very few are left" (NIV).

Does God fight nations? Yes, He does. Zechariah 14:2–3 states that He will fight all nations that come against Jerusalem.

Yes, America is cursing Israel. Why would we not allow the only democracy in the Middle East to join us in fighting Iraq? Because we feared the anti-Semitic nations in the area, those who hate Israel, and we were afraid they would cut off the oil that lubricates our economy.

President Abraham Lincoln saw the Civil War as the judgment of God on a prejudiced nation. In a similar context, in 1917, when the Balfour Declaration proclaimed a miraculous prophetic event of the reestablishment of a Jewish homeland in Palestine, not only would the State Department reject it, but the U.S. government, caving in to anti-Semitic pressure, would go on to pass a major act restricting immigration in the 1920s. The irony of it all is that Hitler did not come into power until 1933, and yet an immigration policy that would keep Russian Jews out of America would be used also to keep German, Polish, and other Jews trying to escape Hitler's "final solution" out of America. The door was shut before Jews even had a chance to knock.

Founded in 1915, the Ku Klux Klan had reached its greatest support by 1920. The 1920s saw the Ku Klux Klan sweep across America like a plague, thanks to the support of anti-Semitic figures like Henry Ford, who also financed an American reprinting of the *Protocols of the Elders of Zion*. Senator Ellison Smith of South Carolina, in a speech titled "Shut the Door," proclaimed in 1924:

> I think we now have sufficient population in our country for us to shut the door and to breed up an unadulterated American citizenship. I recognize that there is a dangerous lack of distinction between people of a certain nationality and a breed of a dog . . . Without offense, but with regards to the salvation of our own, let us shut the door and assimilate what we have and let us breed pure American citizens and develop our own American resources.[20]

I am firmly convinced that the judgment of God came on America over America's anti-Semitic plague, in which a Christian nation would coldly close its heart and its ears to the cries of six million Jews—more than a million of whom were children.

The stock market crashed on Black Friday, October 29, 1929. America went from the most amazing prosperity in world history to date—the Roaring Twenties—to become an economic dust bowl as the plague of the Great Depression swept the nation. The country's demeanor (in popular songs of the times) went from "We're in the Money," to "Brother, Can You Spare a Dime?"

However, God had been trying to get America's attention for more than a century before this tragedy, through what was called the Great Awakening, led by evangelists like Jonathan Edwards, George Whitefield, and Gilbert Tennent. But still America hardened its heart.

The Word of God declares, "I will bless them that bless thee, and curse him that curseth thee."[21] Just as Abraham Lincoln proclaimed that the Civil War was God's judgment for the bigotry behind slavery, the Great Depression was God's judgment for the bigotry of anti-Semitism—"[I will] curse him that curseth thee." Anti-Semitism was buried in the soul of America and God cursed America for it—"He that touches you touches the apple of my eye."[22] Some of the seeds of the same anti-Semitism that fed and fueled the Holocaust are alive and well in twenty-first-century America, no matter how dormant they appear.

A battle is being fought between darkness and light, Babylon and Jerusalem. This is a sure sign that Jesus is coming soon! The Bible says: "And the sons of Issachar, men who understood the times."[23] God is calling prophetically to the remnant that understands the times.

For more than two decades I have seen this battle coming and have been crying out. I did it in Geneva in 1988, in Madrid in 1991, at the White house in 1993, and with books such as *The Jerusalem Scroll* in 1999. But the vast majority of Christians have laughed at what I was saying in disbelief (as in the times of Noah). The laughter stopped on September 11.

The battle has not been won. Judgment is heading to America like a tidal wave. Only the remnant that hears what the Spirit is saying can stop this coming holocaust. America is cursing what God has blessed (Israel) and blessing what God has cursed (in rebuilding Babylon). Does the Bible reveal what will happen to a nation that does this? A thousand percent yes! Is America's future revealed? A thousand percent yes!

Satan hates the Jews and must stop Israel before the Messiah comes and ends his reign. Prophecy declares that Jerusalem will be united and in Jewish hands when the Messiah comes. Satan's goal: to divide Jerusalem and stop the prophetic clock that will seal his doom.

We are living in dangerous days, when men's hearts are failing them for fear! The Bible tells us to be like the wise virgins, not the foolish, and to prepare for His coming. The Bible says we can know the season and times, even if we don't know the day or the hour.

We are in the last days. Look up, for our redemption draws near!

I cannot be silent, and neither can you. The Scriptures call on us to speak out.[24] The battle being fought over Jerusalem is not politics—it's prophecy. It's not a foreign policy battle, but a heavenly battle! When our president says that East Jerusalem and Judea and Samaria are illegal, he is shaking his fist in the face of God Almighty, like ancient Nebuchadnezzar, and challenging Him. The restoration of Israel is not an American gift to God Almighty—it was prophesied to happen! America's very existence, however, is a gift from God Almighty!

America cannot win a battle of defiance against God—no one can! The greatest superpower in world history will wake up one day in total shock, because of our pride and arrogance, as a generation did on Black Tuesday when the Great Depression hit, and even worse as America did when September 11 hit—but more than a thousand times worse. We need, instead, to wake ourselves up so that we are ready for that day rather than letting it catch us sleeping.

The church in America by and large is backsliding. It is a prayerless church, a Wordless church that does not fear God. It has become the first church of Sodom. No longer is the church willing to pay the price of discipleship. The means by which grace has been extended to the church—the crucifixion of our Savior—has been cheapened. Dietrich Bonhoeffer said of this practice: "Cheap grace is the deadly enemy of the church. We are fighting today for costly grace. Cheap grace means grace sold on the market like cheapjack wares. The sacraments, the forgiveness of sin, and the consolations of religion are thrown away at cut prices . . . In such a Church the world finds a cheap covering for its sins, no contrition is required, still less any real desire to be delivered from sin . . . cheap grace means the justification of sin without the justification of the sinner . . . it is grace without discipline, grace without the cross, grace without Jesus Christ, living and incarnate."[25]

The Bible warns in Revelation, chapter 22, again and again: "Behold, I am coming quickly!" The church in America mocks the message of the coming of the Lord and does not preach it from its pulpits. The church rejects the prophetic words of Revelation 22:16 that Jesus is the root and offspring of David. Polluted prophets in the pulpits of America are deceiving the sheep, leading them to the slaughter with their demon-inspired replacement theology—the very doctrines that the Protestant Church in Germany embraced. Dr. Kerrl, a friend of Hitler, defined Hitler's brand of "positive Christianity": "True Christianity is represented by the party, and German people are now called by the party and especially the Fuhrer to real Christianity . . . The Fuhrer is the herald of a new revelation."[26]

God's eternal covenant with Israel is mocked. These blind fools fill their Sundays with unscriptural doctrines of man and reject Israel, yet they hold in their hands a Bible written by Jews who all knew the prophetic truths concerning Israel. They beheld with horror September 11 and weeks later went back to sleep, dumbing-down their congregations with sermons that are nothing more than refried beans; messages they copy from their blind heroes rather than from the Holy Word of a Holy God.

Their New Age doctrine from hell that the church is spiritual Israel not only takes away from the Word of God, but also feeds Jew-hatred and is robbing the church of its eternal purpose: the Great Commission of being a witness in Jerusalem, Judea, and Samaria; and of hearing God—instead of blindly cooperating with the powers of darkness intent on destroying America and Israel.

They scoff at prophecy and blindly close their eyes to prophetic signs like the return of the Jews from the ends of the earth to the promised land, the rebirth of Israel in May 1948, the reunification of Jerusalem on June 6, 1967, and Israel's miraculous survival through five wars during her brief modern history. They have exalted the Osama bin Ladens and Arafats, while blindly doing nothing to reach out to the Jews being blown up weekly by such terrorists, thinking it's not their duty to speak out, sitting silently by while such murderers are promoted to diplomat status, only to inspire greater demons of destruction through a gospel of accommodation and appeasement.

Those that buy these lies are writing their own Bible, a Bible whose actions reject the words of a holy and righteous God. It rejects God's eternal promises to Israel and arrogantly says that it is the chosen people. It is a church that is knee-deep in sin, with homosexuals and "New Age" gurus appointed pastors, ridden with adulterers and pornography addicts named to their deacon boards.

Where does the church go from here? In *The Life and Death of Dietrich Bonhoeffer*, Mary Bosanquet wrote:

> There is only one hope for our age, which is so powerless, so feeble, so wretchedly slight and pitiable, and with all this so forlorn; return to the Church, to the place where one man bears up another in love, where one man shares the life of another, where there is fellowship in God, where there is home, where there is love.[27]

Bonhoeffer's source of hope was rooted in God's Word: "I believe that the Bible alone is the answer to all of our questions, and that we need only to ask repeatedly and a little humbly, in order to receive this answer . . . Only if we expect from it the ultimate answers, shall we receive it. That is because the Bible speaks to us."[28]

The curses of Deuteronomy 28 are heading full-speed toward America, and the blessings of Deuteronomy 28 are being snatched away from our land by an angry God who hears the cries of more than forty million unborn children whom America has murdered, all in the name of freedom—babies who were destined to be the prophetic voice of our land, but now their messages to the earth will never be preached because of the powers of hell.

> And for this reason God will send upon them a deluding influence so that they might believe what is false, in order that

they all may be judged who did not believe the truth, but
took pleasure in wickedness. (2 Thessalonians 2: 11–12
NASB)

"Each generation," according to Jacques Ellul, "thinks it has finally
discovered the truth . . . Christianity becomes an empty bottle that suc-
cessive cultures fill with all kinds of things."[29] In the emptying, we
often lose sight of those things that are the most important: the deity
of Christ, the efficacy of the blood of Christ, the deadliness of sin, the
inerrancy of the Word, and the necessity of repentance.

Why is President Bush, a born-again Christian, not honoring the
Word concerning God's promises to the Jews? Could it be that replace-
ment-theology pastors who do not believe the Word of God—men and
women who spend more time on the golf course or at the health clubs
than on their knees—are "dumbing-down" the president and his advisers? Jesus mentioned deception as one of the last signs before His return. The book of Revelation describes a day when the entire world will
be deceived, billions of people, by the spirits of demons.[30] They choose
human favor over the favor of the Lord, wanting to sit next to "great
men" in the White House rather than sit next to Jesus in the New
Jerusalem; fearing if they rock the boat by speaking the truth their
names will be blotted off the president's list, rather than fear their
names will be blotted out of the Lamb's Book of Life.

Yes, we are living in the end times—and Israel is God's alarm clock!
The nations are enraged over this bone in their throat, Israel.[31] Tiny Israel is God's bait to entrap an arrogant, God-despising world, shaking
its fist in the face of Holy God, preferring to boast over rebuilding the
doomed Tower of Babel, eternally cursed by God rather than rebuilding the tabernacle of David by blessing Israel.

Then the LORD will go forth and fight against those nations
as when he fights on a day of battle. On that day his feet
shall stand on the Mount of Olives. (Zechariah 14:2–4 RSV)

The ancient Jewish prophets saw the day we are living in and clearly warned that God would defend Israel and would guard Israel:

> In that day the LORD will defend the inhabitants of Jerusalem, and the one who is feeble among them in that day will be like David, and house of David will be like God, like the angel of the LORD before them. And it will come about in that day that I will set about to destroy all the nations that come against Jerusalem. (Zechariah 12:8–9 NASB)

This book is a wake-up call from heaven.

> ("Blessed is the one who stays awake and keeps his garments, lest he walk about naked and men see his shame.") And they gathered them together to the place which in Hebrew is called Har-Magedon. (Revelation 16:15–16 NASB)

> And there will be a time of distress such as never occurred since there was a nation until that time; and at that time your people, everyone who is found written in the book, will be rescued. (Daniel 12:1 NASB)

> I will make Jerusalem a heavy stone for all the peoples; all who lift it shall grievously hurt themselves. (Zechariah 12:2–3 RSV)

Why must the church stand with Israel? Because God does, and it is part of the church's eternal purpose—and even a promise of mighty power if it would fulfill its great commission regarding Jerusalem, Judea, and Samaria. Albert Einstein, exiled from Germany because he was Jewish, learned the importance of the church. He wrote:

> Being a lover of freedom, when the [Nazi] revolution came I looked to the universities to defend it, knowing that they had always boasted of their devotion to the cause of truth;

but no, the universities were immediately silenced. Then I looked to the great editors of the newspapers, whose flaming editorials in days gone by had proclaimed their love of freedom; but they, like the universities, were silenced in a few short weeks. Only the church stood squarely across the path of Hitler's campaign for suppressing the truth. I never had any special interest in the Church before, but now I feel a great affection and admiration for it because the Church alone has had the courage and persistence to stand for intellectual and moral freedom. I am forced to confess that what I once despised I now praise unreservedly."[32]

Why does Satan fear Israel so much? Because Israel's restoration will trigger the coming of our Lord and Savior. When He returns, Satan's doom is sealed.

Plagues are heading toward America. Saddam moved his weapons of mass destruction and his billions through Syria before the war began. We need to know who has them and disarm them just as we did Iraq, not ignore them. However, it seems everyone bought the lie that they never existed. Look at the evidence, though, and connect the dots. They are still out there, or Saddam would never have given up so much to protect them.

This is the midnight hour. If God's remnant sleeps, America will perish! However, if we choose instead to wake up and be the church again that God called us to be, the hope we have before us is far greater than anything we have seen in the past.

I'm telling you the truth—Jesus is coming back, and He is coming back soon! Just how ready we are for that day will make all the difference in eternity.

CHAPTER SEVENTEEN

Hope for a Restless World

Not until I went into the churches of America and heard her pulpits aflame with righteousness did I understand the secret of her genius and power.

Alexis de Tocqueville
Democracy in America
1835

I am thy fellowservant, and of thy brethren that have the testimony of Jesus: worship God: for the testimony of Jesus is the spirit of prophecy.

Revelation 19:10

As we saw in the parable of the fig tree in chapter two, just as the fig leaves blossoming indicate that summer is near, so do the signs of the times we are seeing today indicate that Jesus is preparing to come back, and come back soon! As He said to His disciples before and after that parable in the book of Luke:

> Now when these things begin to happen, look up and lift
> up your heads, because your redemption draws near . . .
>   But take heed to yourselves, lest your hearts be weighed
> down with carousing, drunkenness, and cares of this life,

and that Day come on you unexpectedly. For it will come
as a snare on all those who dwell on the face of the whole
earth. Watch therefore, and pray always that you may be
counted worthy to escape all these things that will come to
pass, and to stand before the Son of Man. (Luke 21:28,
34–36 NKJV)

Let no one fool you about the times that we live in. If the parable of
the fig tree and the signs of Matthew 24 are not enough for you, look
at one last mile marker given by Daniel: the increase of travel and
knowledge.

The prophet Daniel accurately predicted the kingdoms and governments that would follow ancient Babylon's disappearance from the
world scene in Daniel 2:31–45. Many of Daniel's prophecies have already been fulfilled, and his writings constitute the cornerstone of biblical prophecy. Daniel described a key characteristic of the "end times,"
the period leading up to the return of Jesus Christ to earth, in terms of
man's pursuit of knowledge.

But you, Daniel, shut up the words, and seal the book until
the time of the end; many shall run to and fro, and knowledge shall increase. (Daniel 12:4 NKJV)

Daniel's prediction of "many shall run to and fro" could easily be interpreted as the "rat race" of modern society; most scholars interpret it
as the increase in travel and the speed of travel. Compare our world
today with the world of even one hundred years ago, when traveling by
train at a speed of sixty miles an hour was an incredible feat of man's
invention. We travel today in 747s that can reach over 600 miles an
hour—or even the Concorde, which reached speeds of 1,350 miles per
hour—is no less than mind-boggling. What would Daniel think of
such a day if we could transport him here in a time machine? I think
he would definitely be looking at the skies every few minutes for
Christ's return!

The rate of man's growth in knowledge is accelerating beyond our comprehension as well. Years ago, scientists actually set out to measure the rate of expansion of man's "knowledge database," to put it in modern technological terms. They assumed that all scientific knowledge accumulated by the year AD 1 equaled one unit of information. They estimated that the amount of knowledge man acquired had doubled to two units during the next 1,500 years. But it took only 250 years for man's knowledge to double to four units. From 1750 until 1900, a period of 150 years, knowledge doubled yet again. And throughout the twentieth century the rate of knowledge growth continued to speed up, with the result that it now takes only one to two years for our knowledge database to double.

Think about that for a moment. Everything we know about the latest scientific developments will double *in less than two years.*

Encyclopedias and textbooks are out of date almost as soon as they're in print. Doctors, engineers, physicists, and researchers are forced to specialize, limiting their concentration to a narrowly focused area of knowledge. Even in our own daily lives, it's almost impossible to keep up with the flow of information. Is it any wonder we often feel that we need an advanced degree just to operate the latest gadget?

Not only does this knowledge explosion indicate that we are living in the end times, the *type* of knowledge man has acquired is absolutely mind-boggling. Things that were in the realm of science fiction only a few years ago are now a present reality, and our government, not to mention the average citizen, is woefully unprepared to deal with the moral and ethical implications of these scientific advances.

Consider cloning. The average American was shocked by the news in January 1997 of the birth of Dolly, a lamb cloned from frozen cells of an adult ewe. In the excitement over this startling new technology, scant attention was paid to the fact that Dolly was the sole survivor of 277 cloned sheep embryos. In fact, the scientists who cloned Dolly waited seven months before releasing news of their success because all the other attempts had ended with the production of abnormal embryos or births of sheep with fatal ailments.

With no federal or international legislation to regulate human cloning, scientists are rushing ahead with research that has profound implications for the future of the human race.

A particular question puzzles most Christians when they consider the cloning dilemma. I've struggled with this question myself, and I actually pray that God never allows us to find the answer. The question is this: Would a human clone have a soul?

The Vatican has answered with a resounding "No." The Pontifical Academy of Life, a panel set up by Pope John Paul II, concluded, "The spiritual soul, 'the constitutive kernel' of every human created by God, cannot be produced through cloning."[1]

The "brave new world" imagined by science fiction writers decades ago is here. It's a world in which man has decided to be his own creator. Ironic, isn't it, that we cavalierly abort millions of unborn babies at the same time we are creating human life in a laboratory?

I can't help but think that at some point—perhaps soon—God will intervene to stop humankind's mad pursuit of creating life on its own terms. We are building nothing less than a technological Tower of Babel. In place of ancient Babylon's worship of astrology and the heavens, modern man worships science and technology; but the end result is the same: Humankind is bent on usurping God's role as Creator. And at some point, the Creator will say, "Enough!" and put a stop to man's folly.

The season of Christ's return is definitely near. How are we to prepare for it? Look at this advice from the Scriptures:

> For the grace of God that brings salvation has appeared to all men, teaching us that, denying ungodliness and worldly lusts, we should live soberly, righteously, and godly in the present age, looking for the blessed hope and glorious appearing of our great God and Savior Jesus Christ, who gave Himself for us, that He might redeem us from every lawless deed and purify for Himself His own special people, zealous for good works.
>
> Speak these things, exhort, and rebuke with all authority. Let no one despise you. (Titus 2:11–15 NKJV)

If the church of the United States will stand up as the light Jesus intended us to be, the politics of our nation will right itself. Legislation can't change people's hearts, but the touch of God can! It is more important to have a nation that prays than a president who prays, though, of course, the best formula is to have both.

There is no question we must rise up and do right, and urge our government to do the same, but we also need to be watchful. America is heading for a fateful day—a day that will impact the United States thousands of times more than September 11—but will that day be our destruction or our redemption? What could be more than a thousand times worse than September 11? A multiple terrorist attack using thermonuclear bombs? A natural disaster the size of which we have never seen before? An asteroid hitting the earth? What?

I believe that day will be the day Jesus calls the Christians home. The day the Rapture takes place. Look at how the Scriptures describe that day:

> Why do you stand gazing up into heaven? This same Jesus, who was taken up from you into heaven, will so come in like manner as you saw Him go into heaven. (Acts 1:11 NKJV)

> Behold, I tell you a mystery: We shall not all sleep, but we shall all be changed—in a moment, in the twinkling of an eye, at the last trumpet. For the trumpet will sound, and the dead will be raised incorruptible, and we shall be changed. For this corruptible must put on incorruption, and this mortal must put on immortality. (1 Corinthians 15: 51–53 NKJV)

> For the LORD Himself will descend from heaven with a shout, with the voice of an archangel, and with the trumpet of God. And the dead in Christ will rise first. Then we who are alive and remain shall be caught up together with them in the clouds to meet the LORD in the air. And thus we shall

always be with the LORD. Therefore comfort one another with these words. (1 Thessalonians 4:16–18 NKJV)

Finally, there is laid up for me the crown of righteousness, which the LORD, the righteous Judge, will give to me on that Day, and not to me only but also to all who have loved His appearing. (2 Timothy 4:8 NKJV)

The Rapture is the church's day of greatest hope. We need to see it as such and prepare for it. But we also need to know that it will not be the same for those not caught up in the Rapture. I don't doubt that if you are reading this book, you have probably also read the book *Left Behind* or seen the movie. However, as devastating as the authors of that series portrayed that day, *I don't believe they even got close.*

Today, America has more born-again Christians per capita than any nation in the world. Twenty-three percent of Americans are professing born-again Christians—including the president of the United States—a total of roughly sixty-five million people. Think for a minute: How many people died on September 11? Roughly three thousand. Remember for a moment the painful chaos and mayhem of that day. Remember what it did to our economy, our confidence to fly in an airplane, our confidence to walk down the street, and the thousands of other ways that it touched our lives. Now imagine for a moment sixty-five million Americans vanishing in the twinkling of an eye—people flying planes, driving cars, steering ships, driving trains and subways, manning nuclear power stations and nuclear silos, navigating submarines filled with nuclear missiles, and so on.

How many times more is sixty-five million than three thousand? *More than twenty thousand times.*

Imagine for a moment if such a shock hit our nation today—a shock more than twenty thousand times that of September 11.

Realize, also, if that happened today, it would take our president. Who else would it take? How many members of the Senate? The House? How many judges? How many governors? How many mayors and city council members? How many firemen and policemen? How many military personnel? How many teachers and college professors? How many presidents and CEO's of companies? How many of our nation's leaders would disappear in a day?

What would happen to our economy on such a day? The stock market crash will make 1929 and 1987 look like minor tremors. How many hardworking employees will vanish? The greatest market for goods and services in the world will suddenly be reduced by 23 percent. There will be a glut of consumer goods, and manufacturing will grind to a halt. Prices will plummet to clear the shelves. How many companies will go bankrupt because of that day—or even disappear all together?

Think of this: What if, in the twinkling of an eye, every person of solid moral character *in the world* suddenly disappeared? Who would be left to take control? What would our government do?

Or, even better yet, there wouldn't be enough of America left to matter. What if we took more than 65 million? What if we have a tremendous revival in our land and took 100 million, or 150 million, or more? What if we stepped into the power of God as Paul and the early apostles did and transformed our world with the power of God's love and truth? What if we took the lie of Wahhabism on with the truth of the gospel? What would the future hold for that day if our nation were a Christian nation again? Some may think this impossible, but with God, all things are possible.

Yes, other nations of the earth would be tremendously affected on that day as well. All who claim to be Christians leaving on that day would total roughly two billion people, though what God will see as a true believer on that day is sure to find millions shocked. Yet, because the United States has the highest percentage of Christians on the earth, it is easy to see why the Rapture would affect America more than any other nation.

Yes, this is my hope. Not that the terrorists get us, nor even that we side with Israel in the final battle (though I would greatly prefer that to option one!), but that God gets us—*all of us*. That revival streaks across America and on the final day, so many of us go that there is not enough of America left to fight over.

There is a saying in the military that was made famous by the book and movie *Black Hawk Down*, and that is the subtitle of the book: "No one gets left behind." That needs to be our motto as well as we face the final days: "No one gets left behind."

Peace in our time is up to those of today's generation who are willing to pray for it and act on what heaven says to do about it. Peace for tomorrow depends on the same. What we need now is a church with its eyes on eternity rather than on how the stock market is performing. We need to rise up and be the church going into eternity rather than the church muddled by the past.

God is calling. What will our answer be?

Look at the fig tree—summer is at the door.

Look at the signs of the times as recorded in Matthew 24. Throughout the book, I have talked about these signs, and the major prophetic event that will affect America's destiny and that of the world: the return of Jesus Christ. I would encourage you to read Matthew 24 again.

These signs of the times are as current as today's news. I truly believe that Jesus is coming soon, and the Rapture is near.

What will happen at the Rapture? Jesus put it this way: "Then two men will be in the field: one will be taken and the other left. Two women will be grinding at the mill: one will be taken and the other left. Watch therefore, for you do not know what hour your Lord is coming."[2]

To paraphrase Jesus' words in modern terms, we might say this: "Then two police officers will be on patrol: one will be taken and the other left. Two workers will be in an office cubicle: one will be taken and the other left. Two firefighters will be battling a blaze: one will be taken and the other left. Two college students will be in class: one will be taken and the other left. Two women will be grocery shopping: one will be taken and the other left."

One day you will look into the eastern sky and witness the single greatest event in the history of humankind. You will be blinded with a light brighter than the light that struck the apostle Paul on the road to Damascus. You will see the lightning flash, hear the shout of the archangel, and a heavenly choir will thunder praises to the returning King.

The trumpet will sound, and the King of kings and Lord of lords, the eternal Prince of Peace, will suddenly appear. Marble mausoleums will rip like tissue paper, and every grave on earth that holds the remains of the righteous will split open. Decaying bodies will be changed in the twinkling of an eye, and gravity will lose its hold as the resurrected saints soar into the heavenlies to meet their Savior in the air.

In your new glorified body, you will enter the pearly gates of heaven to be welcomed by the cheers of Abraham, Isaac, and Jacob. Up there, you will see Moses, who stretched forth his hand to divide the Red Sea. There stands John the Revelator, who, while exiled on the Isle of Patmos, saw the Lord in the midst of the seven golden candlesticks. The big fisherman, Peter, and the apostle Paul, who turned the world upside down for Jesus, are part of the welcoming committee. And there will be your loved ones who have gone before: the precious praying mother . . . the godly father . . . the child taken at an early age . . . the husband . . . wife . . . brother . . . sister.

Suddenly a hush falls on the gathering throng. All of heaven turns in unison to look on Him who redeemed us from our sins . . . and we shall behold Him!

On the hill called Mount Calvary in the city of Jerusalem, Jesus was nailed to a rough-hewn, man-made cross and there suspended between heaven and earth. He became our sacrificial Lamb who freely gave His blood, and through that precious crimson stream purchased our redemption so we could be called the sons of God.

It was in this same city where our resurrected Lord conquered death, hell, and the grave. It was here that He rose from the dead in triumphant victory, and in His glorified body adorned the city of Jerusalem and blessed His faithful followers with His presence. And it was outside the city of Jerusalem that He promised to return to gather His saints.

Some people will be ready for Christ's return, and others will be caught by surprise. The ones who are ready will be snatched away (raptured) to be with Christ; the others will be left here to face the judgment of God.

But that begs the question: Do you know where you will be on that day? Will you be among those who go, or those who are left behind? Are you sure?

If you are not, what you need to do is pray a prayer just like this one to make sure you are among those who go:

> Lord Jesus,
>
> I invite You into my life as my Lord and Savior. I repent of my past sins.
>
> I ask You to forgive me. Thank You for shedding Your blood on the cross to cleanse me from my sin and to heal me. I receive Your gift of everlasting life and surrender all to You.
>
> Thank You, Jesus, for saving me.
>
> I will follow You all the days of my life. Amen.

Now we need to see how many others we can encourage to pray a similar prayer to begin the last revival on the earth before Jesus comes. Eternity is at hand. The return of Christ will be the greatest prophetic event in America's history, indeed the history of the world, and chances are that you will have a ringside seat. We need to be preparing to hear that final trumpet call of God.

> The foundations of the wall of the city were garnished with all manner of precious stones. The first foundation was jasper; the second, sapphire; the third, a chalcedony; the fourth, an emerald; the fifth, sardonyx; the sixth, sardius; the seventh, chrysolyte; the eighth, beryl; the ninth, a topaz; the tenth, a chrysoprasus; the eleventh, a jacinth; the twelfth, an amethyst. (Revelation 21:19–20)

> The city had no need of the sun, neither of the moon, to shine in it: for the glory of God did lighten it, and the Lamb is the light thereof. And the nations of them which

are saved shall walk in the light of it: and the kings of the earth do bring their glory and honor into it. And the gates of it shall not be shut at all by day: for there shall be no night there. (Revelation 21:23–25)

*****

If you made a commitment to Christ while reading this book, please write to me at P.O. Box 210489, Bedford, TX 76095. I would like to send you a gift to help you grow in your faith. I will also be happy to suggest a good church for you to attend.

If you are a pastor and God has spoken to your heart concerning the message on the second coming of Christ, please contact me concerning a speaking engagement.

Afterword

On April 14, 2004, President George W. Bush, standing alongside Israeli Prime Minister Ariel Sharon, announced a dramatic change in U.S. policy regarding the Middle East peace process. This is, perhaps, the most significant and prophetic change in Middle East policy since Harry S. Truman signed the document on May 14, 1948, that recognized the rebirth of the State of Israel.

President Bush courageously set aside decades of liberal policies supported by six previous presidents, the State Department, the European Union, the UN, and the Arab League.

1. President Bush stated that Israel would not have to return to its pre–1967 borders. This is a prophetic and historical move.
2. President Bush addressed the very heart of the Middle East crisis: the refugees. Earlier in this book, I stated that this dilemma had to be resolved in order for peace to come. Mr. Bush clearly stated that neither the Palestinians who lost land in 1948, nor their descendants, could return to Israel. They could, however, return to the Palestinian territories. Had they been allowed to return to Israel, the nation would have become another Lebanon. The president's courage in reversing the "right of return" policy is a bold move, and it provides Israel with the assurance that terrorists in Lebanon would not be imported into major Israeli cities.
3. President Bush recognized Israel's right to retain some key West Bank settlements as part of any peace accord with the Palestinians.
4. President Bush supported Israel's right to fight terrorism.

There was no valid political reason or benefits for the president to make these decisions:

1. It all but guaranteed his loss of the Muslim vote in America (which is as large as the Jewish vote).
2. The fact remains that the Jewish community in America traditionally votes for the Democratic ticket.
3. Power brokers in the Middle East, with all their petrodollars, will do everything in their power—economically and politically—to keep President Bush from reelection. (I am convinced there was no political motivation in President Bush's decision. His evangelical support base was still strong. I believe his decision was based upon his integrity, moral character, and, above all, his faith.)

When President Bush was at a nadir in the polls, when he was being brutally attacked by the liberal media, when the war in Iraq was at its lowest point, and when the 9/11 Commission was attempting to undermine his integrity, with character and courage, he made a biblically based, moral decision to stand with the nation of Israel. I believe this decision by President George W. Bush was prophetic, and will echo throughout eternity.

APPENDIX A

Bibles and Scripture Passages Used at Presidential Inaugurations[1]

President	Date	Edition
George Washington	1789	Genesis 49:13[2] (Masonic Bible); opened at random due to haste
George Washington	1793	Not known
John Adams	1797	Not known
Thomas Jefferson	1801, 1805	Not known
James Madison	1809, 1813	Not known
James Monroe	1817, 1821	Not known
John Q. Adams	1825	Not known
Andrew Jackson	1829, 1833	Not known
Martin Van Buren	1837	Proverbs 3:17[3]
William H. Harrison	1841	Not known
John Tyler	1841	Not known
James K. Polk	1845	Not known
Zachary Taylor	1849	Not known
Millard Fillmore	1850	Not known
Franklin Pierce	1853	Affirmed instead of swearing the oath; did not kiss Bible
James Buchanan	1857	Not known
Abraham Lincoln	1861	Opened at random
Abraham Lincoln	1865	Matthew 7:1; 18:7; Revelation 16:7[4]
Andrew Johnson	1865	Proverbs 21

Ulysses S. Grant	1869	Not known
Ulysses S. Grant	1873	Isaiah 11:1–3[5]
Rutherford B. Hayes	1877	Privately, no Bible; publicly, Psalm 118:11—13
James A. Garfield	1881	Proverbs 21:1[6]
Chester A. Arthur	1881	Privately, no Bible; Psalm 31:1–3
Grover Cleveland	1885	Psalm 112:4–10; Bible opened by chief justice and by chance it fell to this psalm[7]
Benjamin Harrison	1889	Psalm 121:1–6
Grover Cleveland	1893	Psalm 91:12–16
William McKinley	1897	2 Chronicles 1:10; Bible given to him by Methodist church congregation[8]
William McKinley	1901	Proverbs 16
Theodore Roosevelt	1901	No Bible
Theodore Roosevelt	1905	James 1:22–23
William Howard Taft	1909	1 Kings 3:9–11
Woodrow Wilson	1913	Psalm 119
Woodrow Wilson	1917	Privately, not known; publicly, Psalm 46[9]
Warren G. Harding	1921	Micah 6:8 (Washington Bible)
Calvin Coolidge	1923	Not known
Calvin Coolidge	1925	John 1
Herbert C. Hoover	1929	Proverbs 29:18
Franklin D. Roosevelt	1933, 1937, 1941, 1945	1 Corinthians 13
Harry S. Truman	1945	Closed Bible held in left hand; right hand on upper cover[10]
Harry S. Truman	1949	Matthew 5:3–11 and Exodus 20:3–17[11]
Dwight D. Eisenhower	1953	Psalm 127:1 (Washington Bible) and 2 Chronicles 7:14 (West Point Bible)[12]
Dwight D. Eisenhower	1957	Privately, not known; publicly, Psalm 33:12[13] (West Point Bible)
John F. Kennedy	1961	Closed Bible[14]

Lyndon B. Johnson	1963	Missal[15]
Lyndon B. Johnson	1965	Closed family Bible[16]
Richard M. Nixon	1969, 1973	Two family Bibles, both open to Isaiah 2:4[17]
Gerald R. Ford	1974	Proverbs 3:5–6[18]
James E. Carter	1977	Family Bible open to Micah 6:8[19]
Ronald W. Reagan	1981, 1985	Mother's Bible opened to 2 Chronicles 7:14[20] (Both privately and publicly in 1985)
George H. W. Bush	1989	Washington's Masonic Bible opened at random in the center; family Bible on top opened to Matthew 5
William J. Clinton	1993	King James Bible, given to him by grandmother, opened to Galatians 6:8
William J. Clinton	1997	King James Bible, given to him by grandmother, opened to Isaiah 58:12[21]
George W. Bush	2001	Closed family Bible[22]

APPENDIX B

An Index of Ancient Prophecies

Israel is the nation most often mentioned in the Bible. Do you know what nation is second? It's Iraq! However, that is not the name used in the Bible. The names used in the Bible are: Babylon, Land of Shinar, and Mesopotamia. The word "Mesopotamia" means "between two rivers"—more precisely, between the Tigris and Euphrates Rivers.

The name "Iraq" means "country with deep roots." Indeed, Iraq is a country with deep roots. That is very significant in the Bible. Here's why:

No other nation, except Israel, has more history and prophecy associated with it than Iraq.

Prophecies: Curses on nations that reject God and His Word

Genesis 27:29	Malachi 1:14	Deuteronomy 30:1
Genesis 18:18	Genesis 22:18	Genesis 26:4
Psalm 72:17	Isaiah 61:9	Jeremiah 4:2
Malachi 3:12	Galatians 3:8	Deuteronomy 28:14–68
Joel 3:16		

Prophecies: God fighting against nations that reject His Word

Jeremiah 1:19	Jeremiah 15:20	Jeremiah 21:4
Jeremiah 21:5	Jeremiah 32:5	Jeremiah 34:1, 7
Jeremiah 34:22	Daniel 10:20	Daniel 11:7, 11
Zechariah 14:2–3	Acts 5:39	Revelation 2:16
Genesis 12:1–3		

Prophecies: Curses on nations that attempt to divide the land of Israel

Zechariah 7:3   2 Samuel 7:10   Genesis 25:23
Genesis 17:4–9   Genesis 28:13   Zechariah 2:8
Jeremiah 12:14   Amos 9:14–15

Prophecies: Nations that conspire together to divide the land of Israel

Psalm 83:1–18

Prophecies: Nations blessed for blessing Israel

Genesis 18:18   Genesis 22:15–18   Genesis 26:4
Genesis 27:29   Psalm 72:17   Isaiah 61:9
Jeremiah 4:2   Malachi 3:12   Galatians 3:8
Genesis 12:1–3   Isaiah 2:3   Isaiah 62:1–7
Psalm 128:5   Deuteronomy 28:10–13

Prophecies: Curses on the nations that come against Jerusalem

Zechariah 12:1–6   Zechariah 2:8   Revelation 16:12–16

Prophecies: Specially chosen by God

2 Chronicles 6:6   Psalm 135:21   2 Chronicles 37:7

Prophecies: Protected by God

Isaiah 31:3   2 Samuel 24:16   2 Kings 19:34–34
Zechariah 2:5   Psalm 121:4–8   2 Chronicles 12:7

Described as prophecies

Psalm 48:2   Jeremiah 22:8   Psalm 122:3
Psalm 46:4   Isaiah 60:14   Matthew 5:5
Isaiah 1:21, 26   Zechariah 8:3   Isaiah 62:12
Nehemiah 11:1   Jeremiah 3:17   Psalm 48:12
Isaiah 33:30   Zechariah 7:3

Prophecies fulfilled

Jeremiah 20:5

Isaiah 64:10

Isaiah 2:3

1 Kings 14:25–26

Isaiah 7:1

2 Kings 19:1–37

2 Kings 25:1–30

Jeremiah 9:11

Isaiah 44:26–28

Isaiah 40:9

2 Kings 14:13–14

2 Kings 16:5

2 Kings 23:33–35

Jeremiah 29:1–8

Jeremiah 26:18

Zechariah 9:9

Luke 19:42–44

2 Chronicles 12:1–4

2 Kings 18:17

2 Kings 24:10–11

Prophecies: Jerusalem and the nations

2 Chronicles 32:23

Isaiah 66:20

Jeremiah 4:16

Joel 3:1

Zechariah 9:10

Luke 21:24

Psalm 79:1

Jeremiah 3:17

Ezekiel 5:5, 8

Micah 4:2

Zechariah 12:3, 9

Luke 24:47

2 Chronicles 33:9

2 Chronicles 34:14

Ezekiel 26:2

Zechariah 8:22

Zechariah 14:2, 12, 14, 16

Psalm 125:1–2

Future prophecies

Matthew 24:21, 29

Isaiah 2:3

Matthew 24:6–15

Jeremiah 33:7–8

Revelation 2:12

Revelation 21:1, 2, 10

Prophecies declaring the land and eternal covenant

Genesis 17:4–9

Psalm 89:28–37

Psalm 102:12–13

Jeremiah 30:3

Genesis 15:18–21

Psalm 105:8–11

Isaiah 49:15

Ezekiel 28:25–26

2 Chronicles 37:7

Genesis 13:14–15

Amos 9:14–15

Ezekiel 36:24

Prophecies: The Messiah's return to Jerusalem

Psalm 102:15

Zechariah 14:1–3

Prophecies: The rebirth of Israel in 1948

Isaiah 66:8–13

Prophecies: The temple site

Isaiah 14:12–15   Isaiah 2:2–4   Daniel 8:23–25

Prophecies: The return of the Jews to Israel

Isaiah 49:22   Isaiah 43:6   Ezekiel 11:1
Amos 9:14–15   Isaiah 11:12   Jeremiah 29:10–14

Prophecies: Babylon (Iraq)

Eden in Iraq: Genesis 2:10–14
Adam and Eve created: Genesis 2:7–8
Satan's first appearance: Genesis 3:1–6
Nimrod established Babylon: Genesis 10:8–9
Tower of Babel built: Genesis 11:1–4
Confusion of languages: Genesis 11:5–11
Abraham's hometown: Genesis 11:28–12:5; Acts 7:2–4
Isaac's bride from Iraq: Genesis 24:3–4, 10
Jacob in Iraq: Genesis 27:42–45; 31:38
First world empire: Daniel 1:1–2; 2:36–38
Daniel tested: 2 Kings 24; Daniel 2:49; 3:12–30; 6
Greatest revival in history: Jonah 3
Book of Esther: Esther
Book of Nahum: Nahum
Prophecies in Revelation: 9:13–16; 16:16–19; 17; 18
Fall of Babylon: Daniel 14:8
Judgment: Ezekiel 37; 38; Isaiah 13:1, 6, 19; 14:22–23
Daniel's Prophecies: Isaiah 14:22–23; Daniel 2:44; 9:24–26; 9:27; 11:31

Prophecies: The Promised Messiah

He will be born of a virgin: Isaiah 7:14
Place of His birth: Micah 5:2
Rachel weeps for her murdered children: Jeremiah 31:15
He will be called out of Egypt: Hosea 11:1
The Spirit's anointing: Isaiah 11:2
Triumphant entry into Jerusalem: Zechariah 9:9
Betrayed by His friend: Psalms 41:9; 55:12–14

Forsaken by His disciples: Zechariah 13:7
The price of His betrayal: Zechariah 11:12

Prophecies: The Returning Messiah

The Judge: Psalm 98:9
The builder who appears in glory: Psalm 102:16
Son of Man and kingdom claimer: Daniel 7:13
Glorious One from the Father: Matthew 16:26–27; Titus 2:11–15; Hebrews 9:24–28
Claims His throne: Matthew 19:28
Prophetic timeline of His appearing: Matthew 24; Mark 13; Luke 21
Bridegroom: Matthew 25:1–2
Judges His servants: Matthew 25:13–30; 2 Timothy 4:1
His appearing in the clouds: Matthew 26:64; Mark 14:62
Reward for denial: Mark 8:38; Luke 9:26; 2 Peter 3
Ready for His coming: Luke 12:35–48; Luke 17:20–37; 18:8
The ten talents: Luke 19:11–28
The promise of God's anointing: John 1:51
The promise of His return: John 14:3; 14:18; 14:28; Acts 1:10–11
Promised refreshing: Acts 3:19–21
Wait for His coming: 1 Corinthians 1:4–8; 1 Thessalonians 1:19
Judge not: 1 Corinthians 4:5
In remembrance: 1 Corinthians 11:26
Behold, He comes: 1 Corinthians 15:23; 16:22; Philippians 3:10; Revelation 16:15
Rejoice: 2 Corinthians 1:14
The Day of the Lord: Philippians 1:6–10
Watching for Him: Philippians 3:20–21; 1 Timothy 6:13–15; Hebrews 10:25
With Him: Colossians 3:3–5
The joy of His coming: 1 Thessalonians 2:19
Blameless: 1 Thessalonians 3:13; 5:23; Hebrews 10:22
The Rapture: 1 Thessalonians 4:13–18; 5:1–10; 2 John 7; Jude 14–15; Revelation 1:17; 2:25; 3:3; 14:14–16
The revelation: 2 Thessalonians 1:7–10; 1 Peter 4:13; 5:1–4
The reward: 2 Timothy 4:8
Satan defeated: 2 Thessalonians 2:1–8

Patience: Hebrews 10:35–37; James 5:7–8; 1 Peter 1:7; 1:13
Confidence: 1 John 2:28
Like Him: 1 John 2:2–3; 3:2–3
Even so, come quickly: Revelation 22:20

Bibliography

Aarons, Mark, and John Loftus. *Unholy Trinity: The Vatican, The Nazis, and the Swiss Banks.* New York: St. Martin's Griffin, 1991.

Adams, Lawrence E. *Going Public: Christian Responsibility in a Divided America.* Grand Rapids, MI: Brazos, 2002.

Albright, Madeleine. *Madam Secretary: A Memoir.* New York: Miramax, 2003.

Aldrich, Gary. *Thunder on the Left: An Insider's Report on the Hijacking of the Democratic Party.* Fairfax, VA: Patrick Henry Center, 2003.

Ambrose, Stephen E. *D-Day June 6, 1944: The Climactic Battle of World War II.* New York: Simon & Schuster, 1994.

Baer, Robert. *Sleeping with the Devil: How Washington Sold Our Soul for Saudi Crude.* New York: Crown, 2003.

Barrett, David B., and Todd M. Johnson. *World Christian Trends A.D. 30–A.D. 2200: Interpreting the Annual Christian Megacensus.* Pasadena, CA: William Carey Library, 2001.

Barton, David. *The Bulletproof George Washington.* Aledo, TX: Wall-Builders, 1990.

———. *Original Intent: The Courts, the Constitution & Religion.* Aledo, TX: WallBuilders, 2000.

Bass, Warren. *Support Any Friend: Kennedy's Middle East and the Making of the U.S–Israel Alliance.* New York: Oxford University Press, 2003.

Bennett, William J. *Why We Fight: Moral Clarity and the War on Terrorism.* Washington, DC: Regnery, 2002.

Beschloss, Michael. *The Conquerors: Roosevelt, Truman and the Destruction of Hitler's Germany, 1941–1945.* New York: Simon & Schuster, 2002.

Black, Conrad. *Franklin Delano Roosevelt: Champion of Freedom.* New York: Public Affairs, 2003.

Bodansky, Yossef. *The High Cost of Peace: How Washington's Middle East Policy Left America Vulnerable to Terrorism.* Roseville, CA: Forum, 2002.

Buchanan, Patrick J. *The Death of the West: How Dying Populations and Immigrant Invasions Imperil Our County and Civilization.* New York: Thomas Dunne; St. Martin's, 2002.

Chesler, Phyllis. *The New Anti-Semitism: The Current Crisis and What We Must Do About It.* San Francisco, CA: Jossey-Bass, 2003.

Cockburn, Andrew and Leslie. *Dangerous Liaison: The Inside Story of the U.S.–Israeli Covert Relationship.* New York: HarperCollins, 1991.

Colson, Charles, and Ellen Vaughn. *Being the Body.* Nashville: W Publishing, 2003.

Coulter, Ann. *Treason: Liberal Treachery from the Cold War to the War on Terrorism.* New York: Crown Forum, 2003.

Crismier, Charles. *Renewing the Soul of America: One Person at a Time . . . Beginning with You.* Richmond, VA: Elijah Books, 2002.

Cuddy, Dennis Laurence. *September 11 Prior Knowledge: Waiting for the Next Shoe to Drop.* Oklahoma City, OK: Hearthstone, 2002.

Dershowitz, Alan M. *The Case For Israel.* Hoboken, NJ: John Wiley & Sons, 2003.

———. *Why Terrorism Works: Understanding the Threat, Responding to the Challenge.* New Haven and London: Yale University Press, 2002.

Eben, Abba. *Personal Witness: Israel Through My Eyes.* New York: Putnam's, 1992.

Ehrenfeld, Rachel. *Funding Evil: How Terrorism Is Financed—and How to Stop It.* Chicago: Bonus, 2003.

Evans, Michael D. *Israel: America's Key to Survival.* Plainfield, NJ: Logos International, 1981.

———. *Jerusalem Betrayed: Ancient Prophecy and Modern Conspiracy Collide in the Holy City.* Dallas, TX: Word, 1997.

———. *Jerusalem DC: (David's Capital).* Euless, TX: Bedford, 1984.

———. *Let My People Go.* New York: Nelson Resource Management, 1985.

———. *The Prayer of David in Times of Trouble.* Shippensburg, PA: Treasure House, 2003.

———. *The Return.* Nashville: Thomas Nelson, 1986.

———. *Save Jerusalem.* Euless, TX: Bedford, 1995.

———. *Why Americans Should Support Israel.* Euless, TX: Bedford, 2003.

Evans, Mike, and Robert Wise. *The Jerusalem Scroll.* Nashville: Thomas Nelson, 1999.

Friedlander, Saul. *Nazi Germany and the Jews, Volume 1: The Years of Persecution, 1933–1939.* New York: HarperCollins, 1997.

Friedman, Norman. *Terrorism, Afghanistan, and America's New Way of War.* Annapolis, MD: Naval Institute Press, 2003.

Gold, Dore. *Hatred's Kingdom: How Saudi Arabia Supports the New Global Terrorism.* Washington, DC: Regnery, 2003.

Grose, Peter. *Israel in the Mind of America.* New York: Knopf, 1984.

Gunnip, Randy. *The Mystery of Eternity.* Colleyville, TX: Harvest Time, 1998.

Hagee, John. *Attack on America: New York, Jerusalem, and the Role of Terrorism in the Last Days.* Nashville: Thomas Nelson, 2001.

———. *From Daniel to Doomsday: The Countdown Has Begun.* Nashville: Thomas Nelson, 1999.

Halberstam, David. *War in a Time of Peace: Bush, Clinton, and the Generals.* New York: Scribner, 2001.

Hannity, Sean. *Let Freedom Ring: Winning the War of Liberty Over Liberalism.* New York: Regan, 2002.

Hatch, Alden. *General Ike: A Biography of Dwight David Eisenhower.* Chicago: Henry Holt, 1964.

Hausner, Gideon. *Justice in Jerusalem.* New York: Herzl, 1966.

Hazony, Yoram. *The Jewish State: The Struggle for Israel's Soul.* New York: Basic, 2000.

Hedding, Malcolm. *Understanding Israel.* Oklahoma City: Zion's Gate International.

Hersh, Seymour M. *The Price of Power: Kissinger in the Nixon White House.* New York: Summit, 1983.

———. *The Samson Option: Israel's Nuclear Arsenal and American Foreign Policy.* New York: Vintage, 1991.

Herzl, Theodor. *The Jewish State.* Originally translated by Sylvie d'Avigdor, and published by Nutt, London, 1896. Jacob M. Alkow, ed. (1943 edition). New York: Dover, 1988.

Hitchcock, Mark. *Is America in Bible Prophecy?* Sisters, OR: Multnomah, 2002.

Junger, Sebastian. *The Perfect Storm: A True Story of Men Against the Sea.* New York: W.W. Norton, 1997.

Kent, Phil. *The Dark Side of Liberalism: Unchaining the Truth.* Augusta, GA: Harbor House, 2003.

Kepel, Gilles. *Jihād: The Trail of Political Islam.* Translated by Anthony F. Roberts. Cambridge, MA: Belknap Press of Harvard University Press, 2002.

Keyton, Dr. Bree M., and Stephen T. Keyton. *America: Repent or Perish.* Oklahoma City: Hearthstone, 2002.

Kissinger, Henry A. *Crisis: The Anatomy of Two Major Foreign Policy Crises.* New York: Simon & Schuster, 2003.

LaHaye, Tim. *Faith of Our Founding Fathers: A Comprehensive Study of America's Christian Foundations.* Green Forest, AR: Master, 1994.

————. *The Merciful God of Prophecy: His Loving Plan for You in the End Times.* Wheaton, IL: Warner Faith, 2002.

LaHaye, Tim, and Jerry B. Jenkins. *Are We Living in the End Times?: Current Events Foretold in Scripture . . . and What They Mean.* Wheaton, IL: Tyndale, 1999.

Lenczowski, George. *American Presidents and the Middle East.* Durham, NC: Duke University Press, 1990.

Lewis, Bernard. *What Went Wrong?: The Clash Between Islam and Modernity in the Middle East.* New York: Perennial, 2002.

Limbaugh, David. *Persecution: How Liberals Are Waging War Against Christianity.* Washington, DC: Regnery, 2003.

Lindsey, Hal. *Apocalypse Code.* Palos Verdes, CA: Western Front, 1997.

Loftus, John, and Mark Aarons. *The Secret War Against the Jews: How Western Espionage Betrayed the Jewish People.* New York: St. Martin's Griffin, 1994.

Lowry, Rich. *Legacy: Paying the Price for the Clinton Years.* Washington, DC: Regnery, 2003.

Meacham, Jon. *Franklin and Winston: An Intimate Portrait of an Epic Friendship.* New York: Random House, 2003.

Miniter, Richard. *Losing bin Laden: How Bill Clinton's Failure Unleashed Global Terror.* Washington, DC: Regnery, 2003.

Morris, Dick. *Off with Their Heads: Traitors, Crooks & Obstructionists in American Politics, Media & Business.* New York: Regan, 2003.

Mowbray, Joel. *Dangerous Diplomacy: How the State Department Threatens America's Security.* Washington, DC: Regnery, 2003.

Organski, AFK. *The $36 Billion Bargain: Strategy and Politics in U.S. Assistance to Israel.* New York: Columbia University Press, 1990.

Pipes, Daniel. *The Hidden Hand: Middle East Fears of Conspiracy.* New York: St. Martin's, 1996.

Posner, Gerald. *Why America Slept: The Failure to Prevent 9/11.* New York: Random House, 2003.

Ruben, Barry, ed. *Revolutionaries and Reformers: Contemporary Islamist Movements in the Middle East.* Albany: State University of New York Press, 2003.

Sanders, Ronald. *The High Walls of Jerusalem: A History of the Balfour Declaration and the Birth of the British Mandate for Palestine.* New York: Holt, Rinehart & Winston, 1983.

Savage, Michael. *The Savage Nation: Saving America from the Liberal Assault on Our Borders, Language, and Culture.* Nashville: WND, 2002.

Schlink, Basilea M. *Israel: My Chosen People.* London: Kanaan, 1995.

Schoenbaum, David. *The United States and the State of Israel.* New York: Oxford University Press, 1993.

Sperry, Paul. *Crude Politics: How Bush's Oil Cronies Hijacked the War on Terrorism.* Nashville: WND, 2003.

Spiegel, Steven L. *The Other Arab-Israeli Conflict: Making America's Middle East Policy, from Truman to Reagan.* Chicago: University of Chicago Press, 1985.

Stockman-Shomron, Israel. *Israel, the Middle East, and the Great Powers: Studies in the Contemporary History and Politics of the Middle East and the Arab-Israel Conflict.* Jerusalem: Shikmona, 1984.

Tal, Eliyahu, and Jack Padwa. *You Don't Have to Be Jewish to Be a Zionist: A Review of 400 Years of Christian Zionism.* Israel: TalPeter, 2000.

Thomas, Hugh. *Suez.* New York: Harper & Row, 1967.

Timmerman, Kenneth R. *Preachers of Hate: Islam and the War on America.* New York: Crown Forum, 2003.

Victor, George. *Hitler: The Pathology of Evil.* Dulles, VA: Brassey's, 1998.

Warren, Rick. *The Purpose Driven Church: Growth Without Compromising Your Mission & Mission.* Grand Rapids, MI: Zondervan, 1995.

Weinstien, Allen, and Hoshe Ma'oz, eds. *Truman and the American Commitment to Israel.* Jerusalem: Magnes, 1981.

Wurbrand, Richard. *Tortured for Christ.* Bartlesville, OK: Living Sacrifice, 1967, 1998.

Notes

Chapter One: In the Eye of the Prophetic Storm

1. "Address by U.S. President Bill Clinton to the Knesset," October 27, 1994. Online at: http//www.mfa.gov.il/mfa//go.asp?MFAH0bz20. Accessed November 28, 2003. "Remarks by President and Prime Minister Netanyahu in Exchange of Toast," December 13, 1998. Online at: http://clinton3. nara.gov/WH/New/mideast/19981214-14375.html. Accessed November 28, 2003. President Clinton quoted this on many different occasions to audiences concerned with the future of Israel, but at times interchanged the word "forget" for "abandon." I have used the latter word here because it seems the more commonly used in the quotation than "forget."

2. It is interesting that two presidents in recent history also opted to use a Masonic Bible as they took the oath of office: George H. W. Bush (41), and George W. Bush (43). George Herbert Walker Bush took the oath with his family Bible opened to Matthew 5 and placed on top of the same Masonic Bible used by George Washington in 1789. His son George Walker Bush wanted to use the same Masonic Bible, but due to inclement weather, a family Bible was substituted.

3. Mark Gaffney, *Dimona, The Third Temple: The Story Behind the Vanunu Revelation* (Beltsville, MD: Amana, 1989).

4. Webster G. Tarpley and Anton Chaitkin, *George Bush, The Unauthorized Biography*, Chapter 7 (Skull and Bones: The Racist Nightmare at Yale). Online at www.tarpley.net/bush7.html. Accessed: February 2, 2004.

5. Tom Robbins, "The Lesson: Incident at the Towers, 1993," *New York Daily News*, December 9, 1998, in Richard Miniter, *Losing bin Laden: How Bill Clinton's Failure Unleashed Global Terror* (Washington, DC: Regnery, 2003), 19.

6. Miniter, *Losing bin Laden*, xvi, xix.

7. White House Report, "Clinton on Life, Career, Decisions" (Friday, August 11, 2000). Online at: http://usembassy-australia.state.gov/hyper/2000/0811/epf501.htm. Accessed: November 26, 2003.

8. Patrick J. Buchanan, *The Death of the West: How Dying Populations and Immigrant Invasions Imperil Our Country and Civilization* (New York: St. Martin's Press), 5.

9. Martin Luther King Jr. (1929–68), U.S. clergyman, civil rights leader. *Strength to Love* (Philadelphia: Fortress, 1963), pt. 4, ch. 3.

10. Yossef Bodansky, *The High Cost of Peace: How Washington's Middle East Policy Left America Vulnerable to Terrorism* (Roseville, CA: Forum, 2002), 9–10.

11. 2 Chronicles 6:6 NIV.

12. David B. Barrett and Todd M. Johnson, *World Christian Trends A.D. 30–A.D. 2200: Interpreting the Annual Christian Megacensus* (Pasadena, CA: William Carey Library, 2001), 243–44. According to the totals of the chart on these pages, about 6 million Christians died as martyrs to their faith out of the 40 to 55 million killed during World War II.

13. October 8, 2001.

14. Online at: http://www.netanyahu.org/statofforisp.html. Accessed: January 21, 2004.

Chapter Two: America and the Fig Tree

1. Genesis 18:17.

2. Jeremiah 29:10.

3. Rick Ross, "Cults: Public Perceptions vs. Research," July 1998. Online at: http://www.rickross.com/reference/general/general431.html.

4. United States Geological Survey, "Earthquakes with 1,000 or More Deaths from 1900." Online at: http://neic.usgs.gov/neis/eqlists/eqsmajr.html. Last updated: October 23, 2003. Accessed: January 3, 2004. USGS, "Most Destructive Known Earthquakes on Record in the World: Earthquakes with 50,000 or More Deaths." Online at: http://neic.usgs.gov/neis/eqlists/eqs-mosde.html. Last updated: October 23, 2003. Accessed: January 3, 2004.

5. David B. Barrett and Todd M. Johnson, *World Christian Trends A.D. 30–A.D. 2200: Interpreting the Annual Christian Megacensus* (Pasadena, CA: William Carey Library, 2001), 229.

6. Online at www.pollingreport.com/religion.html. Accessed: November 10, 2003.

7. Matthew 28:19–20 NKJV.

8. Matthew 24:33–34 NKJV.

9. Isaiah 18:2 NIV.

10. See Ezekiel 38:13.

11. See Revelation 12:13–17.

12. This list is from Mark Hitchcock, *Is America in Bible Prophecy?* (Sisters, OR: Multnomah, 2002), 27–28, though I have changed some of the Scripture references to verses that more clearly represent his points.

13. Psalm 33:12 NKJV.

14. Proverbs 14:34 NIV.

Chapter Three: A Christian Nation

1. President John Adams, October 11, 1798 (address to the military). Online at: http://www.hartungpress.com/fyi/Quotes.htm. Accessed: January 21, 2004.

2. Thomas Jefferson, "Commerce between Master and Slave," 1782. Available online at http://douglassarchives.org/jeff_a51.htm.

3. *Holy Trinity Church v. United States.* 143 U.S. 457, 465 (February 29, 1892).

4. Ibid., 471.

5. See Michael D. Evans, *Why Christians Should Support Israel* (Euless, TX: Bedford, 2003), 43.

6. David Barton, *The Bulletproof George Washington* (Aledo, TX: Wallbuilders, 1990), 35, 44, 50, 57.

7. Peter Grose, *Israel in the Mind of America* (New York: Knopf, 1984), 5.

8. George Washington, "Letter to Jews of Newport, Rhode Island," 1790, in Kenneth R. Timmerman, *Preachers of Hate: Islam and the War on America* (New York: Crown Forum, 2003), xi.

9. 2 Corinthians 5:17.

10. William F. Shirer, *The Rise and Fall of the Third Reich* (New York: Simon & Schuster, 1960), 98.

11. Grose, *Israel in the Mind of America*, 5.

12. Ibid.

13. Isaiah 18:1–2.

14. Isaiah 18:2, 7.

15. Scholars today believe that Isaiah 18 refers to Cush—Egypt as we know it today. Though Pastor MacDonald may have misinterpreted this Scripture, his call to action was still a godly one. It was the first step in the American conscience toward supporting the rebirth of the nation of Israel.

16. Grose, *Israel in the Mind of America*, 9.

17. Ibid.

18. Ibid., 15.

19. Ibid.

20. Ibid., 20.

21. Ibid., 23–24.

22. Adolf Hitler, *Mein Kampf*, trans. Ralph Manheim (Boston: Houghton Mifflin, 1943), 161.

23. Shirer, *The Rise and Fall of the Third Reich*, 349.

24. Ibid., 77.

25. Ibid., 1056.

26. Ibid., 1069.

27. Ronald Lewin, *Hitler's Mistakes* (New York: Quill, William Morrow, 1948), 15–16.

Chapter Four: Presidents in Prophecy

1. William Eugene Blackstone, "The Blackstone Memorial, 1891." Online at http://www.amfi.org/blackmem.html. Accessed: October 21, 2003.

2. Thomas Jefferson, "Commerce between Master and Slave," 1782. Available online at http://douglassarchives.org/jeff_a51.htm.

3. Peter Grose, *Israel in the Mind of America* (New York: Knopf, 1984), 25–26.

4. John F. Walvoord, "Foreword" to William E. Blackstone, *Jesus Is Coming: God's Hope for a Restless World*, 3rd printing of an updated edition (Grand Rapids, MI: Kregel, 1989), 8.

5. Blackstone, *Jesus Is Coming*, 161.

6. Ibid., 171, 175.

7. Grose, *Israel in the Mind of America*, 45.

8. William E. Currie, "God's Little Errand Boy."

9. Victor Frankl, *The Doctor and the Soul: Introduction to Logotherapy*

(New York: Knopf), xxi, quoted in Ravi Zacharias, *Can Man Live Without God?* (Dallas: Word, 1994), 25.

10. Blackstone, "The Blackstone Memorial, 1891."

11. Ibid.

12. Hilton Obenzinger, "In the Shadow of 'God's Sun-Dial': The Construction of American Christian Zionism and the Blackstone Memorial." Online at: http://www.stanford.edu/group/SHR/5-1/text/obenzinger.html. Last updated: February 27, 1996. Accessed: October 21, 2003.

13. Moshe Davis, "Reflections on Harry S. Truman and the State of Israel," in Allen Weinstien and Hoshe Ma'oz, eds., *Truman and the American Commitment to Israel.* (Jerusalem: Magnes, 1981), 83.

14. Grose, *Israel in the Mind of America*, 41.

Chapter Five: A Prophetic Struggle

1. Edward R. Lyman, online at http://www.quotesland.com/view.php?do=view&full_quotes=yes&author_id=3176. Accessed: January 24, 2004.

2. Alex Bein, "Theodor Herzl: A Biography," in Theodor Herzl, *The Jewish State.* Originally translated by Sylvie d'Avigdor, and published by Nutt, London, 1896. Jacob M. Alkow, ed. (1943 edition) (Mineola, NY: Dover, 1988), 34.

3. Herzl, *The Jewish State*, 157.

4. Ronald Sanders, *The High Walls of Jerusalem: A History of the Balfour Declaration and the Birth of the British Mandate for Palestine* (New York: Holt Rinehart & Winston, 1983), 27–28.

5. Grose, *Israel in the Mind of America*, 24–25.

6. Ibid., 48–49.

7. Ibid., 67.

8. The Balfour Declaration, November 2, 1917. Online at: http://www.mfa.gov.il/mfa/go.asp?MFAH00pp0. Accessed: January 21, 2004.

9. Michael D. Evans, *Israel, America's Key to Survival* (Plainfield, N.J.: Logos International, 1981), 125–6.

10. Ibid., 69–70.

11. Ibid.

12. Grose, *Israel in the Mind of America*, 81.

13. Ibid., 82.

14. Sanders, *The High Walls of Jerusalem*, 637.

15. Michael Beschloss, *The Conquerors: Roosevelt, Truman and the Destruction of Hitler's Germany, 1941–1945* (New York: Simon & Schuster, 2002), 44.

Chapter Six: A Deadly Lack of Conviction

1. Martin Niemoller, online at: http://internet.ggu.edu/university_library/if/Niemoller.html. Accessed: October 21, 2003

2. Webster G. Tarpley and Anton Chaitkin, *George Bush, The Unauthorized Biography*, Chapter 7 (Skull and Bones: The Racist Nightmare at Yale). Online at www.tarpley.net/bush7.html. Accessed: February 2, 2004.

3. Frau Forester Nietzsche, *The Life of Nietzsche* (New York: Sturgis & Walton, 1921), 2:656.

4. Klaus Sholder, *Die Kirchen und das Dritte Reich*, vol. 1, *Borgeschichte und Zeit der Illusionen 1918–1934* (Frankfurt am Main, 1977), pp. 338ff., in Saul Friedlander, *Nazi Germany and the Jews, Volume 1: The Years of Persecution, 1933–1939* (New York: HarperCollins, 1997), 42.

5. William F. Shirer, *The Rise and Fall of the Third Reich* (New York: Simon & Schuster, 1960), 111.

6. Martin Luther, "On the Jews and their Lies," 1543. Online at: http://www.flholocaustmuseum.org/history_wing/antisemitism/reformation.cfm. Accessed: December 18, 2003.

7. "Theological Myth," p. 113, in Freidlander, *Nazi Germany and the Jews*, 45.

8. *Microsoft® Encarta® Encyclopedia 2000* (Redmond, WA: Microsoft Corporation, 1993–99), s.v., "Hitler, Adolf."

9. Friedlander, *Nazi Germany and the Jews*, 62–63.

10. Ibid., 64.

11. David Kranzler, "The Jewish Refugee community of Shanghai, 1938–1945," *Wiener Library Bulletin* 26 (1972–73): 28ff., in Friedlander, *Nazi Germany and the Jews*, 303.

12. *Microsoft® Encarta® Encyclopedia 2000*, s.v., "Holocaust."

13. *Foreign Relations of the United States, 1938*, vol. 1 (Washington, DC, 1950), 740–41, in Friedlander, *Nazi Germany and the Jews*, 248.

14. Roosevelt cable to Myron Taylor, *Documents on American Foreign Relations, 1939*, vol. 2 (Boston: World Peace Foundation), 66, in Gideon Hausner, *Justice in Jerusalem* (New York: Herzl, 1966), 229.

15. Waite, *Adolf Hitler*, 29.

16. Dalia Ofer, *Escaping the Holocaust: Illegal Immigration to the Land of Israel, 1939–1944* (New York, 1990), chapter 1; Yehuda Bauer, *Jews for Sale? Nazi-Jewish Negotiations 1933–1945* (New Haven, CN, 1994), chap. 3, in Friedlander, *Nazi Germany and the Jews*, 304.

17. Bernard Wasserstein, *Britain and the Jews of Europe, 1939–1945* (Oxford, 1988), 40, in Friedlander, *Nazi Germany and the Jews*, 304.

18. Michael Barak, e-mail to Renata Valar, February 22, 2002.

19. *Parade* magazine (December 7, 2003), 6.

20. Seymour M. Hersh, *The Samson Option: Israel's Nuclear Arsenal and American Foreign Policy* (New York: Vintage, 1991), footnote on 127.

21. Peter Grose, *Israel in the Mind of America* (New York: Knopf, 1984), 120–21.

22. Michael Beschloss, *The Conquerors: Roosevelt, Truman and the Destruction of Hitler's Germany, 1941–1945* (New York: Simon & Schuster, 2002), 54.

23. "Henry Morgenthau, Jr. (1891–1967)." Online at http://www.pbs.org/wgbh/amex/holocaust/peopleevents/pandeAMEX97.html. Accessed: October 26, 2003.

24. Beschloss, *The Conquerors: Roosevelt, Truman and the Destruction of Hitler's Germany, 1941–1945*, 38.

25. Ibid., 43.

26. Ibid., 53.

27. Ibid., 54.

28. Grose, *Israel in the Mind of America*, 128.

29. Randolph Paul and John Pehle, "Report to the Secretary on the Acquiescence of This Government in the Murder of The Jews." Online at http://www.pbs.org/wgbh/amex/holocaust/filmmore/reference/primary/some report.html. Accessed: October 26, 2003.

30. Ibid.

31. Beschloss, *The Conquerors: Roosevelt, Truman and the Destruction of Hitler's Germany, 1941–1945*, 57.

32. Ibid., 58.

33. Gideon Hausner, *Justice in Jerusalem* (New York: Herzl, 1966), 240.

34. Grose, *Israel in the Mind of America*, 154.

Chapter Seven: The Olive Tree Replanted

1. Allen Weinstien and Hoshe Ma'oz, eds., *Truman and the American Commitment to Israel* (Jerusalem: Magnes, 1981), 5.

2. Peter Grose, *Israel in the Mind of America* (New York: Knopf, 1984), 159.

3. Ibid., 190 (also see page 337).

4. Walter Isaacson and Evan Thomas, *The Wise Men* (New York: Simon & Schuster, 1986), 452, in A.F.K. Organski, *The $36 Billion Bargain: Strategy and Politics in U.S. Assistance to Israel* (New York: Columbia University Press, 1990), 26.

5. Michael Beschloss, *The Conquerors: Roosevelt, Truman and the Destruction of Hitler's Germany, 1941–1945* (New York: Simon & Schuster, 2002), 224 (also see page 351).

6. UNSCOP was made up of eleven countries: Australia, Canada, Czechoslovakia, Guatemala, Holland, India, Iran, Peru, Sweden, Uruguay, and Yugoslavia.

7. Andrew and Leslie Cockburn, *Dangerous Liaison: The Inside Story of the U.S.-Israeli Covert Relationship* (New York: HarperCollins, 1991), 19.

8. Abba Eban, *Personal Witness: Israel Through My Eyes* (New York: Putnam's, 1992), 151–52.

9. Grose, *Israel in the Mind of America*, 293.

10. The Golan Heights were part of Syria at this time.

11. Cockburn, *Dangerous Liaison*, 22.

12. John Fitzgerald Kennedy, Inaugural Address, January 20, 1961. Online at: http://www.yale.edu/lawweb/avalon/presiden/inaug/kennedy.htm. Accessed: November 6, 2003.

13. Walter Eytan, *The First Ten Years: A Diplomatic History of Israel* (New York: Simon & Schuster, 1958), 209ff., in Schoenbaum, *The United States and the State of Israel*, 79.

14. Warren Bass, *Support Any Friend: Kennedy's Middle East and the Making of the U.S–Israel Alliance* (New York: Oxford University Press, 2003), 144.

15. Seymour M. Hersh, *The Samson Option: Israel's Nuclear Arsenal and American Foreign Policy* (New York: Vintage, 1991), 96.

16. Ibid., 146.

17. Ibid., 158.

18. Yitzhak Rabin, *The Rabin Memoirs* (Boston, 1979), 100, in Schoenbaum, *The United States and the State of Israel*, 167.

19. Thomas F. Kranz, "Robert F. Kennedy Assassination (Summary)," for the Federal Bureau of Investigation and made available by the Freedom of Information Act (March 1977), 17.

20. Ibid., 10.

21. Ibid., 15.

22. Ibid., 6.

23. Hersh, *The Samson Option*, 177.

24. Ibid., 127.

25. Ibid., 143–44.

26. Ibid., 223.

27. Seymour M. Hersh, *The Price of Power: Kissinger in the Nixon White House* (New York: Summit, 1983), 234.

28. Henry Kissinger, *Years of Upheaval* (Boston: Little, Brown, 1982), 948, in Organski, *The $36 Billion Bargain*, 29.

29. Organski, *The $36 Billion Bargain*, 31.

30. Bass, *Support Any Friend*, 246.

Chapter Eight: Reviving Ishmael

1. Founding Inscription, Dome of the Rock, Jerusalem, Online at http://www.bibleplaces.com/domeofrock.htm. Accessed: January 22, 2004.

2. "Letter to an Anti-Zionist Friend," Rev. Martin Luther King Jr., *Saturday Review* XVLII (August 1967): 76.

3. Abdulhak Adnan, *La Science chez les Turcs ottoman* (Paris: 1939), 87, 98–99, in Bernard Lewis, *What Went Wrong?: The Clash Between Islam and Modernity in the Middle East* (New York: Perennial, 2002), 7.

4. Lewis, *What Went Wrong?*, 9.

5. Albert Hourani, *Arabic Thought in the Liberal Age, 1798–1939* (Oxford: Oxford University Press, 1970), 37, in Dore Gold, *Hatred's Kingdom: How Saudi Arabia Supports the New Global Terrorism* (Washington, DC: Regnery, 2003), 19.

6. Gold, *Hatred's Kingdom*, 26–27.

7. Ibid., 13.

8. Mark 12:17.

9. Nadav Safran, *Saudi Arabia: The Ceaseless Quest for Security* (Cambridge: Harvard University Press, 1985), 58, in Gold, *Hatred's Kingdom*, 60.

10. Nawaf E. Obaid, "Improving U.S. Intelligence Analysis on the Saudi

Arabian Decision-Making Process" (Master's Thesis, John F. Kennedy School of Government, Harvard University, 1998), 13, in Gold, *Hatred's Kingdom*, 60.

Chapter Nine: Exporting Hate

1. A convocation of world leaders was held in Jerusalem beginning on October 11, 2003. The purpose of the meeting was to discuss how to win the war on terrorism through moral clarity. Transcripts were made of all the addresses and are held by Dmitry Radyshevsky, executive director, The Michael Cherney Foundation. Further references to remarks offered during the summit are taken from these transcripts.

2. Nadav Safran, *Saudi Arabia: The Ceaseless Quest for Security* (Cambridge: Harvard University Press, 1985), 58, in Dore Gold, *Hatred's Kingdom: How Saudi Arabia Supports the New Global Terrorism* (Washington, DC: Regnery, 2003), 87. Safran's source was the Saudi Arabian Ministry of Petroleum and Natural Resources.

3. The State Department's U.S. Commission on International Religious Freedom was the first government agency to step forward publicly and finger Saudi Wahhabism as a "strategic threat" to the United States. See Tom Carter's article "Saudis' Strict Islam called a 'Threat,'" *Washington Times* (November 19, 2003). Online at http://www.washtimes.com/world/20031118-113127-4259r.htm. Accessed: November 26, 2003.

4. Timmerman, *Preachers of Hate*, 66.

5. Safran, *Saudi Arabia*, 221, in Gold, *Hatred's Kingdom*, 119. Safran's source was the Saudi Arabian Ministry of Petroleum and Natural Resources.

6. Gold, *Hatred's Kingdom*, 126.

7. Blaine Hardin, "Saudis Seek U.S. Muslims for their Sect," *New York Times*, October 20, 2001, in Gold, *Hatred's Kingdom*, 126.

8. Reza F. Safa, *Inside Islam* (Orlando, FL: Creation House, 1997).

9. Andrew and Leslie Cockburn, *Dangerous Liaison: The Inside Story of the U.S.-Israeli Covert Relationship* (New York: HarperCollins, 1991), 194.

10. Gold, *Hatred's Kingdom*, 127.

11. Tom Carter, "Saudis; Strict Islam called a 'Threat,'" *Washington Times* (November 19, 2003). Online at http://www.washtimes.com/world/2003 1118-113127-4259r.htm. Accessed: November 24, 2003.

12. IslamOnline.net, "Sudanese Islamist Group to Look for Office Abroad." Online at http://www.islam-online.net/iol-english/dowalia/news-

14-2-2000/topnews5.asp. Created: February 14, 2000. Accessed: November 26, 2003.

13. Daniel Pipes, "The Danger Within: Militant Islam in America," *Commentary* magazine, November 2001.

14. White House Report, "Clinton on Life, Career, Decisions" (Friday, August 11, 2000). Online at: http://usembassy-australia.state.gov/hyper/2000/0811/epf501.htm. Accessed: November 26, 2003.

Chapter Ten: Treason

1. Abraham Lincoln. Online at: http://lincoln.thefreelibrary.com/. Accessed: January 22, 2004.

2. See Luke 2.

3. Simon Tisdall, "Symbolic gesture seals hopes to end blood and tears" *Guardian Unlimited* (September 14, 1993). Online at: http://www.guardian-century.co.uk/1990-1999/Story/0,6051,112648,00.html. Accessed: November 30, 2003.

4. Ambassador Dore Gold, an interview with Amnon Lord, October 2003.

5. Elliot Engel, address during the Jerusalem Summit: Building Peace on Truth, October 12–14, 2003.

6. Alan M. Dershowitz, *Why Terrorism Works: Understanding the Threat, Responding to the Challenge* (New Haven and London: Yale University Press, 2002), 2.

7. Yoram Etinger, an interview with Amnon Lord, October 25, 2003.

8. Tal Silberstein, an interview with Amnon Lord, November 2, 2003.

9. Yossef Bodansky, *The High Cost of Peace: How Washington's Middle East Policy Left America Vulnerable to Terrorism* (Roseville, CA: Forum, 2002), 223.

10. Tal Silberstein, an interview with Amnon Lord, November 2, 2003.

11. *New Yorker* (March 24, 2003).

12. Ibid.

Chapter Eleven: Lunatics, Liberals, and Liars

1. Abraham Lincoln. Online at: http://lincoln.thefreelibrary.com/. Accessed: January 22, 2004.

2. Report of the United States Commission on National Security (Hart-Rudman Report), January 31, 2001; online at: http://www.nssg.gov./Reports/reports.htm.

3. Joel Mowbray, *Dangerous Diplomacy: How the State Department Threatens America's Security* (Washington, DC: Regnery, 2003), 9–10.

4. "Saudi ambassador accuses Iraq war opposers of 'chutzpah,'" Associated Press, December 13, 2003. Marc Rouleau, "Cynicism of the Saudis," *New York Sun*, November 27, 2002; http://www.nysun.com/sunarticle.asp?artID=362; NewsMax.com; http://www.newsmax.com/archives/articles/2002/12/7/170251.shtml; PR Watch.org; March 21, 2002, http://www.prwatch.org/spin/March_2002.html.

5. "Saudi Arabia tries to improve its image among Americans," *New York Times*, August 28, 2002.

6. "Saudis Spend Millions to Make You Like Them"; NewsMax.com; October 28, 2003.

7. Cited by Daniel Pipes in "What Riyadh Buys [in Washington]"; *New York Post*; December 11, 2002.

8. Amnesty International: "Saudi Arabia: An urgent reform of the criminal justice system is needed," AI Index: MDE 23/005/2003 (Public); News Service No: 187; August 8, 2003; http://web.amnesty.org/library/Index/ENGMDE230052003?open&of=ENG-SAU.

9. Mortimer B. Zuckerman, "Graffiti on History's Walls," *U.S. News & World Report*, vol. 135, no. 15 (November 3, 2003), 47–48.

Chapter Twelve: The Battle Lines Are Drawn Through the Heart of Jerusalem

1. Mark Gaffney, *Dimona, The Third Temple: The Story Behind the Vanunu Revelation* (Beltsville, MD: Amana, 1989).

2. Sam Orbaum, "Jerusalem's Guest Book," *Jerusalem Post*, March 24, 2000.

3. 2 Chronicles 33:7.

4. 2 Chronicles 7:14.

5. See chapter 15 for more information on sales to these countries.

6. Seymour M. Hersh, *The Samson Option: Israel's Nuclear Arsenal and American Foreign Policy* (New York: Vintage, 1991), 20.

7. Ibid., 119.

8. Ibid., 121.

9. Ibid.

10. Judges 16:28.

11. Judges 16:30.

12. Hersh, *The Samson Option*, 9.

13. Yossef Bodansky, *The High Cost of Peace: How Washington's Middle East Policy Left America Vulnerable to Terrorism* (Roseville, CA: Forum, 2002), 568.

14. Joby Warrick, "Dirty Bomb Warheads Disappear," *Washington Post*, December 7, 2003.

15. George Santayana, *The Life of Reason*, Volume 1, 1905.

Chapter Thirteen: Our Nation's Issue of the Twenty-first Century: Winning the War on Terror

1. Terminology that is often used to describe the Jews and their allies in the Islamist documents. See for example Dore Gold, *Hatred's Kingdom: How Saudi Arabia Supports the New Global Terrorism* (Washington, DC: Regnery, 2003), 231.

2. For information on transcripts of the Jerusalem Summit, see chapter 8, note 5.

3. Glenn Kessler, "US Penalizes Israel in Loan for West Bank Construction," *Washington Post*, November 26, 2003. Connie Bruck, "Back Roads—How Serious Is the Bush Administration About Creating a Palestinian State?" *New Yorker*, December 15, 2003.

4. "Jerusalem Embassy Relocation Act," The Jewish Virtual Library. Online at: http://www.us-israel.org/jsource/Peace/Jerusalem_Relocation_Act. html. Accessed: December 13, 2003.

5. Mortimer B. Zuckerman, "Graffiti on History's Walls," *U.S. News & World Report*, vol. 135, no. 15, 50.

6. Ibid., 48.

7. Ibid., 50.

8. Gold, *Hatred's Kingdom*, 246.

9. Acts 1:8 NKJV.

Chapter Fourteen: The "New" Anti-Semitism

1. Thomas Jefferson, "Commerce between Master and Slave," 1782. Available online at http://douglassarchives.org/jeff_a51.htm. (Emphasis added.)

2. Abraham Lincoln, "Second Inauguration Address." Available online at: http://www.law.ou.edu/hist/lincoln2.html. Accessed December 22, 2003.

3. John Loftus and Mark Aarons, *The Secret War Against the Jews: How Western Espionage Betrayed the Jewish People* (New York: St. Martin's Griffin, 1994), 71.

4. Robert Parry, "Springtime for Appeasers," online at http://www.consortiumnews.com/1999/120299a.html; accessed March 11, 2004.

5. Loftus and Aarons, *The Secret War Against the Jews,* 58.

6. Secretary of State John Foster Dulles in February 1957 quoted on p. 99 of Donald Neff, *Fallen Pillars* (Washington: Institute for Palestine Studies) Update, 2002.

7. "Speech by Prime Minister Mahathir Mohamad of Malaysia to the Tenth Islamic Summit Conference, Putrajaya, Malaysia," (October 16, 2003). Complete text of the speech available online at: http://www.adl.org/Anti_semitism/malaysian.asp. Accessed: December 22, 2003.

8. *Der Parteitag der Arheit vom 6 bis 13 September 1937: Offizieller Bericht uber den Verlauf des Reichsparteitages mit samtlichen Kongressreden* (Munich, 1938), p. 157, in Saul Friedlander, *Nazi Germany and the Jews, Volume 1: The Years of Persecution, 1933–1939* (New York: HarperCollins, 1997), 184–85.

9. Ibid., 177.

10. Gerald Fleming, *Hitler and the Final Solution* (Berkeley: University of California Press, 1984), 17, in George Victor, *Hitler: The Pathology of Evil* (Dulles, VA: Brassey's, 1998), 123.

11. Phyllis Chesler, *The New Anti-Semitism: The Current Crisis and What We Must Do About It* (San Francisco, CA: Jossey-Bass, 2003), 218–23.

12. *The Palestine Times* 114 (December 2000).

13. Associated Press (March 25, 2000).

14. Ahmad Abu Halabiya, "Friday sermon in Gaza mosque on October 13, 2000," broadcast live on Palestinian Authority TV. Zuckerman, "Graffiti on History's Walls," *U.S. News & World Report,* 48.

15. "EU Threatens to Cut Aid Over Anti-Semitic Texts in PA," "*Mein Kampf* in East Jerusalem and the Palestinian Authority," "Palestinian Author-

ity Anti-Semitism Since the Hebron Accord," "Palestinian Press Continues Incitement in Violation of Road Map," "Palestinian Textbooks," "Palestinians Use Crosswords to Negate Israel"; all of above cited in Jewish Virtual Library, 2004; Dr. Mitchell G. Bard, director; http://www.us-israel.org/jsource/anti-semitism/palantoc.html.

16. "The disease of the century," official Palestinian Authority daily, *Al Hayat al-Jadida*; December 28, 1999; "A Compendium of Hate: Palestinian Authority Anti-Semitism Since the Hebron Accord"; Special Report, Israel Government Press Office; Jerusalem, December 16, 1997.

17. "Hitler is a youth idol, *Mein Kampf* is a bestseller," by Amos Nevo, *Yediot Aharonot* daily, March 10, 2000.

18. "Official Palestinian TV: Kill Jews," by Itamar Marcus, Palestinian Media Watch, April 30, 2003.

19. Quotation of Sif Ali Algeruan in *Al Hayat al-Jadida*, the official daily newspaper of the Palestinian Authority, from "Hitler is a Youth Idol, *Mein Kampf* is a Bestseller," article by Amos Nevo, *Yediot Aharonot*, March 10, 2000.

20. Reports are available online at: http://eumc.eu.int/.

21. Manley Philips, February 20, 2002.

22. *Courierra de la Sera* (April 12, 2002).

23. "A Campaign of Hatred," by Yair Sheleg, in *Indymedia UK*, July 23, 2003. Online at: http://www.indymedia.org.uk/en/2003/07/274659.html.

24. Robert S. Wistrich, "Islamic Judeophobia: An Existential Threat," reproduced in http://www.therightroadtopeace.com/infocenter/doc/RobertS Wistrich-Judeophobia.doc, 2003.

25. Geffrey B. Kelly, "The Life and Death of a Modern Martyr" *Christian History* 4 (1991): 8.

26. See Psalm 122:6.

Chapter Fifteen: Blessings and Cursings

1. Genesis 3:1.

2. Quoted in *The Peace Encyclopedia*: Zionism; www.yahoodi.com/peace/zionism.html.

3. Online at http://www.informationclearinghouse.info/article4950.htm.

4. Jimmy Carter, "For Israel, Land or Peace," *Washington Post* (November 26, 2000).

5. *New York Times* (December 1, 2003).

6. U.S. Senate Congressional Record, 1977 to 1988.

7. Donald Wagner, "Christian Zionism," five-part series in *Daily Star* (Lebanon); October 7, 2003. Online at: http://198.133.233.21/stopthe killing/christian_zionism_donald_wagner.htm.

8. Remarks in New York City on receiving the Charles Evans Hughes Gold Medal of the National Conference of Christians and Jews, March 23, 1982. Online at: http://www.us-israel.org/jsource/US-Israel/presquote.html.

9. Address to the nation on United States policy for peace in the Middle East (September 1, 1982). Online at: http://www.us-israel.org/jsource/US-Israel/presquote.html.

10. Remarks at a White House meeting with Jewish leaders (February 2, 1983). Online at: http://www.us-israel.org/jsource/US-Israel/presquote.html.

11. Remarks at the Welcoming Ceremony for President Chaim Herzog of Israel (November 10, 1987). Online at: http://www.us-israel.org/jsource/US-Israel/presquote.html.

12. Remarks following a meeting with former national security officials (October 5, 1981). Online at: http://www.reagan.utexas.edu/resource/speeches/1981/81oct.htm.

13. Question-and-answer session at a working luncheon with out-of-town editors (October 16, 1981). Online at: http://www.reagan.utexas.edu/resource/speeches/1981/101681b.htm.

14. (September 1, 1982). Online at: http://www.reagan.utexas.edu/resource/speeches/1982/82sep.htm.

15. The morning after the Sabra and Shatilla massacres of Palestinians by Christian militias, Reagan blamed Israel (September 18, 1982). Online at: http://www.reagan.utexas.edu/resource/speeches/1982/91882a.htm.

16. Address in the Knesset by Prime Minister Menachem Begin, June 29, 1982; Israel Ministry of Foreign Affairs, Foreign Relations, Historical Documents, VOLUME 8: 1982–1984; http://www.mfa.gov.il/mfa/go.asp? MFAH0ibx0.

17. US Code; TITLE 22 > CHAPTER 61 ANTI-TERRORISM > Sec. 5201 (The Anti-Terrorism Act of 1987).

18. *Israel's Foreign Relations*, Selected Documents, Volumes 11–12:

1988–1992, Message from President Reagan to Prime Minister Shamir, December 22, 1988; http://www.mfa.gov.il/mfa/go.asp?MFAH0j330.

19. George H. W. Bush, Address to the UN, September 23, 1991. Online at: http://www.freelists.org/archives/news/09-2002/msg00021.html.

20. Letter to George Klein of NYC March 19, 1992, in *All the Best*, 552–54.

21. Statement by the prime minister's office on Israel's Position on the Peace Talks (December 1, 1991). Online at: http://domino.un.org/UNIS-PAL.NSF/0/0ed8f0566763bda8852560f200663a61?OpenDocument.

22. Mitchell G. Bard, *U.S.-Israel Relations: Looking to the Year 2000*. DC: AIPAC, 1991; the American Jewish Committee and *The Near East Report*. Online at: http://www.us-israel.org/jsource/US-Israel/bdaygreet.html.

23. Clinton's reply after Israeli Ambassador Shoval presented his credentials (September 10, 1998). Online at: http://www.us-israel.org/jsource/US-Israel/presquote.html.

24. Washington press conference (December 23, 1996); Associated Press.

25. Washington press conference (July 1, 1999); Associated Press.

26. Remarks by the president to the American Jewish Committee (May 3, 2001), National Building Museum, Washington, D.C. Online at: http://www.whitehouse.gov/news/releases/2001/05/20010504.html.

27. Address to the National Commemoration of the Days of Remembrance (April 19, 2001). Online at: http://www.whitehouse.gov/news/releases/2001/04/20010424-3.html.

28. "President Bush Discusses Iraq Policy at Whitehall Palace in London, England"; the White House, Office of the Press Secretary; November 19, 2003; http://www.whitehouse.gov/news/releases/2003/11/20031119-1.html.

29. *New York Times* (November 27, 2003).

30. The Federation of American Scientists, Arms Sales Monitoring Project; http://www.fas.org/asmp/library/armsmonitor.html.

Chapter Sixteen: Our Nation's Future: A Rude Awakening or a Great Awakening?

1. Richard Wurbrand, *Tortured for Christ* (Bartlesville, OK: Living Sacrifice, 1967, 1998), 78.

2. Conway, *The Nazi Persecution of the Churches*, 220.

3. 2 Kings 22:11–13.

4. See Romans 1:21–32.

5. Shirer, *The Rise and Fall of the Third Reich*, 226.

6. Robert G. Waite, *Adolf Hitler: The Phychopathic God* (New York: Basic, 1977), 17.

7. Eberhard Behtge, *Dietrich Bonhoeffer* (New York: Harper & Row, 1970), 191.

8. Suster, *Hitler: The Occult Messiah*, 77.

9. Quoted from David Hunt, *Peace, Prosperity and the Coming Holocaust* (Eugene, OR: Harvest House, 1983), 141.

10. J. S. Conway, *The Nazi Persecution of the Churches* 1933–1945 (New York: Basic, 1968), 48.

11. Richard Pierard, "Radical Resistance," *Christian History* 10, No. 4 (1991): 30.

12. Donald Sklar, *Gods and Beasts: The Nazis and the Occult* (New York: Dorset, 1977), 53.

13. Oswald J. Smith, "My Visit to Germany," *Defender* 11 (September 1936): 15; quoted in David A. Rausch, *A Legacy of Hatred* (Chicago: Moody, 1984), 101.

14. Conway, *The Nazi Persecution of the Churches*, 15.

15. Shirer, *The Rise and Fall of the Third Reich*, 238.

16. Ibid., 239.

17. Gerald Suster, *Hitler: The Occult Messiah* (New York: St. Martin's, 1981), 135.

18. Waite, *Adolf Hitler*, 16.

19. Rousas J. Rushdoony, *Law and Liberty* (Fairfax, VA: Thoburn, 1971), 73.

20. Speech by Ellison DuRant Smith, April 9, 1924, *Congressional Record*, 68th Congress, 1st Session (Washington, DC: Government Printing Office, 1924), vol. 65, 5961–5962.

21. Genesis 12:3.

22. See Zechariah 2:8.

23. See 1 Chronicles 12:32.

24. See Isaiah 62:1.

25. Dietrich Bonhoeffer, *The Cost of Discipleship*, trans. C. Kaiser (New York: Macmillan, 1949), 45–46.

26. Shirer, *The Rise and Fall of the Third Reich*, 239.

27. Mary Bosanquet, *The Life and Death of Dietrich Bonhoeffer* (London: Hodder and Stoughton, 1968), 65.

28. Ibid., 109.

29. Jacques Ellul, *The Subversion of Christianity* (Grand Rapids: Erdmans, 1986), 18.

30. See Revelation 16:12–16.

31. See Revelation 11:16–18 NASB.

32. Cited in Arthur C. Cochrane, *The Church's Confession Under Hitler* (Philadelphia: Westminster, 1962), 40.

Chapter Seventeen: Hope for a Restless World

1. Associated Press, dateline Vatican City, June 24, 1997.

2. Matthew 24:40–42 NKJV.

Appendix A: Bibles and Scripture Passages Used at Presidential Inaugurations

1. Library of Congress Web site, "Bibles and Scripture Passages Used by Presidents in Taking the Oath of Office." Online at: http://memory.loc.gov/ammem/pihtml/pibible.html. Accessed: January 5, 2003.

2. Clarence W. Bowen, *The History of the Centennial Celebration of the Inauguration of George Washington* (NY, 1892), 72 (illustration).

3. Listed in the files of Legislative Reference Service, Library of Congress, source not given.

4. John Wright, *Historic Bibles in America* (NY, 1905), 46.

5. List compiled by clerk of the Supreme Court, 1939.

6. One source (*Chicago Daily Tribune*, September 23, 1881, p. 5) says that Garfield and Arthur used the same passage, but does not indicate which one.

7. Stilson Hutchins, *The National Capitol* (Washington, 1885), 276.

8. *Harper's* magazine, August 1897.

9. Senate Document 116, 65th Congress, 1st Session, 1917.

10. *New York Times*, April 13, 1945, 1, col. 7.

11. *Facts on File*, January 16–22, 1949, 21.

12. *New York Times*, January 21, 1953, 19.

13. *New York Times*, January 22, 1957, 16.

14. *New York Times*, January 21, 1961, 8, col. 1.

15. Booth Mooney, *The Lyndon Johnson Story*, 1.

16. Office of the clerk of the Supreme Court via phone July 1968.

17. *Washington Post*, January 20, 1969, A1.

18. *New York Times*, August 10, 1974, p. A1.

19. *Washington Post*, January 21, 1977, A17.

20. White House Curator's Office.

21. *Washington Post*, January 21, 1997, A14.

22. Inauguration staff. George W. Bush had hoped to use the Masonic Bible that had been used both by George Washington in 1789, and by the president's father, George H. W. Bush, in 1989. This historic Bible had been transported, under guard, from New York to Washington for the inauguration but, due to inclement weather, a family Bible was used instead.

Acknowledgments

I wish to thank my publisher Warner Faith for their confidence and for their support of this project. There are only two words to describe the Warner Faith team—Dream Team. I am especially grateful to my publisher at the Time Warner Book Group, Rolf Zettersten. I affectionately refer to him as Mr. "I" for his intelligence, integrity and incisiveness.

I am also extremely grateful to my principal editor, Steve Wilburn. The greatest fear of any author is that his editor will pull the arms and legs off the baby (the book), all in the name of journalistic integrity. Working with Steve Wilburn was a pure delight. He did not destroy the "baby"; rather his diligence and his amazing gift were used to massage the muscles of the manuscript until the baby was running like a track star. For that I am most appreciative.

A special thanks to the Warner Faith marketing team, Lori Quinn, Andrea Davis, and Preston Cannon; you are the best.

A special thanks goes to Ilan Chaim for his marvelous research assistance, and my gratitude for those in Jerusalem. I must not forget two of my dearest and oldest friends whose wisdom and passion have been the inspiration for this book, and many others: Binyamin Netanyahu (former Prime Minister) currently Minister of Finance, and Ehud Olmert, Jerusalem's former Mayor, and current Vice Premier of Israel, and Minister of Industry and Trade. I also wish to thank Yossef Bodansky, Daniel Pipes, and Richard Perle with whom I shared the platform at the Jerusalem Summit. All three were walking encyclopedias of knowledge on the subject.

I also wish to honor three giants who are no longer with us. They are the reason I began this journey three decades ago: Prime Minister Menachem Begin, Dr. Reuben Hecht, Senior Advisor to the Prime Minister, and Isser Harel, founder of Mossad, Israeli intelligence. These great men generously gave an enormous amount of their time to me. They helped me to understand the extreme seriousness of the subject, not only as it relates to Israel, but to America and the world.

Above all, I wish to thank my Executive Assistant, Lanelle Young, who does a magnificent job in everything she pursues. She has been of immeasurable help on this manuscript.

To my dear friend, Rick Killian, I can only say, "What would I have done without you. You have been my right hand. Your help on this project has been invaluable."

I also wish to express my appreciation to my attorney/agent Tom Winters. No one could ever have a better agent than Tom. There is no way this book would have happened without Tom. I must also say, "thank you," to Tom's Executive Assistant, Debby Boyd. Her faith in me has been a source of enormous strength.

My dear friend, Dr. Mike Atkins, deserves my thanks and appreciation for his wisdom, and creative assistance.

Special thanks to my darling daughter, Rachel. This marvelous vision began the very week Rachel informed me she was pregnant with her first child. Amazingly, the birthing of this book has coincided with the birth of Rachel's son, Ethan, my beloved grandson. Rachel has faithfully been there during her entire pregnancy. She and I have both been pregnant, I with this book, and she with Ethan.

I wish to express gratitude to my hero—a man who has influenced my life more than any other. He has always been my hero. I knew that he was destined for greatness, and wished to be named after him. I had my name changed. I added the middle name, David, to my name when he was born—my beloved son, Michael David Evans. His faith in me, my vision, and in this book has been enormous. He constantly encouraged me: "You can do it, Dad." "I believe in you." "You're my hero."

Finally, a book project of this magnitude demands a grueling work schedule. Most of all, I'm indebted to my beloved wife, Carolyn. Without her patience, compassion, encouragement, and sacrifice, there would be no possible way I could have achieved this.

This book is dedicated to a handful of leaders among millions who are the moral glue of the twenty-first century that holds our nation together:

Dr. Don Argue
Ms. Kay Arthur
Dr. Mark L. Bailey
Rev. Jerry Barnard
Dr. Ron Benefiel
Rev. M. Wayne Benson
Rev. Reinhard Bonnke
Mr. Claud Bowers
Dr. James Bridges
Dr. Kermit Bridges
Ms. Vonette Bright
Dr. Mac Brunson
Rev. Keith Butler
Rev. Happy Caldwell
Rev. Charles Capps
Dr. Mark Chinonna
Dr. David Yongi Cho
Dr. David Clark
Dr. Charles Paul Conn
Rev. Kenneth Copeland
Ms. Ann Coulter
Dr. Paul Crouch
Rev. Jim Cymbala
Dr. James Dobson
Rev. Creflo Dollar
Dr. James Draper
Dr. Ronald L. Ellis
Mr. Stewart W. Epperson
Rev. Des Evans
Dr. Tony Evans
Dr. Jerry Falwell
Mr. Joseph Farah
Rev. David Flower
Rev. Jentezen Franklin
Dr. J. Don George
Dr. Billy Graham

Dr. Franklin Graham
Dr. Jack Graham
Dr. John Hagee
Dr. Ted Haggard
Dr. Kenneth Hagin, Jr.
Dr. Lanny Hall
Rev. Mac Hammond
Mr. Sean Hannity
Dr. Jack Hayford
Mr. Ron Hembree
Mr. Eric Hogue
Rev. Larry Huch
Rev. Bill Hybels
Bishop T. D. Jakes
Dr. David Jeremiah
Dr. D. James Kennedy
Ambassador Alan Keyes
Dr. Byron D. Klaus
Dr. Tim LaHaye
Mr. Henry Lamb
Mr. Marcus Lamb
Rev. James Leggett
Mr. David Limbaugh
Mr. Rush Limbaugh
Rev. Hal Lindsey
Bishop Eddie Long
Mrs. Anne Graham-Lotz
Dr. Erwin W. Lutzer
Mr. Bill McCartney
Ms. Michelle Malkin
Dr. Gerald Mann
Dr. John C. Maxwell
Mr. Michael Medved
Dr. James Merritt
Dr. R. Albert Mohler, Jr.
Dr. Miles Munroe

Rev. Steve Munsey
Rev. Joel Osteen
Ms. Star Parker
Rev. Rod Parsley
Bishop G. E. Patterson
Dr. Ron Phillips
Dr. Glen Plummer
Dr. Richard Roberts
Dr. Pat Robertson
Rev. James Robison
Dr. Adrian Rogers
Dr. Hiram E. Sanders
Dr. Laura Schlessinger
Mr. Jay Sekulow
Ms. Barbara Simpson
Dr. Robert B. Sloan, Jr.
Rev. Chuck Smith
Dr. Robert H. Spence
Dr. Charles Stanley
Mr. Mark Steyna
Mr. Steven Strang
Mr. Steven Sumrall
Dr. Charles Swindoll
Mr. Cal Thomas
Dr. Thomas Trask
Rev. Casey Treat
Dr. Jack Van Impe
Dr. Kenneth Ulmer
Dr. Paul Walker
Dr. Jon R. Wallace
Dr. Rick Warren
Rev. Randy and
    Paula White
Dr. Ed Young

Index

About the Author

Michael David Evans is an award-winning journalist who has served as a confidant to leaders in the Middle East for more than two decades. He is one of the most sought-after Middle East analysts by the networks in the United States. He has appeared on hundreds of network television and radio shows including *Good Morning America, Nightline, Crossfire, The Good Morning Show* (Great Britain), *Fox and Friends, CNN World News, NBC, ABC,* and *CBS.*

Mr. Evans has been one of the most popular speakers worldwide, having spoken face-to-face to more than one million people a year during the past decade. He is chairman of the board of many enterprises, including the Corrie ten Boom Foundation in Holland and the Jerusalem Prayer Team (to which more than three hundred of America's top leaders such as Rev. Joel Osteen, Dr. Jack Hayford, Dr. Paul Crouch, Mrs. Anne Graham Lotz, Dr. Jerry Falwell, Dr. Pat Robertson, Mr. Joseph Farah, Ms. Kay Arthur, Dr. Tim LaHaye, Dr. John C. Maxwell, Dr. John Hagee, Dr. Jack Graham, Dr. Stephen Olford, Mr. Bill McCartney, and Mr. Steve Strang have lent their support).

Mr. Evans is also the author of the *New York Times* best seller *Beyond Iraq: The Next Move.* Millions throughout the world have seen the television specials he has hosted. Mr. Evans's prime-time television specials have received national awards on thirteen different occasions. These specials have included celebrity guests Kathie Lee Gifford, Evander Holyfield, Deion Sanders, Steve Allen, Gavin MacLeod, James Garner, Pat Boone, Monty Hall, and Jayne Meadows.

As a writer, he has been published in the *Wall Street Journal, Newsweek,* and numerous publications. He is a member of the National Press Club. Mr. Evans has covered world events for more than two decades.

Mr. Evans's wife, Carolyn, is the chairwoman and founder of the Christian Woman of the Year Association. Ruth Graham, Elizabeth Dole, Mother Teresa, and other distinguished women are among the recipients who have been honored during the past fifteen years. The executive committee is comprised of a number of prominent women including Dr. Cory SerVaas, owner of the *Saturday Evening Post*.